Cottage Meeting

RESOURCE GUIDE

FOR PERSONAL, FAMILY, AND COMMUNITY STUDY

ISBN
979-8-88680-023-4

Printed in the United States of America
First edition 2012
Second edition 2022

Contents

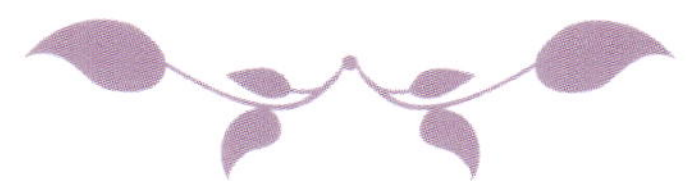

Dear Ladies,

We are so excited to have this opportunity to introduce you to the Cottage Meeting Project. Over the years, as we have participated in Cottage Meetings ourselves, we have personally witnessed the powerful influence this program can have on the hearts and minds of all those who participate. And the influence it has on our nation is immeasurable.

The Cottage Meeting Project is a simple program with profound results because it focuses on the home and begins with the very heart of America: moms! "The hand that rocks the cradle" isn't just a cute saying; it is an immortalized fact. The mothers of a country mold its citizens, determine its institutions, and shape its destiny. There is no person who has greater influence on society than a mother, and there is no place that has greater influence than the home. That is exactly why the Cottage Meeting Project is so successful in creating a foundation of liberty: it begins with women, and is centered in the home.

We encourage you to take time to read through the Hostess Guide to familiarize yourself with the program and how it works. The Hostess Guide is available on the MFA website and included in the back of this book. Whether you choose to host a Cottage Meeting or not, this Resource Guide is an excellent resource for you and your family, and we hope, as you read through the information provided, you will see just how easy it is to host a Cottage Meeting in your own home—and we hope you will.

We know, from our own experiences, that as you participate in this program, you will gain a wealth of knowledge and understanding that will infuse you with hope and inspire you with direction. The relationships you establish through Cottage Meeting groups will provide comfort and strength as you shore each other up and learn and grow together. As Cottage Meeting groups continue to form throughout the nation, we will strengthen our communities and create networks of freedom and virtue. Pockets of liberty will emerge all across America, and by one woman, one home, one cottage meeting a time, we will heal our land!

It is our sincere hope and desire that you will join us in the Cottage Meeting Project. And together, as we enrich our individual lives, we will build a brighter tomorrow as we strengthen our homes, enhance our communities, and secure the blessings of liberty for ourselves and our posterity, one home and one family at a time.

Kimberly Fletcher

President & Founder, Moms for America®

> *Perhaps our job is not necessarily to win this fight but to prepare the ground; to make the soil fertile and sow the seeds so that Liberty may thrive when the battle is done.*
>
> ~ KrisAnne Hall

Which hope we have as an anchor of the soul, both sure and steadfast...

-Hebrews 6:19

PRESENTATION ONE

Anchored in Hope

PREPARATION

To prepare yourself to lead this presentation, please review and consider the following material:

- Read "Coming Full Circle" provided in the supplemental materials section of this presentation

- Obtain a copy of the film *Monumental: In Search of America's Treasures* (available in the MFA online store and included in the Hostess Kit)

- Watch the film Monumental prior to your meeting

- Read "Anchored in Hope" provided in the supplemental materials section of this presentation

- Read "Introduction" in *The 5000 Year Leap*

PURPOSE

The purpose of this presentation is to introduce participants to Moms for America®, provide an overview of the MFA mission, and introduce the four cornerstones of liberty.

KEY POINTS

- The blessings of liberty are secured and maintained as citizens focus on God, Family, The Founder's Constitution, and Virtuous and Moral Leadership

- The Cottage Meeting Project is designed to teach and encourage these four cornerstones in homes across America

- Home is the place so save society and heal America

- Our Founding Families had a powerful formula for fostering and preserving liberty

Home Assignment

Read first chapter of *Raising Patriots: Restoring Our Garden of Liberty*

Personal Study

Read "Coming Full Circle" in Supplemental Material of this Presentation

Family Enrichment

Watch the film *Monumental* as a family. See if you can discover any unique or "hidden" monuments in your area.

MEETING OUTLINE

Welcome & Gathering

We recommend starting your meeting with a prayer and the Pledge of Allegiance.

Show Video: "Hope for America" (available in Hostess Resource Center)

Why is hope essential for success in any endeavor?

What must we do to qualify for help from God? (See Bible references-2 Chronicles 7:14, Isaiah 61:1, 1 Corinthians 9:10, 2 Corinthians 3:17, Galatians 5:1)

Group Discussion

Discuss as a group the "Founders' Formula" and "Anchored in Hope" using the following resources

Show Video: Show the clip "Founders' Formula" from the film *Monumental: In Search of America's Treasures.* (Available in the Hostess Resource Center on the MFA website)

Summarize the Article: "Anchored in Hope" and introduce the Four Cornerstones of Freedom:

1. Look to God
2. Look to Family
3. Look to the Constitution
4. Look for Moral & Virtuous Leaders

What role can mothers play in the preservation of liberty?

Read & Discuss: "Coming Full Circle" article in the supplemental materials section of this presentation.

Share this quote by Sogyal Rinpoche:

"Light must come from inside. You cannot ask the darkness to leave; you must turn on the light."

How can we be the light in the darkness?

Summary

Summarize your thoughts and share why you feel starting a Cottage Meeting is so important and the powerful impact it can have on our nation.

- Give the Home Assignment for the next meeting

- Announce date, time, and location for next meeting

ADDITIONAL PRESENTATION IDEAS

If you would like to hold additional meetings on this topic, here are some ideas:

Show Movie: *Monumental: In Search of America's National Treasure* starring Kirk Cameron. In the film, actor Kirk Cameron takes you on a journey through time to discover the Founders formula for freedom.

Because this is such a powerful movie that promotes the message of this presentation, we suggest setting up a separate movie night to share the film so you can discuss it at your next regular meeting. You can also have everyone view the film on their own and discuss in a follow-up meeting. *Monumental* traces the heroic and harrowing travels of the early Pilgrims and encounters the unlikely men and women who risked everything for liberty. You'll experience the stories of faith that guided education, government, and civic life and hear from inspiring leaders on simple and practical ways to keep America's ideals alive, beginning at home. This is a high-energy patriotic film that unites us in a celebration of America's story of faith and freedom!

MINI COTTAGE IDEAS

Mini Cottages are designed especially for moms of preschoolers and moms who work full-time jobs. Moms simply read and/or watch the same materials at home, on their own, then meet together once a week in a playdate or over lunch during the workday to discuss what they read. The articles and videos are short and can usually be read and/or viewed in less than hour. Below are some suggestions to host mini cottage discussions under the "Anchored In Hope" theme.

- Plan a movie night and watch the film *Monumental: In Search of America's Treasures* together

- Read the short book *Raising Patriots: Restoring Our Garden of Liberty*

- Read "Coming Full Circle" and watch the video "Hope for America" provided in the supplemental materials section of this presentation

- Read "Anchored in Hope" provided in the supplemental materials section of this presentation

- Watch the Video Clip "Founders Formula" from the film *Monumental* (Available in the Hostess Resource Center on the MFA website)

- Read "After America, There's No Place to Go" provided in the supplemental materials section of this presentation

COTTAGE MEETING BOOK CLUB

For those who like the book club format, we've compiled a list of great books to help you gain an appreciation for and foundational understanding of the concepts presented in "Anchored in Hope."

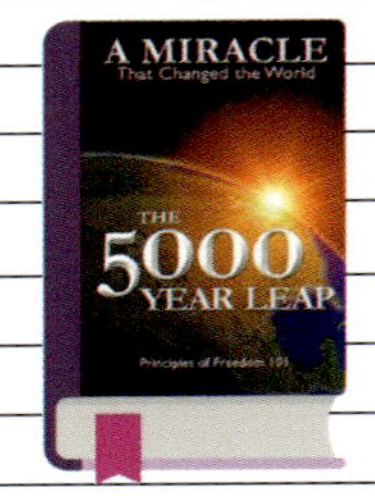

The 5000 Year Leap: A Miracle That Changed the World by W. Cleon Skousen

The nation the Founders built is now in the throes of a political, economic, social, and spiritual crisis that has driven many to an almost frantic search for modern solutions. The truth is that the solutions have been available for a long time—in the writings of our Founding Fathers. Discover the 28 Principles of Freedom our Founding Fathers said must be understood and perpetuated by every people who desire peace, prosperity, and freedom. Learn how adherence to these beliefs during the past 200 years has brought about more progress than was made in the previous 5000 years. These 28 Principles include The Genius of Natural Law, Virtuous and Moral Leaders, Equal Rights—Not Equal Things, and Avoiding the Burden of Debt. This is a core book used throughout the Cottage Meeting Project. It is the perfect book to launch a Cottage Meeting Book Club. A list of general discussion questions is available on the Moms for America® website.

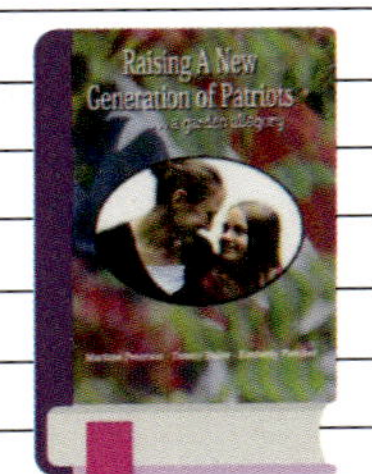

Raising Patriots: Restoring Our Garden of Liberty by Marlene Petersen, Tamy Hulse, and Kimberly Fletcher

A companion book to the Cottage Meeting Resource Guide. It is required reading for all hostesses and should be highly encouraged among group participants. The book gives a very good overview of the principles presented in the first 12 introductory presentations and expanded on through the Cottage Meeting program. The book is a short easy that takes just 30-60 minutes to read. It is available as a free download through the Moms for America® website and can be purchased in hard copy from our web store. A hard copy of the book is included in the Hostess Kit.

COTTAGE MEETING FOR KIDS

Cottage Meeting for Kids is a liberty promoting program for the entire family and focused on children from preschool aged to teens. It is full of great stories and fun activities to help children gain a love of liberty. Families can join together each month for an Activity Day to share the concepts they've learned and enhance them through group activities. Here are some ideas to promote the concepts presented in "Anchored in Hope."

- Watch the film *Monumental* together as a family.

- Treasure Scavenger Hunt—In the spirit of the film, you can do a scavenger hunt with other families. You can make it a treasure hunt with clues or just a simple scavenger hunt for specific items. You can talk about why the items are on the list after they find them. These could include:

☐ American Flag	☐ Candle
☐ Bible	☐ Map of United States
☐ Constitution	☐ Statue of Liberty
☐ Heart	☐ Liberty Bell
☐ Star	

Book List

Here is a great list of books you can read together as a family to help your children gain an appreciation for the blessings of liberty and the miracle of America:

The 4th of July Story
by Alice Dalgliesh

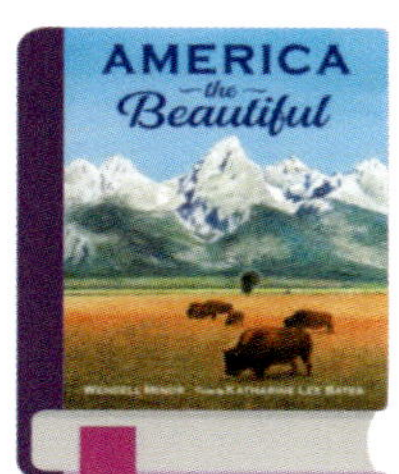

America the Beautiful
by Wendell Minor

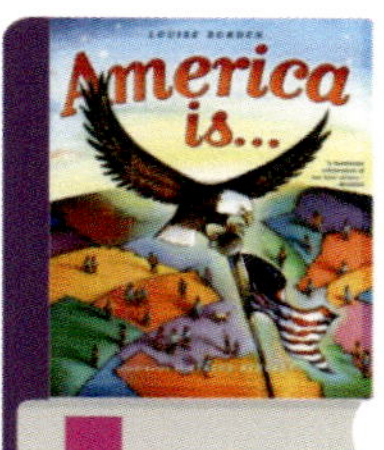

America Is…
by Louise Borden

Liberty
by Lynn Curlee

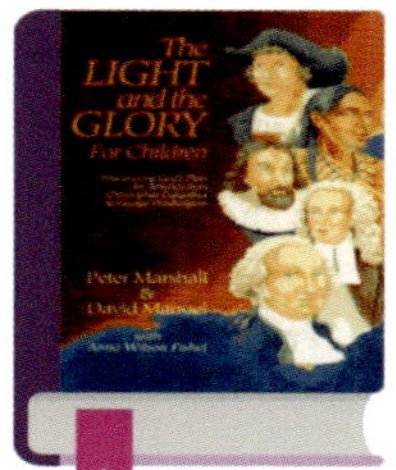

The Light and the Glory for Children
by Peter Marshall & David Manuel

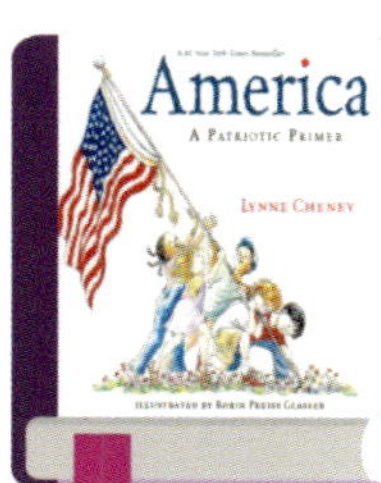

America: A Patriotic Primer
by Lynne Cheney

The Flag We Love
by Pam Munoz Ryan

A Is for America
by Devin Scillian

When Washington Crossed the Delaware
by Lynne Cheney

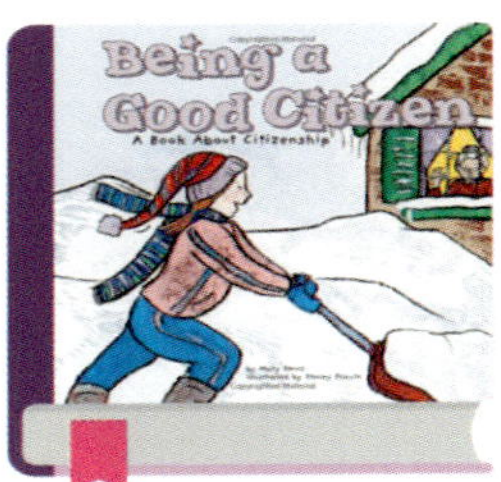

Being A Good Citizen
by Mary Small

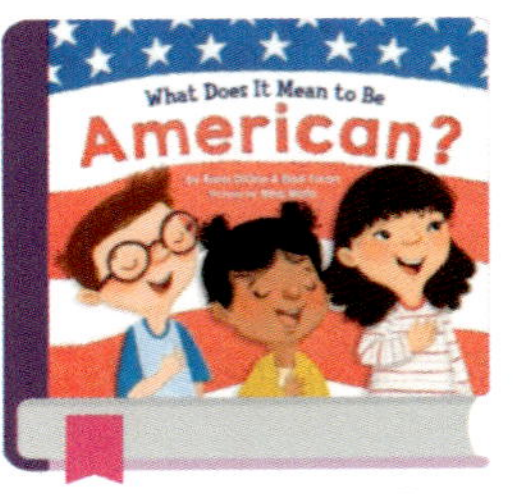

What Does It Mean to Be American
by Rana DiOrio & Elad Yoran

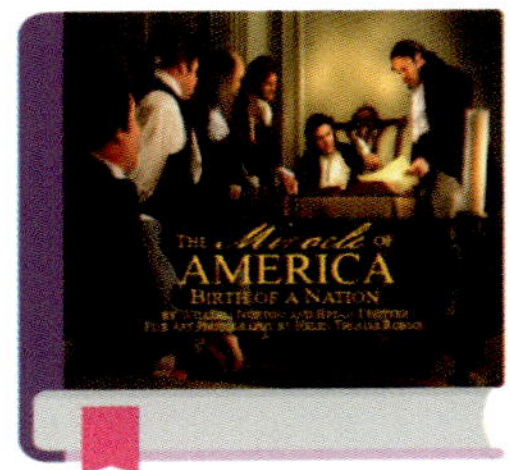

The Miracle of America
by William Norton & Brian Trotter

SUPPLEMENTAL MATERIALS

Coming Full Circle

BY KIMBERLY FLETCHER, FOUNDER, MOMS FOR AMERICA®

In 2004, I founded *Moms for America* in a living room in a small town in Ohio with 26 women. My goals were simple: give voice and value to the moms of America, promote America's history and heritage, and teach women how to be actively involved as citizens without sacrificing their families. In the years since our founding, I have a learned so many things and met so many amazing people, but I must admit, I was quite surprised at where the experiences of the last few years have led me as now I find myself coming full circle.

I started *Moms for America* out of a deep concern for our country and the direction we are headed—a concern I am sure many of us feel. In the beginning, I was convinced that the best way to fix all our problems was to give women a platform where they could voice their values. I just knew that once the media realized there were millions of women in America who had something to say they would want to know what it was. And when our elected leaders realized that all these women had an opinion on legislative matters, they would surely vote the way we wanted. What I learned, however, was that the media had no desire to hear anything we had to say and our elected officials didn't seem to think we were smart enough to have an opinion on anything.

> *The problem isn't with Congress, the media, or even government; the problem is that Liberty is homegrown and not enough people are growing it.*

I then decided the problem was the media. Our elected officials were listening to the media, and the media was obviously biased and not listening to us. So, I started a campaign to get an evening news program on the Fox affiliate stations like the other major networks had. Surely, I thought, if there was a Fox News evening news program on local Fox stations across the country it would provide competition to the biased network media and allow more people in America access to "real" news. Six months into that campaign, after collecting thousands of signatures on petitions and getting the attention of executives at Fox News (including Roger Ailes himself), I found myself on the phone with the Affiliate Relations executive in Hollywood, California. He informed me that no amount of signatures would ever be enough to convince the Fox Network to do this. Six months and over five thousand signatures later, I concluded that trying to solve our problems through the media was a grand waste of time and concluded public policy was the answer. So began focusing my efforts on effecting public policy.

I participated in several Family Lobby Days and even organized some of my own. I collaborated with groups and individuals who were introducing policy as well as speaking out against bad policy. I testified before our state legislature on numerous bills for and against, wrote letters and made phone calls to my members of Congress, and even went to Washington to visit them in person, since that is where they always seemed to be.

After all my efforts, I found that it was nearly impossible to get any kind of meeting with my congressman or Senators. The state legislators put on a good act on Lobby Day. We got a few smiles, pats on the head, and our children went home with coloring books as souvenirs. The bills I testified for were almost always dead-on-arrival, and the ones I testified against, well, the legislators flat out told me they were going to pass them anyway.

That is when I concluded the real problem in America was that the wrong people were in office, and we needed better people serving at all levels of government. So, I got involved in elections. I volunteered on campaigns; I registered voters and passed out voter information throughout our neighborhood and at the polls on Election Day. We won some elections and lost others, and all in all, it was a very good experience, but it also taught me a valuable lesson—it doesn't matter how good a candidate is, or how much he respects the Constitution if the voters don't value either. And that is when it hit me; that is when I realized that the place where I have the greatest impact on our nation is the place where I have always been—at home.

The more I thought about it, the more I realized that I was spending all my efforts trying to fix what I thought

was the problem when, in reality, they were only symptoms of it. The problem isn't with Congress, the media, or even government; the problem is that Liberty is homegrown and not enough people are growing it.

We have outsourced our training in liberty and virtue.

For decades now, we have counted on the schools, churches, media, and community to influence our children for good. Is it working? Are you happy with the results? Liberty doesn't begin in Congress; it begins at home. Everything outside the home is a resource for the family not a replacement for it. Winston Churchill said, *"There is no doubt that it is around the family and the home that all the greatest virtues, the most dominating virtues of human society, are created, strengthened and maintained."* I know this to be true.

We cannot preserve liberty and change the course of our nation if we don't start with our own hearts and in our own homes. We are raising the future leaders, reporters, entertainers, teachers, policy makers, and voters in our homes today. How can we expect liberty and virtue to prevail if we don't start there?

That is the truth that has brought me full circle.

There are already so many groups and organizations out there to help support Americans in all those other areas. The Liberty movement has provided a wealth of support and resources, but the one place that was lacking was the place that matters most, the place where liberty begins—the home.

So, we at *Moms for America* have completely redirected our focus to dedicate all our efforts to that place where we, as women, have the greatest impact, where our voice has the highest value, and where our intrinsic influence can literally change the course of our nation and preserve liberty for generations to come. And with your help, will continue to grow and flourish; because while we know that elections, public policy and an active citizenry are all vitally important in preserving liberty, we know, from our own experience, that the place it all begins is in the home!

Anchored in Hope

BY TAMMY HULSE, FORMER VICE PRESIDENT, MOMS FOR AMERICA®

As the mighty Mississippi River wanders through the city of Minneapolis, the water travels through a series of rapids and falls. To accommodate boat travelers, a lock system has been built to safely bring the boats to a lower water level. An observation deck has been built for those who would like to watch the lock fill with water, receive a boat, drain the water, and then let it out the other side. One day, those who came to observe this day-to-day routine witnessed something out of the ordinary.

A gentleman in a fishing boat had missed the turn for the lock and got caught in a current that was swiftly taking him towards the falls. The people watched, terrified, wondering what they could do to help. As the boat approached the falls, somehow it got lodged between two rocks. Time had been suspended as the man in the fishing boat stopped with his boat tilting at a severe angle at the brink of the falls. Those who observed at the side quickly called for help and tried to find a way to assist the gentleman. The man in the boat was left with a view of rushing water all about him and a perfect awareness of the impending doom if his boat were to become dislodged. Fears were raging, yet everyone could see that a panic response resulting in sudden movements could easily dislodge the boat and send it over the falls.

I had the opportunity to watch the rescue effort on the news. A helicopter was brought in, and a rescue worker secured himself to a harness and cable where he would be lowered from the helicopter to the boat, retrieve the gentleman, and lift him to safety. To help the man in the boat remain calm and understand his role in this rescue effort, other workers were involved in talking to him over a loudspeaker.

They spoke of hope and reassurance as they redirected this man's thinking from the water rushing about him to the helicopter and rescue worker above. Directions were given with clarity and optimism. The man focused his attention on what he needed to do. The rescue workers showed their courage and skill as they carefully lifted this man to safety. Cheers of gratitude and relief were expressed as the rescue workers and victim were brought to shore safe and sound.

This rescue operation was successful because both the rescuers and the victim recognized what needed to be done for a safe recovery. The rescue team was well-trained, and they knew the harness and cable were completely trustworthy. Every effort was made to keep the victim's attention focused on the rescuers above and not on the destructive forces that were surrounding him. By shifting the focus away from the problem and towards the solution, all participants were anchored in the hope of success.

What is hope? The dictionary defines hope as a belief, even a confidence, that the future event is attainable. In my personal life, I have discovered that hope is a powerful energy force that keeps us moving forward despite the obstacles that may confront us. Hope is an anchor during the winds of adversity. Hope is the antidote for discouragement and despair. Hope is the fuel that propels us towards success.

How do we find hope? The incident with the man in the boat suggests two vital steps. First, we must shift our focus from the problem to the solution. When the gentleman in the boat could only see the force of the water that surrounded him, his fear intensified. But when he shifted his attention to the rescuers above, a feeling of hope gave him courage to hang on and do his part. Second, we must recognize that our solution is trustworthy. We need to have confidence that the plan will work. By identifying and executing a viable solution, we pave the way for hope to pour into our souls.

Today, freedom loving Americans are bombarded with fears and concerns for the future of their liberties. As we watch the news and the actions of our elected officials, our attention is turned to the turbulent waters that may engulf us. If we are not careful, these challenges may distract us and divert our focus away from the true source of hope.

Wouldn't it be nice to have someone standing at the sidelines of our lives with a loudspeaker to help us keep a proper focus? We certainly won't find that in the news. It seems that the objective of the media is to keep our attention focused on the problems. One of the tactics of those who seek to overthrow liberty is to bombard the public with more problems than they can possibly resolve effectively. In contrast to the daily rhetoric of the media, the objective of *Moms for America* is to speak of solutions and reassurance and to redirect the attention of mothers and fathers to the true source of hope in America. We understand that a people who are filled with fear and panic can easily be persuaded, but a people well anchored in hope cannot be overcome. If we could stand on the shore with a loudspeaker, we would shout out four specific things to look to that will engender and sustain hope:

Look

1. *Look to God*
2. *Look to Family*
3. *Look to the Constitution*
4. *Look for Moral & Virtuous Leaders*

1. Look to God as the source of our freedoms and blessings. The God of our Fathers was instrumental in establishing this free government, and we must look to Him to help us preserve it. In a day when men and governments are debating over who has authority to bestow "rights" upon the people, we must stand firm in the truth found in our Declaration of Independence, which states that *"all men are created equal, that they are endowed by their Creator with certain unalienable rights, that among these are Life, Liberty, and the pursuit of Happiness."*

Moms for America provides several resources to keep our focus on the God of our Fathers, our Creator and source of all blessings. The Bible is one of these resources. Bible reading by our Founding Fathers was instrumental in the establishment of this free land. Bible reading today will be instrumental in preserving it. The Bible is filled with true stories about God's dealings with mankind and about mankind's dealings with each other. The Story Bible is available for purchase on our website. The presentation of the Story Bible from the King James Version, in story format and chronological order, lays a perfect foundation for personal and family study. Families will also enjoy reading the Freedom Series, a 12-volume set of history books, to discover how our Founding Fathers exercised faith in God and dedicated themselves to daily study of the Bible.

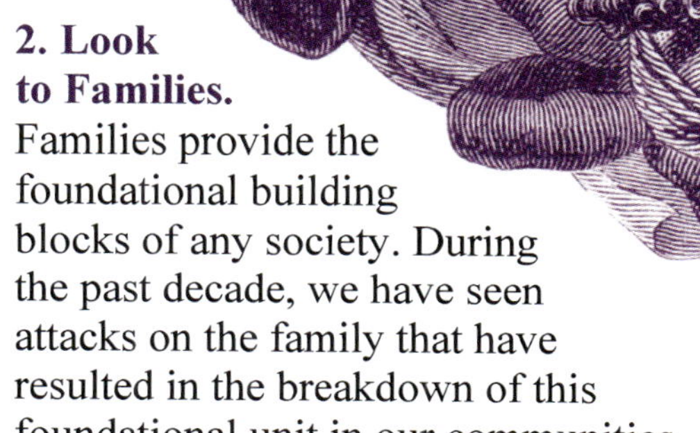

2. Look to Families. Families provide the foundational building blocks of any society. During the past decade, we have seen attacks on the family that have resulted in the breakdown of this foundational unit in our communities.

Moms for America encourages fathers to fulfill their role with compassion and love. We encourage mothers to fulfill their role by creating a home environment that nurtures and inspires its members to achieve their full potential. We encourage parents to spend time with their children to build positive relationships, to teach faith in

God, and to nurture a love of family, community, and country. We know there is no place like home to restore hope in America.

We provide many resources to help parents maintain a clear focus on creating quality family life in their own homes. The American Heritage Center on the *Moms for America* website has several resources to teach parents how they can bring the family together to learn about and remember America's great heritage, to preserve the American legacy in their own family values and traditions, and to secure the future by raising a new generation of patriots who are devoted to the cause of liberty.

3. Look to the US Constitution as written by our Founding Fathers.

The Biblical prophet Hosea said, *"My people are destroyed for lack of knowledge."* We must not let that happen in America. The United States became a great nation by following correct principles. She will remain a great nation if we can hold fast to the truth. There are two things we can do.

First, we must study and learn for ourselves the principles in the Constitution from the viewpoint of our Founding Fathers. Just as the rescuers of the man in the boat looked to the integrity of the harness and

cable system, we can look to the U.S. Constitution as equipment we can trust. The original document was inspired by God and is based on correct principles. During the past century, the original Constitution has been changed by amendments and creative judicial interpretation. These changes have weakened the unique and strong government provided by our Founders. If we the people understood this great document from the viewpoint of the Founders and insisted that our government officials be governed by it, many of the problems we see today would resolve themselves. We need to understand our equipment and use it wisely.

Second, we must also teach our children about the spiritual roots of this great nation. Our American heritage is deeply rooted in correct principles. It has been bequeathed to us by our forebears and must be handed down to each succeeding generation with great care. The Freedom Series is a 12-volume set of books that is a compilation of many historical accounts and events that made this country great. They are written in a manner that even children will understand and cherish the message they contain. We invite you to visit the American Heritage Center on our website. Click on *America— Share the Story* to discover the many resources and stories available to families who seek to preserve the legacy of American freedom.

4. Look for moral and virtuous leaders. Edmund Burke once said, *"All that is necessary for the triumph of evil is for good men to do nothing."* America has an abundance of good men and women. They serve as leaders in their schools, in their

communities, in their churches, and in their businesses. We need these good men and women to step up and guide their neighbors and communities in civic responsibility. Good leadership begins at a local level, within the homes of America. If virtuous parents insist on a high moral standard at a community level, that influence will have a powerful impact at a state and national level.

America is sailing through some rough waters and all indicators suggest that the battle between good and evil, between tyranny and liberty, will increase in its intensity. We believe moms are in a pivotal position to determine the outcome of this battle. When mothers choose to anchor themselves to the principles that engender hope, their families will follow suit and be a mighty force in the battle for liberty. There is no place like Home to restore Hope in America.

As we listen to news filled with stories of fear and discouragement, we must make a conscious effort to shift our focus and remember to **Look to God, Look to Family, Look to the Constitution, Look to Moral and Virtuous Leaders.**

By focusing on these four cornerstones, fear will transform to faith, apathy will turn into resolve, and despair will be converted into hope. Please join us at *Moms for America* and become part of the solution as we work together to secure the blessings of liberty for ourselves and our posterity.

After America, There's No Place to Go

BY KIMBERLY FLETCHER, FOUNDER, MOMS FOR AMERICA®

Kitty Werthmann was born and raised in Austria. She spent seven years of her life under Hitler's rule and five years under Russian Communist rule. In 1950, Kitty came to America. The first thing she saw when the ship came into harbor was the Statue of Liberty—an image she has never forgotten.

Kitty spent her first night in America in a hotel. The next morning, she asked the concierge for directions to the nearest police station, which he told her was within walking distance. Kitty walked to the police station and told the desk sergeant she wanted to register.

The desk sergeant asked what she was talking about. Kitty repeated, "I want to register," she said, "so you will know where I am. How will you find me if I break the law?"

"Don't worry, Lady," the sergeant replied, "if you break the law we'll find you. Now get out of here!"

Kitty walked outside quite perplexed. She looked up at the clear blue sky wondering, "What kind of country is this?" And then she realized.

"All of a sudden," she said, "it dawned on me. It's freedom!"

Many Americans favor comfort and security over liberty. The great Scottish freedom-fighter William Wallace would chide us with the same words he used for his countrymen, *"...you choose base slavery with safety rather than honest liberty with danger."*

If a love of liberty is not the overriding desire of our hearts, we will follow the same path of destruction as other great civilizations who made the same fatal choice. The great historian Sir Edward Gibbons spoke of the downfall of Greek civilization, *"In the end, more than they wanted freedom, they wanted security. They wanted a comfortable life, and they lost it all- security, comfort and freedom. When...the freedom they wished for was freedom from responsibility, then Athens ceased to be free."*

Immigrants like Kitty know what despotism is because they lived it.

They know what freedom is because they found it in America. The United States is that light on the hill that is the hope of the world. For those of us blessed to be born here, let us preserve this last bastion of hope and never let freedom slip from our grasp.

In the immortal words of Ronald Reagan, *"You and I have a rendezvous with destiny. We will preserve for our children this, the last best hope of man on earth, or we will sentence them to take the first step into a thousand years of darkness. If we fail, at least let our children and our children's children say of us we justified our brief moment here. We did all that could be done."*

The future of America, of freedom itself, is in our hands.

Kitty Werthmann's full story can be found in her article, *"Don't Let Freedom Slip Away"* in the Hostess Resource Center.

We the People: A Matter of the Heart

BY KIMBERLY FLETCHER, FOUNDER, MOMS FOR AMERICA®

We the People! Those words have echoed through our nation in a ground swell over the last few years. We've seen them on posters and placards, written them on brochures and flyers, and heard them shouted at rallies and town halls all over America, but do we really know what they mean? Do we really understand what we are saying?

When the Founders penned those words, they knew what they meant, all of America knew what they meant, and so did a King who lashed out at the words, knowing they would mean the eventual end of his Kingdom. The whole world sat in curious awe waiting to see what would happen in America, waiting with great anticipation to witness the answer to the unthinkable question—can man really govern himself?

That was the question that resonated through the hearts of men all over the world for centuries. Can men really govern themselves? The world, in general, did not believe so. For most of human history, people were ruled by those who were stronger, wealthier, or had more clout. Tyranny and slavery ruled the world; survival of the fittest determined who ruled.

As rulers would change or power would shift, tyranny always reared its ugly head. Sometimes the tyranny was instantaneous; other times, it crept in slowly or took a different shape so it wasn't recognized right away. But soon the people saw it for it what it was, somebody would rise up and cry "Freedom!" and the people would follow their new ruler—or rulers—to something they were sure would be better. But all they did was trade one ruling class for another in hopes of a just master.

Through the annals of time, we can see the results of these trades—from the Senate to Caesar, Czar to Lenin, Lenin to Stalin, King Louis 16th to Napoleon, the Qing Dynasty to Communist China, Yellow Emperor to Red Dictator, Wilhelm II to the Weimar Republic, and the Weimar Republic to Adolph Hitler. All through history, we see it repeated over and over again. The people face intense tyranny, they rise up against it, embrace the new leaders, a new tyranny creeps in, and the people still suffer. So why is America so different? Why is it, after years of history repeating itself, that the United

States of America broke the chains of tyranny and became a free people? The answer is in that powerful phrase—We the People! But, more importantly, what kind of people we were. Or in other words, what did our heart look like?

The people who came to America came with a spirit of adventure, a hope for something better, and a desire to work and sacrifice for that something better. And no group was more committed than the Pilgrims—who were willing to give all, suffer

all, and sacrifice all for the freedom to believe, worship, and raise their children in peace. This small band of emigrants, the heirs of the age of enlightenment, were the beneficiaries of the blessings of the reformation. Their belief in God and the Bible and their devotion to their families were deeply rooted in their hearts. And their heart is what guided their actions.

Our heart isn't just a place for emotions. It is the engine that empowers us to act and think—the place to process all of life's experiences. It is the *"seat of understanding; the power of producing"* (Noah Webster's 1828 Dictionary). Just as the engine of a car gives power to the vehicle to move, the engine of the soul gives man the power to act and choose. Our emotions merely serve as indicators to the condition of our heart—just as the instrument panel on the car serves as an indicator to the condition of an engine.

So, if we are going to heal America, we need to repair the engine that drives us—we need a mighty change of heart! We must take the time to read past the first three words of the preamble that we've been shouting on deaf ears and embrace the part that states "secure the blessings of liberty to ourselves and our posterity."

Secure is a strong word. It doesn't mean to dabble, preserve, or sustain. Webster's 1828 Dictionary defines it as *"safe; free from danger of being taken by an enemy; to guard effectively from danger; to make safe."* Liberty cannot be secured by a president, a Congress, or a government. It can only be secured by We the People—in our own hearts. Through our book *Raising Patriots: Restoring Our Garden of Liberty* and the presentations shared in the *Cottage Meeting Resource Guide*, you will discover the Founders' formula of success—the key ingredients that led to the rare and blessed gift of freedom.

The things we present in *Raising Patriots* and the *Resource Guide* are the simple solutions to the seemingly never-ending sea of complex problems facing our nation today. But please don't let the word "simple" fool you. These solutions are simple, but they are not easy. They require dedication, commitment, and consistency, but most of all, they require a belief that they will work, that these simple solutions will, in fact, solve our complex problems and not only protect liberty but secure it for generations to come.

We know they work because it is these principles that led to the freedom and prosperity our nation has experienced for over 200 years. We know they work because it is these same principles the Destroyers of Liberty have used to successfully unravel the threads of freedom and virtually dismantle the Constitution that was designed to protect that freedom.

We know it is in the home and family that liberty begins and where the foundation is most securely rooted because the Destroyers of Liberty have launched an all-out assault on the home and family.

We know that a knowledge of our history and heritage is paramount in the preservation of liberty because the Destroyers of Liberty have worked very hard to make history inconsequential, boring, and undesirable.

We know stories touch the heart and pierce the soul like no other medium because the Destroyers of Liberty have done everything they can to remove these stories from our libraries, our homes, and our lives.

We know that beautiful art, music, and literature inspire because the Marxist and Communist Destroyers of Liberty have spent an enormous amount of time distorting art and removing all goodness and beauty from these things.

We know, beyond any doubt, that women play so vital a role in the nurturing of liberty and virtue that, without them and their tender influence, liberty and virtue would cease to exist. And the Destroyers of Liberty know that too, or they wouldn't have spent decades defaming women and tearing down their vital roles as mother and maker of the home. The Destroyers of Liberty have done everything they can to deceive, distract, and devalue women for the sole concentrated purpose of limiting their influence in the home because they are very well aware of how powerful that influence is in determining the future of our nation.

If the solutions we present in the Cottage Meeting Program weren't the answers, then the Destroyers of Liberty wouldn't be working so hard to destroy, disrupt, and distort them. They wouldn't be spending so much time trying to distract us from these things or work so hard to try and convince us they don't matter. The fact is: they do matter, and the Destroyers of Liberty know it.

It is important to understand that America is not the only place where liberty can thrive.

Though it has become uniquely American, Liberty can prosper anywhere under the right conditions, but it is America that God has chosen as the venue for freedom. It is the United States of America where freedom was established and prospered to become an example of truth, virtue, and freedom to the world. America truly is that light on the hill. We are the light and hope of the world. If we fail here, all hope of free men and women in this world will wither away. The experiment the world has been watching with great anticipation for two centuries will have failed. We will have proven that men can not govern themselves, and freedom will cease to exist.

So, we need to ask ourselves, do we really want freedom? Are we, like our Founders, willing to make the sacrifices and exert the energy necessary to secure freedom or are we merely looking for more just masters? Do we really want freedom or do we just want the government to leave us alone? These are the hard questions we need to ask ourselves. And while we are considering the answers, remember that the government left us alone for decades while the Destroyers of Liberty worked their silent destruction behind closed doors, slowly dismantling everything we hold dear.

Yes, the principles we will share are simple; so simple, we have overlooked them for decades. But let us not think them so simple that we dismiss them as irrelevant and allow the Destroyers of Liberty to win by the very means we have scoffed and disregarded.

"We the People" is a powerful phrase, but it is the heart of "we the people" that determines the direction our nation will go; whether freedom will prevail, whether liberty can be secured, whether the experiment will prove that man can, in fact, govern himself.

It took well over a hundred years of parents nurturing seeds of liberty in the hearts of their children to gain this freedom, but once it took root, it sank deep into the hearts of those little boys, who grew to be the men who would pen those immortal words— We the People! That is the power of simplicity. Is it easy? Absolutely not. But is it worth it?

Oh Yes! It is!

RELATED QUOTES

"There are those, I know, who will say that the liberation of humanity, the freedom of man and mind, is nothing but a dream. They are right. It is the American dream."
- Archibald MacLeish

"It may be that the night will close over us in the end, but I believe that morning will come again . . . We are the Lantern Bearers, my friend; for us to keep something burning, to carry what light we can forward into the darkness and the wind."
- Rosemary Sutcliff, The Lantern Bearers (1959)

"it's only when the night is darkest that you can see the light of the stars."
- Elizabeth Hunter

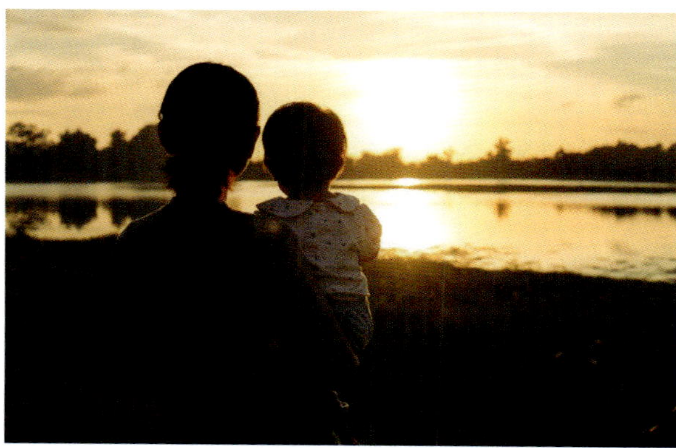

"We do not need more material development; we need more spiritual development.

We do not need more intellectual power; we need more moral power.

We do not need more knowledge; we need more character.

We do not need more government; we need more culture.

We do not need more law; we need more religion.

We do not need more of the things that are seen;

we need more of the things that are unseen.

It is on that side of life that it is desirable to put the emphasis at this present time.

If that side is strengthened, the other side will take care of itself.

It is that side which is the foundation of all else. If the foundation be firm, the superstructure will stand."
- Calvin Coolidge

"Liberty lies in the hearts of men and women; when it dies there, no constitution, no law, no court can save it...While it lies there, it needs no constitution, no law, no court to save it."
- Learned Hand, jurist

"Light must come from inside. You cannot ask the darkness to leave; you must turn on the light."
- Sogyal Rinpoche

"You and I have a rendezvous with destiny. We will preserve for our children this, the last best hope of man on earth, or we will sentence them to take the first step into a thousand years of darkness. If we fail, at least let our children and our children's children say of us we justified our brief moment here. We did all that could be done."
- Ronald Reagan

"Have courage and be kind."
- Disney's Cinderella

"All the darkness in the world cannot extinguish the light of a single candle."
- St. Francis Of Assisi

"Darkness cannot drive out darkness; only light can do that. Hate cannot drive out hate; only love can do that."
- Martin Luther King, Jr.

"There is no darkness so dense, so menacing, or so difficult that it cannot be overcome by light."
- Vern P Stanfill

FROM THE FOUNDERS

"The bosom of America is open to receive not only the Opulent and respectable Stranger, but the oppressed and persecuted of all Nations and Religions; whom we shall welcome to a participation of all our rights and privileges, if by decency and propriety of conduct they appear to merit the enjoyment."
- George Washington

The establishment of Civil and Religious Liberty was the Motive which induced me to the Field - the object is attained - and it now remains to be my earnest wish & prayer, that the Citizens of the United States could make a wise and virtuous use of the blessings placed before them.
- George Washington

"I agree with you that it is the duty of every good citizen to use all the opportunities, which occur to him, for preserving documents relating to the history of our country."
- Thomas Jefferson

There is a price tag on human liberty. That price is the willingness to assume the responsibilities of being free men. Payment of this price is a personal matter with each of us."
- James Monroe

Journal

"You and I have a rendezvous with destiny. We will preserve for our children this, the last best hope of man on earth, or we will sentence them to take the first step into a thousand years of darkness. If we fail, at least let our children and our children's children say of us we justified our brief moment here. We did all that could be done.

-Ronald Reagan

No Place Like Home

"There is no doubt that it is around the family and the home that all the greatest virtues, the most dominating virtues of human society, are created, strengthened and maintained."

~Winston Churchill

PREPARATION

To prepare yourself to lead this presentation please review and consider the following material:

- Read "Liberty Begins at Home" found in the Supplemental Materials of this presentation

- View the video *Liberty Begins at Home* provided in the Hostess Resource Center on the Moms for America® website www.MomsforAmerica.us

- View the National Prayer Breakfast speech by Dr. Ben Carson from 2013 (27 minutes)

- Review Principle 26 of the 5000 Year Leap

- Optional: Review Vignette 14.5 in Promises of the Constitution (available in MFA online store)

PURPOSE

The purpose of this presentation is to introduce the significant role of the home and family in society, introduce the Pillars of Liberty, and established the principle that liberty begins at home.

KEY POINTS

- Home is the center of society and women are the center of the home. What we teach and nurture in the home becomes the future of America

- Mothers have a profound influence in shaping the character of our culture and nation

- Home is our first association with society

- Home is a place of refuge from the storm, whether it comes from political, emotional, spiritual, or moral challenges in society

Home Assignment

Read pages 1-33 of *The 5000 Year Leap*

Personal Study

Read article "Liberty Begins at Home" in the Supplemental Material section of this presentation.

Family Enrichment

Family Art Project: Make a collage of the American Flag. Look for pictures in magazines with red, white, and blue hues. Tear the pictures into pieces, group them by color and glue them onto a paper to create an American Flag.

Fly Kites as a Family: Talk about the importance of the string on the kite, that it will fall to the ground if we let go of the string. This can be likened to government—as long as we hold onto correct principles we are free. If we let go of those principles, our country will fall.

MEETING OUTLINE

Welcome & Gathering

We recommend starting your meeting with a prayer and the Pledge of Allegiance.

Show Video: "Liberty Begins at Home" (available in Hostess Resource Center)

What is the Pattern of Liberty our Founding Families left us?

How can family promote the cause of liberty? (See Bible References James 1:25, Titus 2:4, Leviticus 10:11, Deuteronomy 11: 19)

What types of dangers come to a society from the breakdown of the family? How did the Founding Fathers of America define the family? (See Principle 26 of The 5000 Year Leap)

Group Discussion

Discuss as a group the importance of the home using the following resources:

Read and Discuss: *"Liberty Begins at Home"* provided in the Supplemental Materials section of this presentation.

Use the "Pillars of Liberty" graphic included in the Supplemental Materials to introduce the Pillars of Liberty.

The Foundation of Liberty, created by our Founding Families, was nurtured in the home as parents planted seeds of Faith, Virtue, and Patriotism—the Three Pillars of Liberty. By following this same formula, we too can build a strong nation capable of sustaining freedom. The principles shared in *Moms for America's* core book, *Raising Patriots: Restoring Our Garden of Liberty* presents a good overview of how we can nurture a foundation of liberty in our homes.

How can families work together to "keep the Republic" as suggested by Benjamin Franklin?

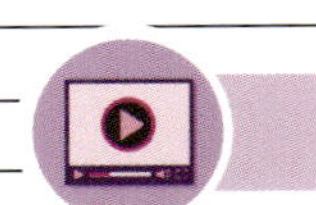

Show the Video: Speech by Dr. Ben Carson from the 2012 National Prayer Breakfast (Available in the Hostess Resource Center on the MFA website)

Dr. Carson spoke of the importance of education, the influence of his mother, and the vital need to return to the principles and values that made America the freest, most prosperous nation on earth. Dr. Carson's speech was so impressive that it went viral. Many people, however, lashed out at Dr. Carson's words saying they were "inappropriate." When asked about the negative feedback in an interview Dr. Carson responded, "I always pray before I give a speech, and I ask God to give me the right things to say, and I think that it's very rare these days for people to speak the truth. Everybody wants to get along, and in the meantime, the fabric of our nation is being destroyed."

What influence did Dr. Carson's mother have on his life?

How can we teach our children to speak and stand for truth?

Summary

Summarize your thoughts on the principles discussed in this presentation.

- Give the Home Assignment for the next meeting

- Announce date, time and location for next meeting

ADDITIONAL PRESENTATION IDEAS

Show Movie: *Agenda: Grinding America Down* by Curtis Bowers. This is a great follow up film to *Monumental*.

Monumental presents the formula America was founded on to preserve freedom. *Agenda* proves the case by demonstrating that formula contains those very things that Marxists and Communists have been using to destroy freedom and the Constitution by redefining American values.

You can show the film as a regular meeting or plan a separate movie night. You can also have everyone view the film on their own and discuss in a follow-up meeting.

You can also discuss the 45 Communist Goals from the book *The Naked Communist* provided in the Supplemental Materials of this presentation. The Communist Goals were introduced into the Congressional Record in 1963.

Suggested Reading:

"You Can Call the 2020 Election Anything You Want but Don't Dare Call It Conspiracy" (article from Townhall.com. Link is provided in the Hostess Resource Center)

None Dare Call it Conspiracy by Gary Allen

The Naked Communist by W. Cleon Skousen

A Warning to the West by Aleksandr Solzhenitsyn

MINI COTTAGE IDEAS

Mini Cottages are designed especially for moms of preschoolers and moms who work full-time jobs. Moms simply read and/or watch the same materials at home, on their own, then meet together once a week in a playdate or over lunch during the workday to discuss what they read. The articles and videos are short and can usually be read and/or viewed in less than hour. Below are some suggestions to host mini cottage discussions under the "Liberty Begins at Home" theme.

- Plan a movie night and watch the film *Agenda* together.

- View the Video of Ben Carson's Speech at the National Prayer Breakfast (video link available in the Hostess Resource Center)

- Read "Simplicity with Perseverance" provided in the supplemental materials section of this presentation.

- Read "Liberty Begins at Home" provided in the supplemental materials section of this presentation. Review the "Pillars of Liberty" handout.

COTTAGE MEETING BOOK CLUB

For those who like the book club format, we've compiled a list of great books to help you gain an appreciation and foundational understanding of the concepts presented in "There's No Place Like Home."

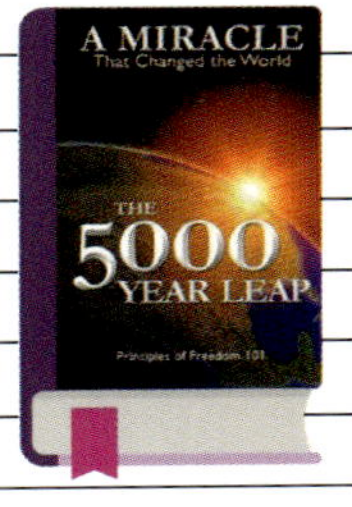

The 5000 Year Leap: A Miracle That Changed the World by W. Cleon Skousen

The nation the Founders built is now in the throes of a political, economic, social, and spiritual crisis that has driven many to an almost frantic search for modern solutions. The truth is that the solutions have been available for a long time—in the writings of our Founding Fathers. Discover the 28 Principles of Freedom our Founding Fathers said must be understood and perpetuated by every people who desire peace, prosperity, and freedom. Learn how adherence to these beliefs during the past 200 years has brought about more progress than was made in the previous 5000 years. These 28 Principles include The Genius of Natural Law, Virtuous and Moral Leaders, Equal Rights—Not Equal Things, and Avoiding the Burden of Debt. This is a core book used throughout the Cottage Meeting Project. It is the perfect book to launch a Cottage Meeting Book Club. A list of general discussion questions is available on the Moms for America® website.

None Dare Call it Conspiracy by Gary Allen

This book is a primer for anyone who wishes to understand the basic workings of the global network of Insiders that is determined to wield power over all of mankind in the coming New World Order. The story is true. The names have not been changed to protect the guilty. This book may have the effect of changing your life. After reading this book, you will never look at national and world events in the same way again.

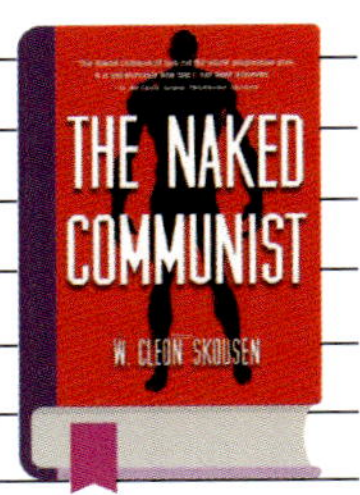

The Naked Communist by W. Cleon Skousen

Soon after its quiet release during the height of the Red Scare in 1958, *The Naked Communist: Exposing Communism and Restoring Freedom* exploded in popularity, selling almost two million copies to date and finding its way into the libraries of the CIA, the FBI, the White House, and homes all across the United

States. From the tragic falls of China, Korea, Russia, and the UN to the fascinating histories of Alger Hiss, Whittaker Chambers, Elizabeth Bentley, and General MacArthur, *The Naked Communist* lays out the entire graphic story of communism—its past, present, and future.

A Warning to the West by Aleksandr Solzhenitsyn

Alexander Solzhenitsyn's *Warning to the West* includes the texts of the Nobel Prize-winning author's three speeches in the United States in the summer of 1975—his first major public addresses since his expulsion from the Soviet Union in 1974—on June 30 and July 9 to trade-union leaders of the AFL-CIO in Washington, D.C., and in New York City, and on July 15 to the United States Congress; and also the texts of his BBC interview and radio speech, which sparked widespread public controversy when they were aired in London in March 1976.

COTTAGE MEETING FOR KIDS

Cottage Meeting for Kids is a liberty promoting program for the entire family and focused on children from preschool to teens. It is full of great stories and fun activities to help children gain a love of liberty. Families can join together each month for an Activity Day to share the concepts they've learned and enhance them through group activities. Here are some ideas to promote the concepts presented in "Liberty Begins at Home." You can find additional ideas, outlines and activities on the Moms for America® website under "Cottage Meetings for Kids."

- Watch the PBS Series *Liberty Kids* with your children (The video series is available to view online on YouTube or Amazon Prime. You can also purchase the series on DVD).

- Watch *Schoolhouse Rock: America Rock* (This video can be purchased online. Video segments are also available on the MFA website under Cottage Meetings for Kids).

- Bake cookies using a recipe or make a simple handcraft following instructions with your children. Explain why patterns are important to follow to create the finished product you want. What happens when you don't follow the pattern or recipe?

- Plant seeds in a garden or garden box. Discuss with your children why you plant certain seeds, what they need to grow and why you need the right seeds to get the plants you want (example: if you plant cucumber seeds you will get cucumbers not tomatoes).

- Play the song "Coming to America" by Neil Diamond. Why do so many people around the world want to come to America?

- Read the book *The Miracle of America: Birth of A Nation* with your children. There is also a coloring book that compliments the book. The children can color while you tell the stories.

Book List

Great books to read with your children to promote the ideas presented in this presentation and nature a love of liberty in the hearts of your children.

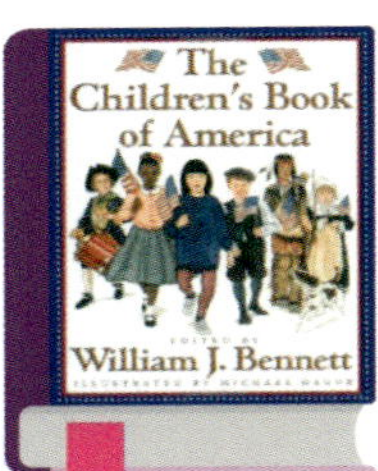

***The Children's Book
of America***
by William J. Bennett

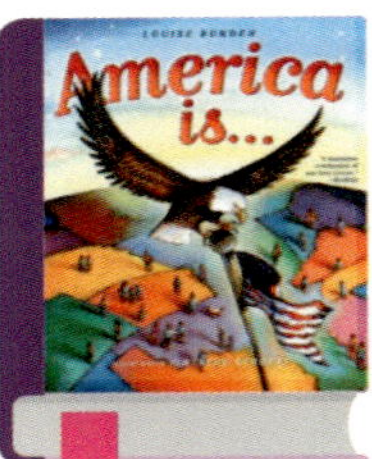

America Is…
by Louise Borden

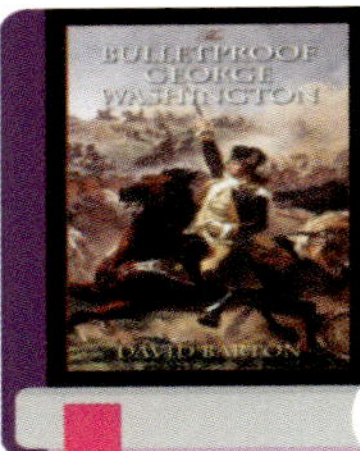

***The Bulletproof
George Washington***
by David Barton

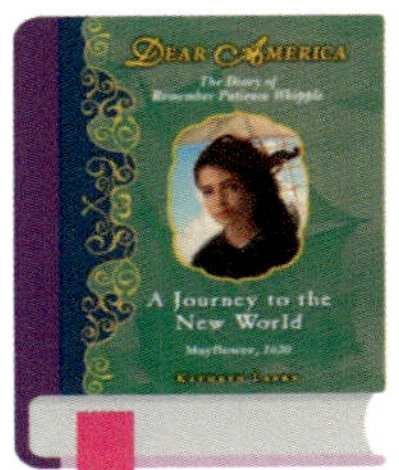

***Dear America: A Journey
to the New World***
by Kathryn Lasky

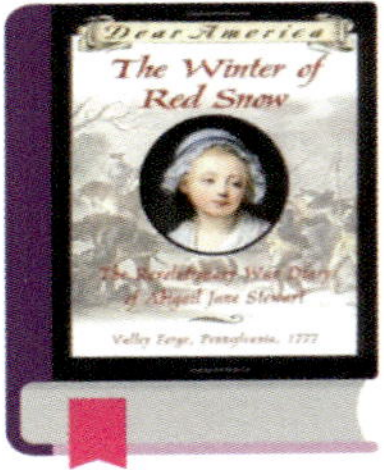

***Dear America: The
Winter of Red Snow***
by Abigail Jane Stewart

Patriots in Petticoats
by Patricia Edwards Clyne

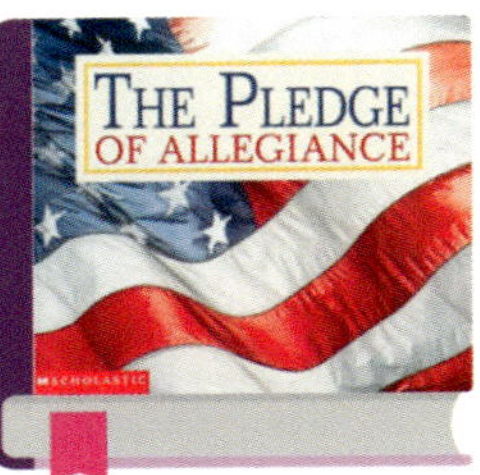

***The Pledge of
Allegiance***
by Francis Bellamy

The Miracle of America
by William Norton &
Brian Trotter

SUPPLEMENTAL MATERIALS

Liberty Begins at Home

In 1787, after a long hot summer of deep debates and negotiations, Congress approved the Constitution of the United States of America. As Benjamin Franklin left Independence Hall, a woman approached him and asked, *"Sir, what did you give us?"* To which Mr. Franklin replied, *"A Republic ma'am, if you can keep it."* How profound his words were.

Benjamin Franklin knew how hard it would be to keep the Republic. He knew how easy it would be for men in power to usurp power and authority (not granted them) if we were not vigilantly watching. He knew how easy it would be for us to forget what the Republic was about and the ideas that made it strong if we were not constantly reminding ourselves. He knew how easy it would be for us to start looking to the government to solve our problems and save us from ourselves. He knew "keeping" the Republic would mean hard work, a firm understanding of the principles of liberty, and an unwavering commitment to preserve them. Benjamin Franklin knew what a challenge it would be to sustain a Republic, but he fervently believed that if ever there were a people who could do it, it would be us.

After two centuries of freedom, we have certainly done better than any other nation, country, or empire, but we have definitely not done our due diligence in keeping the Republic. In fact, the Republic our Founders left to us is hardly recognizable anymore. All the things our Founding Fathers feared, warned us about, and tried so desperately to protect us against are the very things we are facing today.

There has been a lot of talk about democracy lately. Democracy seems to be the new buzz word in the world, but I often wonder if the countries currently mulling around the idea of democracy really understand what it means? Even more, do Americans understand what it means? In this revival of liberty we are experiencing in our country today, I think these are questions every American should be asking themselves. So today, I'd like to share what Democracy means to me.

I think Benjamin Franklin defined it best when he said, "Democracy is two wolves and a lamb voting on what to have for lunch. Liberty is a well-armed lamb contesting the vote."

Our Founding Fathers realized the oppression of a Monarchy, but they were also aware of the failings of a Democracy. And while the world looks to America as a symbol of democracy, it is the combination of self-governance and representative leadership that is the secret of America's success. America is not a democracy, it is a Democratic Republic—the divinely perfect combination to promote freedom and protect individual liberties.

If we are to have a discussion about what Democracy means, we must first understand what it is and what it is not. The American experiment is much more than a form of government; it is an ideal. It is the belief that man can, in fact, govern himself, and if he will not, then the experiment fails. But, like Benjamin Franklin, our Founders truly believed it could be done and that we would do it.

Many people are blaming the predicament of our country on the president, his administration, Congress, and the government in general, but in reality, those things are not the problem but merely symptoms of it. You can't rid a garden of noxious weeds simply by cutting the stems; you have to go to the root. The problem in our country today is not an out of control government, the problem is that Americans are not acting American—we are not embracing our divine heritage of liberty, we don't know our magnificent, providential history, and we are not fulfilling our civic responsibility. The harsh reality is, if we don't like what's going on in our nation today, we only have ourselves to blame.

We are a government of the people and by the people not just for the people. If we the people are not "by the people," if we are not willing to do our civic duty and watch over government, then corruption will take root and consume our nation until we the people are strangled right out of existence. If we the people are not willing to be "of the people" and run for elected office, then there will be plenty of self-serving, power-hungry individuals who will. If we the people

are not fostering a love of liberty in our own homes and our own hearts, then we will never understand and embrace the principles of liberty our nation was founded on. If we are not willing to sacrifice our lives, our fortunes, and our sacred honor to preserve liberty and sustain the Constitution then freedom in America will cease to exist. We are the reason we are in the state we are in. And we are the only ones who can pull us out of it.

It is true, there have been many forces working against us feverishly trying to destroy this last bastion of hope for the world, but in the end, we are the keepers of the flame—not the schools, not Congress, not the media. If our schools aren't teaching our children about America's history and heritage, then we need to be doing it. If the media is not going to present truth and facts, then we need to. It is not the government's job to raise and teach our children; it is ours. We cannot count on others to do our job for us, and we cannot legislate our rights and responsibilities away and expect liberty to simply sustain itself in the name of democracy.

If our children are patriots, it is because we raised patriots in our homes. If our children know and understand the Constitution, it is because we taught them. If our children embrace freedom and love their country, it is because we instilled that love in them through our own examples.

Democracy is the embodiment of self-reliance, self-governance, and self-sacrifice, which, simply stated, means the American experiment can only succeed when we are able to govern ourselves in righteousness. As Alexis de Tocqueville so aptly stated, "America is great because she is good, and if America ever ceases to be good, she will cease to be great."

It is not our government, our wealth, or our rich soil that ensures our democracy, it is our goodness. And if American's cease to be good, then the American experiment will have run its course. But goodness has not ceased. It is here, rising up in homes all across America. The spirit of America is alive; it just needs to be awakened.

And that should be our personal quest: to wake up the American people and infuse the light of liberty in their very souls. Every American we convert to Liberty and the Constitution is one American closer to securing a free nation. It is very probable that the day is not far off when our economy will collapse and our government will crumble, but America never will; because America isn't a president or a Congress, it is us! It is We the People. And We the People will rise from the ashes waiving the standard of liberty to the world. Every American who understands and internalizes the principles of liberty will rise up, holding the Constitution firmly in their grip and lead the people of this nation to freedom.

So, when I am asked, what does Democracy mean to me? I answer, it means hope. It means believing in something greater than yourself. It means personal responsibility. And if we don't take that responsibility seriously, instead of explaining to our children what democracy is, we will have to explain what happened to it.

Liberty begins at home. You and I, we hold the keys. We are the keepers of the flame. We must do everything in our power to pass on that flame, to make sure it burns bright, and ensure it continues to be a light on the hill and a beacon of hope to the world. The Constitution is our banner. Raise it high. Because if liberty is to prevail in America, then it will be because of you!

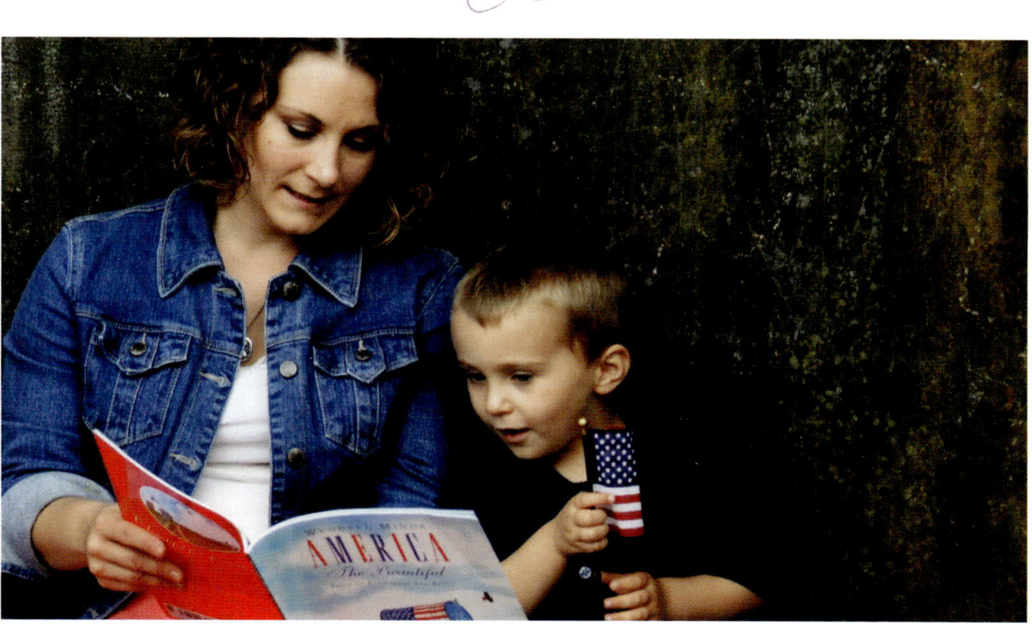

Simplicity with Perseverance

BY KIMBERLY FLETCHER, FOUNDER, MOMS FOR AMERICA®

I stood on the scale staring at the numbers. Two pounds! It couldn't be right. I'd been walking every day, five to six days a week. I was eating healthier and having smaller meals more often. I was even riding my bike to places near my house instead of taking the car. Two months of this, and all I had to show for it was two pounds!

I looked at my husband in exasperation, trying once again to convince him (and me) that liposuction was the answer, and he, once again, lovingly put his arm around me and assured me that persistence in what I was already doing was a much safer way to reach my goal and would have much more lasting results. I knew he was right. I knew it was these simple steps I was already taking that would get me to where I wanted to be, but I also knew that it would not be easy. It would take patience, persistence, consistency, and dedication.

While liposuction definitely seemed the easy way out, I knew the easy way wasn't really a way out at all but just a delay of the same results. I didn't put on sixty pounds on overnight, and I wasn't going to lose it in a day.

Reflecting on this experience, it seems curiously similar to the situation we face in America today. So many of us are looking for those easy answers that will "fix" our nation and get us back on track. But the answers are not easy. They are simple—maybe, we think, too simple—but they are definitely not easy. It took us a hundred years to get where we are as a nation, and we can't turn it around overnight. There is no magical liposuction that will suck out our over-bloated government, balance our budget, or stop the out-of-control spending. It will take patience, persistence, consistency, and dedication, and it has to begin with us!

I know a lot of people who have put their hope in a presidential election, and while it is extremely important that we get involved, it deeply concerns me that so many Americans have convinced themselves that a new face in the White House will fix everything. Corruption, dishonesty, arrogance, and deception are way too entrenched at all levels of government for that to be the case. A change of presidents may slow down the tyranny, it may even kick the stone down the road a little, but it will NOT "fix" America, and it will NOT protect or sustain liberty. No election can do that because the harsh fact is, in a land where our government is chosen by the voice of the people, what we get is a reflection of who we are ourselves.

If we as a people are wicked, we will elect wicked rulers. If we have no understanding or respect for the Constitution, we won't make an effort to vote for someone who does. If we don't reverence God or love our country, why would we care if those we vote for do? So while the easy answer we seek (a change of men) may bring minimal, short-term results, it is the simple answer (a mighty change within ourselves) that will deliver the long term, lasting results we seek. The only way we can truly secure liberty for ourselves and our posterity is to nurture liberty within our own hearts and in our own homes.

Unfortunately, when I tell people this, they tend to discount the idea; some even disregard it as a completely absurd notion. After all, how can reading stories save America? How can having dinner together as a family secure liberty? How can a focus on education fix our government? And yet, history has proven that it does just that.

When I see in their eyes skepticism over the simplicity of the ideas presented in our book *Raising Patriots*, I think of the story of Naaman from the Bible. Naaman was a great and powerful commander in the Syrian army who was stricken with leprosy. He sent his servant to Elisha, the prophet, asking him to come and heal him. Elisha didn't come to Naaman. Instead, he told Naaman's servant to go back and tell his master that if he washed in the river Jordan 7 times he would come out clean. Naaman became angry and was offended that Elisha didn't bother to come himself. He wanted a great miracle, and Elisha didn't come to offer it. Naaman was appalled that Elisha would suggest he do something so ridiculous as bathe in a river, and a dirty one at that, so he disregarded Elisha's council and refused to wash in the Jordan River.

It was Naaman's humble servant, troubled by his master's reaction, who helped him realize the miracle he was dismissing. "...if the prophet had told you to do something great, would you not have done it? How much more then, when he says to you, 'Wash, and be clean'?"

Naaman was humbled by his servant's words. He went down into the River Jordan, washed seven times, and came out clean!

Please don't underestimate the power of simplicity. It is out of small and simple things that great things come about. I know it isn't easy to bring your family together for dinner each night, I know it is a challenge to gather your young ones (and even your older ones) together to read stories, and I know how hard it is be consistent in an age of mounting pressures and chaotic schedules, but I also know it is worth it. It is worth every minute set aside, every opportunity spared.

It only takes a few minutes a day to read a story to our children; just a little juggling to eat dinner together or gather our family and read the Bible together, but it is those simple things, those little moments, that will secure liberty. And one day, in the not so distant future, it will be our sons and our daughters who will serve as leaders, make public policy, teach future generations, and vote in elections. And the kind of people they become will depend on us!

Frederick Douglas once said, "It is easier to build strong children than to repair broken men." We can spend all our time trying to fix the broken men in Washington or we can exert our energies building strong children who will transform Washington.

There is no easy way out of the debacle our nation faces, but there is a simple one. It will require time, dedication, and commitment, but it will bring us the miracle we are seeking, and that will make it all worth it!

Many conservatives have been warning for years that the events facing our nation are not accidental. In his 1958 book *The Naked Communist*, W. Cleon Skousen outlines the Communist plot to destroy American liberty through an all-encompassing strategy to infiltrate every level of our culture. That was a warning. More than 60 years later, we are seeing the results of that strategy with the rise of socialism and the undermining of the American family and the principles of liberty that have preserved our nation since its founding.

Skousen's work has been derided by some as conspiracy theory, but reading his list of Current Communist Goals—excerpted below from *The Naked Communist*—the warnings are not far-fetched or unbelievable. We are witnessing them right now.

Mothers across the country are watching the United States of America disappear before our eyes. We are a republic founded on principles of liberty. The Constitution that protects pur God-given rights is being eroded and undermined with radical legislation and political elites who have seized bureaucratic power never granted to them by the Founding Fathers or "we the people."

We have watched in desperation as election integrity and transparency have been taken away and the legacy of liberty that is the birthright of every American has shrunk. At *Moms for America* we have heard from countless mothers who are feeling stunned and overwhelmed by the destruction of a free nation taking place at such a rapid pace.

Patriotic mothers know that it is not too late to turn the tide. The Communist Goals are coming to fruition, but the fight for the soul of a nation is not over. The women who believe in the mission of *Moms for America* know the power of raising the next generation. We are telling our children the story of America, the freest and most prosperous nation on Earth. We are teaching them the virtues necessary to preserve liberty through self-government. Though flawed and imperfect, our country is the last best hope for liberty and the sanctuary for people seeking freedom in every corner of the world. We are bringing attention to the "Current Communist Goals" in order to rally American mothers to stop the destruction of our nation before it is too late.

Communist Goals (introduced into the Congressional Record in 1963)

EXTENSION OF REMARKS OF HON. A. S. HERLONG, JR. OF FLORIDA IN THE HOUSE OF REPRESENTATIVES Thursday, January 10, 1963 (Congressional Record--Appendix, pp. A34-A35)

Mr. HERLONG.

Mr. Speaker, Mrs. Patricia Nordman of De Land, Fla., is an ardent and articulate opponent of communism, and until recently published the De

Land Courier, which she dedicated to the purpose of alerting the public to the dangers of communism in America. At Mrs. Nordman's request, I include in the RECORD, under unanimous consent, the following "Current Communist Goals," which she identifies as an excerpt from "The Naked Communist," by Cleon Skousen:

CURRENT COMMUNIST GOALS

1. U.S. acceptance of coexistence as the only alternative to atomic war.

2. U.S. willingness to capitulate in preference to engaging in atomic war.

3. Develop the illusion that total disarmament [by] the United States would be a demonstration of moral strength.

4. Permit free trade between all nations regardless of Communist affiliation and regardless of whether or not items could be used for war.

5. Extension of long-term loans to Russia and Soviet satellites.

6. Provide American aid to all nations regardless of Communist domination.

7. Grant recognition of Red China. Admission of Red China to the U.N.

8. Set up East and West Germany as separate states in spite of Khrushchev's promise in 1955 to settle the German question by free elections under supervision of the U.N.

9. Prolong the conferences to ban atomic tests because the United States has agreed to suspend tests as long as negotiations are in progress.

10. Allow all Soviet satellites individual representation in the U.N.

11. Promote the U.N. as the only hope for mankind. If its charter is rewritten, demand that it be set up as a one-world government with its own independent armed forces. (Some Communist leaders believe the world can be taken over as easily by the U.N. as by Moscow. Sometimes these two centers compete with each other as they are now doing in the Congo.)

12. Resist any attempt to outlaw the Communist Party.

13. Do away with all loyalty oaths.

14. Continue giving Russia access to the U.S. Patent Office.

15. Capture one or both of the political parties in the United States.

16. Use technical decisions of the courts to weaken basic American institutions by claiming their activities violate civil rights.

17. Get control of the schools. Use them as transmission belts for socialism and current Communist propaganda. Soften the curriculum. Get control of teachers'

associations. Put the party line in textbooks.

18. Gain control of all student newspapers.

19. Use student riots to foment public protests against programs or organizations which are under Communist attack.

20. Infiltrate the press. Get control of book-review assignments, editorial writing, and policymaking positions.

21. Gain control of key positions in radio, TV, and motion pictures.

22. Continue discrediting American culture by degrading all forms of artistic expression. An American Communist cell was told to "eliminate all good sculpture from parks and buildings, substitute shapeless, awkward and meaningless forms."

23. Control art critics and directors of art museums. "Our plan is to promote ugliness, repulsive, meaningless art."

24. Eliminate all laws governing obscenity by calling them "censorship" and a violation of free speech and free press.

25. Break down cultural standards of morality by promoting pornography and obscenity in books, magazines, motion pictures, radio, and TV.

26. Present homosexuality, degeneracy and promiscuity as "normal, natural, and healthy."

27. Infiltrate the churches and replace revealed religion with "social" religion. Discredit the Bible and emphasize the need for intellectual maturity which does not need a "religious crutch."

28. Eliminate prayer or any phase of religious expression in the schools on the ground that it violates the principle of "separation of church and state." (Remember these goals were published to expose them in 1958. Coincidence?)

29. Discredit the American Constitution by calling it inadequate, old-fashioned, out of step with modern needs, a hindrance to cooperation between nations on a worldwide basis.

30. Discredit the American Founding Fathers. Present them as selfish aristocrats who had no concern for the "common man."

31. Belittle all forms of American culture and discourage the teaching of American history on the ground that it was only a minor part of the "big picture." Give more emphasis to Russian history since the Communists took over.

32. Support any socialist movement to give centralized control over any part of the culture—education, social agencies, welfare programs, mental health clinics, etc.

33. Eliminate all laws or procedures which interfere

with the operation of the Communist apparatus.

34. Eliminate the House Committee on Un-American Activities.

35. Discredit and eventually dismantle the FBI.

36. Infiltrate and gain control of more unions.

37. Infiltrate and gain control of big business.

38. Transfer some of the powers of arrest from the police to social agencies. Treat all behavioral problems as psychiatric disorders which no one but psychiatrists can understand [or treat].

39. Dominate the psychiatric profession and use mental health laws as a means of gaining coercive control over those who oppose Communist goals.

40. Discredit the family as an institution. Encourage promiscuity and easy divorce.

41. Emphasize the need to raise children away from the negative influence of parents. Attribute prejudices, mental blocks and retarding of children to suppressive influence of parents.

42. Create the impression that violence and insurrection are legitimate aspects of the American tradition; that students and special-interest groups should rise up and use ["] united force ["] to solve economic, political or social problems.

43. Overthrow all colonial governments before native populations are ready for self-government.

44. Internationalize the Panama Canal.

45. Repeal the Connally reservation so the United States cannot prevent the World Court from seizing jurisdiction [over domestic problems. Give the World Court jurisdiction] over nations and individuals alike.

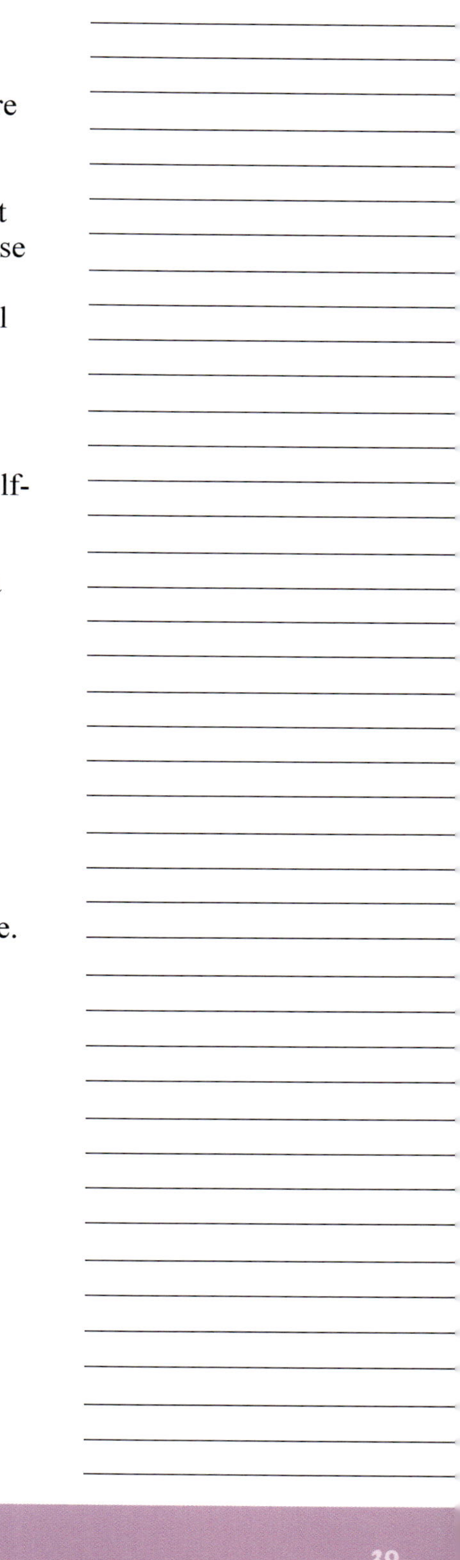

The Pillars of Liberty
LIBERTY
FAITH
VIRTUE
PATRIOTISM
LIBERTY BEGINS AT HOME

RELATED QUOTES

"Very few generations have been granted the role of defending freedom in its maximum hour of danger. This is that moment and you are that generation! Now is the time to defend our freedoms." - **Judge Andrew Napolitano**

"It is easier to build strong children than to repair broken men." - **Frederick Douglas**

"If we could have but one generation of properly born, trained, educated and healthy children, a thousand problems of government would vanish." - **Herbert Hoover**

"A mother's greatest act of Patriotism is manifest in the nurture and care of her own family. By instilling in our children the Faith that God is the author of freedom, and sowing seeds of Virtue in their hearts, we are establishing a foundation of freedom where liberty can grow and prosper." - **Kimberly Fletcher**

"If our country is worth dying for in time of war let us resolve that it is truly worth living for in time of peace." -**Hamilton Fish**

"It has always seemed to me that the great problem is to elevate the nation and place it on a higher level. Two factors, the man and the woman, must co-operate for this end, and it lies especially with the mothers of the people, by slow and strenuous work, to arouse in it a conscious sense of culture and discipline. To the woman, then, we must look for the solution of the problem of humanity. It must come from them as mothers: that is the mission that lies before them." - **Heinrik Ibsen**

"Home…is the great conservator of good, the "seeding place of virtue." It is the origin of all civilization. The laws of a nation are but rescripts of its domestic codes. The words uttered and doctrines taught around the fireside are the influences that shape the destinies of empires." - **C.E. Sargent, Our Home**

"It is the influences of home that live in the life of kingdoms, while parental counsel repeats itself in the voices of republics. We would impress upon the minds of our readers this grand truth, and would that we might thunder it into the ears of all mankind, that a nation is but a magnified home."
- **C.E. Sargent, Our Home**

"The light is what guides you home, the warmth is what keeps you there." - **Ellie Rodriguez**

"There is a magic in that little world, home; it is a mystic circle that surrounds comforts and virtues never known beyond its hallowed limits." - **Robert Southey**

"The strength of a nation derives from the integrity of the home." - **Confucius**

FROM THE FOUNDERS

"All government originates in families, and if neglected there, it will hardly exist in society . . . The foundation of all free government and of all social order must be laid in families. . ."
- **Noah Webster**

"I should be pained to believe that [the American people] have forgotten that agency, which was so often manifested during our Revolution, or that they failed to consider the omnipotence of that God who is alone able to protect them." - **George Washington**

"How little do my countrymen know what precious blessings they are in possession of, and which no other people on earth enjoy?"
- **Thomas Jefferson**

"Those who expect to reap the blessings of freedom, must, like men, undergo the fatigue of supporting it." - **Thomas Paine**

"When once a Republic is corrupted, there is no possibility of remedying any of the growing evils but by removing the corruption and restoring its lost principles; every other correction is either useless or a new evil." - **Thomas Jefferson**

"Posterity, you will never now how much it has cost my generation to preserve your freedom. I hope you will make good use of it." - **John Adams**

"Freedom can exist only in the society of knowledge. Without learning, men are incapable of knowing their rights, and where learning is confined to a few people, liberty can be neither equal nor universal." - **Benjamin Rush**

Journal

"It has always seemed to me that the great problem is to elevate the nation and place it on a higher level. Two factors, the man and the woman, must cooperate for this end, and it lies especially with the mothers of the people, by slow and strenuous work, to arouse in it a conscious sense of culture and discipline. To the woman, then, we must look for the solution of the problem of humanity. It must come from them as mothers: that is the mission that lies before them."
-Heinrik Ibsen

PRESENTATION THREE

Ladies First

"Righteous women in their circle of influence, beginning in the home, can turn the world around."

~Alexis de Tocqueville

PREPARATION

To prepare yourself to lead this presentation please review and consider the following material:

- Read "Gathering Place" provided in the Supplemental Materials of this presentation.

- View the videos "Hands of Heaven" and "Invisible Woman" provided in the Hostess Resource Center on the Moms for America® website www.MomsforAmerica.us

- Read "Women's Influence" chapter excerpt from W*OMEN: America's Last Best Hope* (excerpt provided in Hostess Resource Center)

- Review Principle 8 of the *5000 Year Leap*

- Optional: Review Vignette 13.6 in *Promises of the Constitution* (available in MFA online store)

PURPOSE

The purpose of this presentation is to help women realize their powerful influence in their home and family, the community, and the nation; if we are to heal our nation, we must begin by first educating ourselves.

KEY POINTS

- Women have a divine and essential role in God's plan for his children on earth and were held in reserve as the final and crowning act of the creation

- The role of motherhood is vital to the human race and was first recognized by Adam, who called his companion Eve, because she was the mother of all living

- Men and women both have been endowed by their Creator with certain unalienable rights

Home Assignment

Read "The Gathering Place" included in the Supplemental Materials of this presentation.

Personal Study

Watch the video "The Invisible Woman" in the Cottage Meeting Resources on the MFA website.

Family Enrichment

Honoring Mother: Ask a father or oldest male in the home to take the lead in honoring the mother for 2 weeks. Open the door for her, maintain clean language in her presence, offer assistance. Evaluate the feelings in the home after two weeks.

Read *Patriots In Petticoats*, by Patricia Edwards Clyne, together with your children. Use the Internet to search for pictures and/or locations of the monuments and historic sites mentioned at the end of each chapter. If one of these historic sites is near your home, take a day trip to go and see it.

MEETING OUTLINE

Welcome & Gathering

We recommend starting your meeting with a prayer and the Pledge of Allegiance.

Read or Summarize:

Women are a powerful influence—especially mothers. The mothers of a country mold its citizens, determine its institutions, and shape its destiny. There is no person who has greater influence on society than a mother. There are many examples of the incredible influence of mothers in the lives of their children, but it is rare that these contributions to society are seen by anyone but those in their own family. On rare occasion, however, a book or a movie comes out that celebrates the positive influence of women. *Gifted Hands* is just such a movie.

During the last presentation, we became familiar with Dr. Ben Carson. In this presentation, you have the opportunity to get to know the incredible mother who dramatically influenced his life. Not only did Sonya Carson's son become a world-renowned neurosurgeon, he also spoke very eloquently of the blessings of liberty, the greatness of America—and millions of people all over the world heard him speak. "I not only saw and felt the difference my mother made in my life," said Dr. Carson, "I am still living out that difference as a man."

Sonya Carson is a mother who planted seeds of faith, virtue, and patriotism in the hearts of her sons, and Dr. Ben Carson is the perfect example of the kind of fruit that can come from the tender nurturing of those seeds.

Show Video: *Invisible Woman* (available in Hostess Resource Center)

How does God, the Creator of our earth, view the role of women?

See Bible References Psalms 127:3, 2 Tim. 1: 5-7, Prov. 31:10-31

Read & Discuss (optional): *Promises of the Constitution* - Vignette 13. 6

"If we mean to have heroes, statesmen and philosophers, we should have learned women." - **Abigail Adams**

Show Video: clip from the film *"Generation Zero"* (Available in the Hostess Resource Center)

"The woman...who deserts the cradle in order to help defend civilization against the barbarians may well later meet, among the barbarians, her own neglected child." - **Neal Maxwell**

What does this quote tell us about our role as women and mothers?

How does our influence in the home impact our culture and the future of our nation?

Read or Summarize: "The Gathering Place" provided in the Supplemental Materials of this presentation.

"Freedom is never more than one generation away from extinction. We didn't pass it to our children in the bloodstream. It must be fought for, protected, and handed on for them to do the same, or one day we will spend our sunset years telling our children and our children's children what it was once like in the United States where men were free." - Ronald Reagan

How can we, in our role as mothers, secure the blessings of liberty for future generations?

Summary

Summarize your thoughts on the material covered in this presentation

- Give the Home Assignment for the next meeting

- Announce date, time, and location for next meeting

ADDITIONAL PRESENTATION IDEAS

Show Movie: *Gifted Hands: The Ben Carson Story*

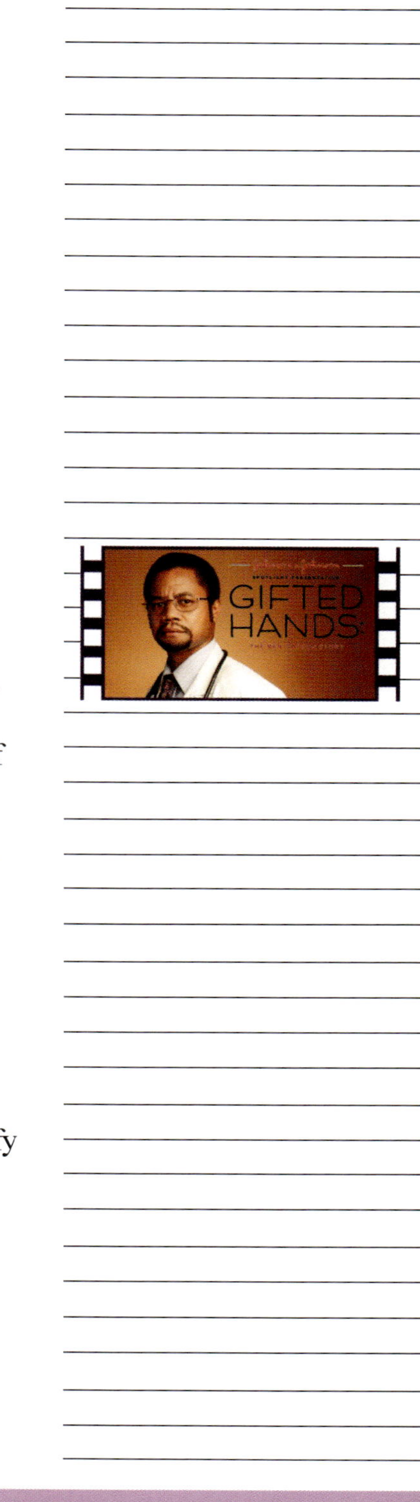

In the "Anchored in Hope" presentation, we highlighted the National Prayer Breakfast speech by Ben Carson. *Gifted Hands* is a feature film depicting his real-life story and the amazing woman who raised him. Cuba Gooding Jr. stars in this true story about a renowned brain surgeon who overcame obstacles to change the course of medicine forever. Young Ben Carson didn't have much of a chance. Growing up in a broken home amongst poverty and prejudice, his grades suffered, and his temper flared. And yet, his mother never lost her faith in him. Insisting he follow the opportunities she never had, she helped to grow his imagination, intelligence and, most importantly, his belief in himself. That faith would be his gift—the thing that would drive him to follow his dream of becoming one of the world's leading neurosurgeons. The film depicts the powerful, true story of the incredible influence of a mother's love. The film is available to purchase online or view on Amazon Prime.

Dr. Glenn Kimber teaches that an "unalienable right" is the right to perform a responsibility given to us by God. Use the following Bible references to identify God-given responsibilities and connect them with unalienable rights:

- Genesis 1:28

- Deuteronomy 11:19, 22, Deuteronomy 13:4

- Isaiah 54:13

- Ephesians 6:4

Discuss the difference between a right and a privilege (Refer to *5000 Year Leap* introduction pages 28-33 and Principle 8).

MINI COTTAGE IDEAS

Mini Cottages are designed especially for moms of preschoolers and moms who work full-time jobs. Moms simply read and/or watch the same materials at home, on their own, then meet together once a week in a playdate or over lunch during the workday to discuss what they read. The articles and videos are short and can usually be read and/or viewed in less than hour. Below are some suggestions to host mini cottage discussions under the "Ladies First" theme.

- Read the short book essay "When Queens Ride By" available to purchase online

- Read "Gathering Place" found in the Supplemental Materials of this presentation.

- View the videos *Hands of Heaven* and *Invisible Woman* provided in the Hostess Resource Center on the Moms for America® website www.MomsforAmerica.us

- Read "Women's Influence" chapter excerpt from *WOMEN: America's Last Best Hope* (excerpt provided in Hostess Resource Center)

- Review & Discuss Principle 8 of the *5000 Year Leap*

COTTAGE MEETING BOOK CLUB

For those who like the book club format, we've compiled a list of great books to help you gain an appreciation and foundational understanding of the concepts presented in "Ladies First."

When Queens Ride By by Agnes Sligh Turnbull, 1926

When Queens Ride By is a charming story illustrating the tremendous impact a woman can have on her family and how the woman truly is the heart of the home. Great inspiration for any woman fee;omg overwhelmed and discouraged by trying to keep everything together. This wonderful story brings new hope and new light. It will touch your heart, make you smile, and renew your courage to move forward with your efforts to make your home a warm and comfortable place for your family to live, love, and prosper. A short 30 minute read, and well worth the time.

It Takes A Mother to Raise A Village by Colleen Down

While the old African proverb of "it takes a village to raise a child" sounds appealing, perhaps the realities of life are more accurately conveyed in the story of *The Little Red Hen*. "Who will help me potty train my child?" asks the mother, "Not I," says the village. "Who will help me clean up this third glass of spilt milk?" asks the mother. "Not I," says the village. "Who will help put braces on my child's teeth?" asks the mother. "Not I," says the village. "Who wants to use my child to further their own political agendas?'" asks the mother. "WE DO," says the village. The irony of motherhood is that there has not been a spokesperson for mothers because those who feel most passionately are simply too busy. Full time Mom, Colleen Down, has decided to ignore her buzzing dryer and ringing phone long enough to stand up and defend those whose profession it is to rock the cradle, and to remind them once again that they truly do have the power to change the world.

WOMEN: America's Last Best Hope by Kimberly Fletcher

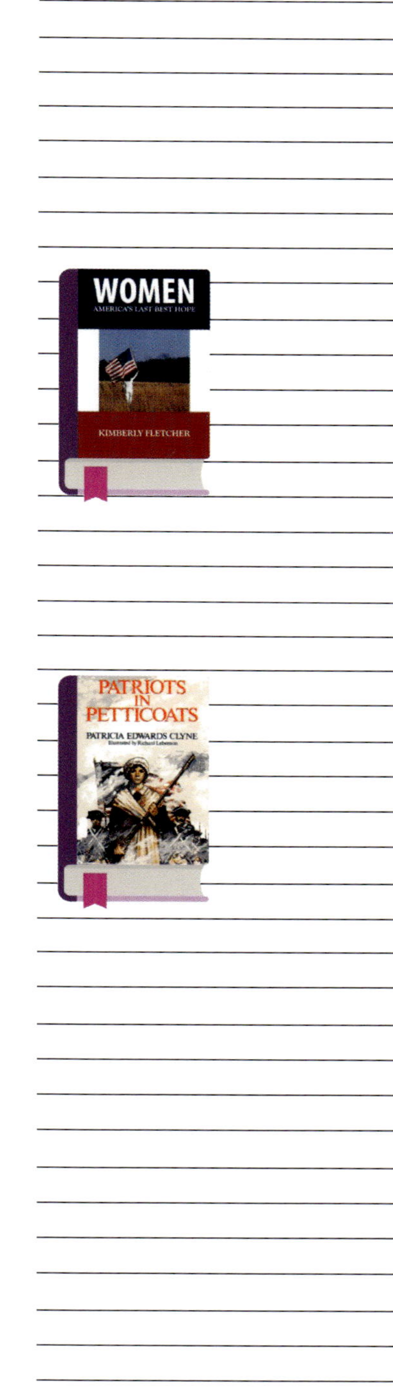

At a time in our history when our nation stands at the pivotal crossroads of enduring freedom or endless servitude, we need to do everything we can to educate and enlighten our citizens on America's history, heritage, and founding principles of liberty, and there is no better place to start than with the women of America. *Women: America's Last Best Hope* is as an educational, inspirational, eye-opening experience—a refreshing outlook presented with a combination of true grit and endearing eloquence that only a woman can get away with. A must read for every woman who is hungering for truth, seeking direction, and yearning for a voice.

Patriots In Petticoats by Patricia Edwards Clyne

The role played by women during the years fighting for this country's independence is little known to most Americans. This is a great primer to get you started. Among those covered in this book are Penelope Barker, Mary Lindley Murray, Margaret Corbin, Sybil Ludington, Lydia Darragh, Nancy Hart, Mary Hays, Sally Townsend, Tempe Wick, Phebe Reynolds, Betty Zane, "Mad Anne" Bailey, and many others. While most people are unfamiliar with these incredible women, after you read their stories, you will come to know and even love them for the women they were and all they did for the cause of liberty.

The book contains more than twenty brief biographies of women who fought for their country's independence. A special feature of the book is that, at the end of each story, you will find information on related historic sites and markers that can be visited today.

NOTE: Make sure and get the version by Patricia Edwards Clyne. There was a newer version written by another author, but it isn't near as good.

COTTAGE MEETING FOR KIDS

Cottage Meeting for Kids is a liberty promoting program for the entire family and focused on children from preschool to teens. It is full of great stories and fun activities to help children gain a love of liberty. Families can join together each month for an Activity Day to share the concepts they've learned and enhance them through group activities. Here are some ideas to promote the concepts presented in "Ladies First." You can find additional ideas, outlines, and activities on the Moms for America® website under "Cottage Meetings for Kids."

- Middle and High School age boys can review the audio "Knighthood: Be A Man" by Dan Ralphs (available in Cottage Resources on the MFA website)

- Great films to watch as a family and discuss are *Follow Me Boys* and *Courageous*

- Create discussion activities to help boys understand how to respect girls/women and girls how to be ladies and respect boys/men (see articles in Cottage Resources under "Ladies First" for ideas)

Recommended Programs to teach Freedom and American Values

- American Heritage Girls (AmericanHeritageGirls.org)

- Trail Life USA for Boys (TrailLifeUSA.com)

- Heroic Youth: Crowned With Virtue Clubs for girls and Mastering Knighthood Clubs for boys. (HeroicYouth.com)

Book & Movie List

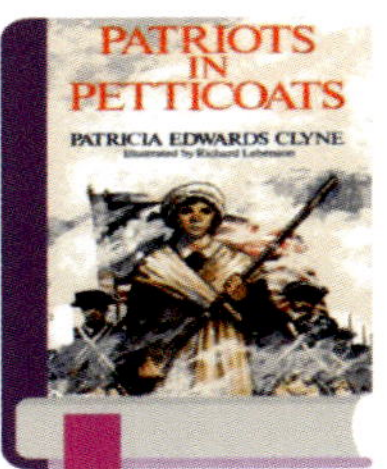

Patriots in Petticoats
by Patricia Edwards Clyne

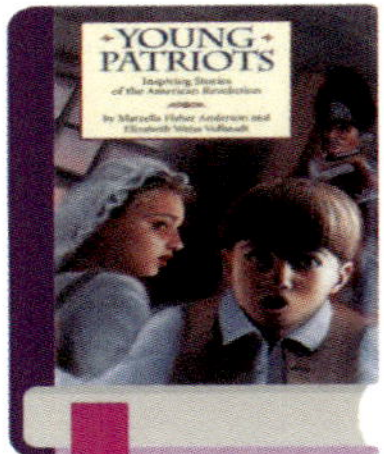

Young Patriots
by Marcella Anderson &
Elizabeth Vollstadt

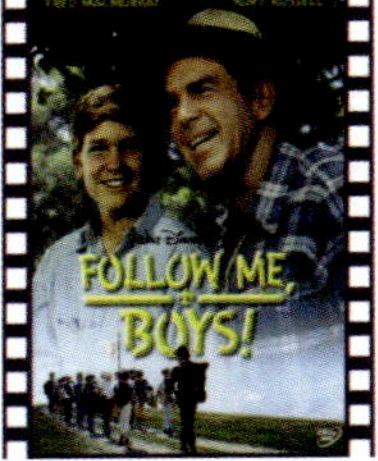

Follow Me Boys (1966)
starring Fred MacMurray

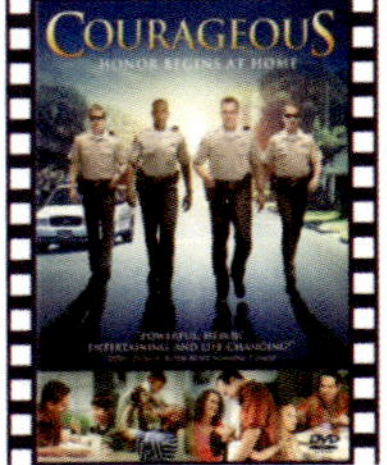

Courageous (2011)
Directed by Alex Kendrick

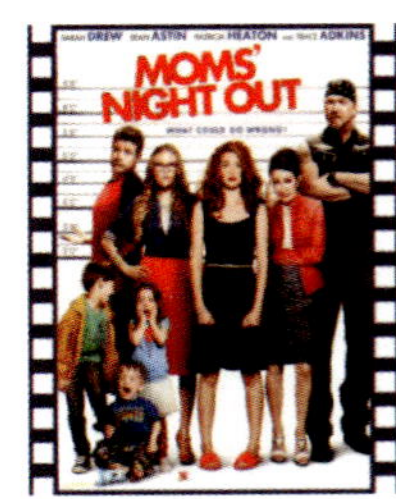

Moms Night Out (2014)
Directed by the Erwin Brothers

SUPPLEMENTAL MATERIALS

The Gathering Place

BY KIMBERLY FLETCHER

When I was a little girl, I spent every summer in a little town called Cowansville an hour north of Pittsburgh, Pennsylvania. The town was named after one of my ancestors, John Cowan, who purchased the land after the Revolutionary War. For over 200 years, our family called the town home. When my mother was growing up, the little town was home to her eleven aunts and uncles and a virtual army of cousins. And at the center of it all was our family homestead where my great-grandparents (Charles and Jesse) lived and where the family gathered for holidays, picnics, and special occasions. It was affectionately known as the Gathering Place, and beautiful memories that would bind the family together for generations were created there.

My great-grandma, known to all as Grandma Jesse, birthed eleven babies in that house. It was the place where her sons would leave to serve in the Second World War and where jubilant celebrations were held upon their safe return. The Homestead sat on a small hill off an old dirt road. Lining the front of the house were eleven soaring pine trees—one for each one of Grandma Jesse's children, which she carefully planted with her own hands. I spent a lot of summers climbing in those trees as a child. My mother told me it was a favorite place for her and her cousins as well.

When my mother was a young girl, my great-grandfather passed away and

Grandma Jesse gave the homestead to my grandfather and decided to move into the old parson's house next to the town church. After Grandma moved from the homestead, it was her oldest daughter, my Aunt Helen, who would open her home as the new family gathering place. And that was the gathering place of my childhood.

Each summer, for as long as I can remember, my parents would drive me to Cowansville, and I would spend several weeks with Grandma Jesse. To this day, when I hear the sweet sound of birds singing in the morning, my mind is taken back to the memory of that little town.

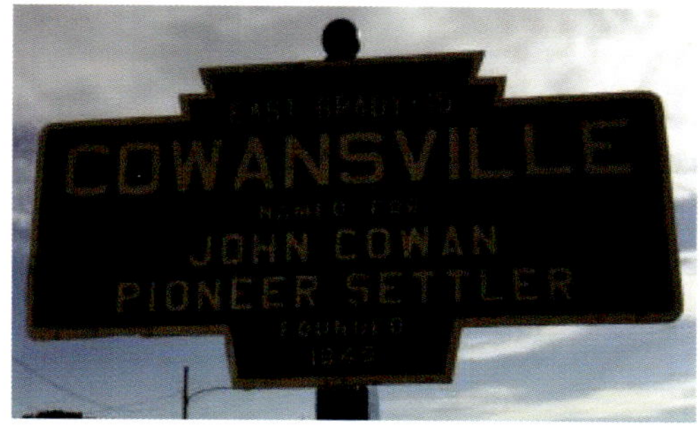

There were a lot of special places in Cowansville, but my favorite was Grandma's front porch. It seemed as if you could see the whole world from there. It was the perfect view to witness the bustle at Uncle George's store across the street. And we had a front row seat to all the campers and travelers driving to Paradise Park to see Minnie Pearl or Roy Clark. The whole Hee-Haw gang performed at the park at one time or another. There were so many things to do and see in the little town, but for me, there was none more magical then Aunt Helen's house.

Aunt Helen's house was a bit of heaven for a little girl with a big imagination and thirst for adventure. The fruit orchards behind the house burst with apples and pears that Aunt Helen converted into delicious pies and preserves. Gathering the fruit was one of my favorite things because they used a wagon pulled by my Uncle's big green tractor. I just plopped in the back and enjoyed the ride.

A small pathway connected the garage (where they kept the tractor) to the house where everyone gathered. Along the pathway was a large white arbor laden with the scent of sweet smelling lilacs that floated through the air all summer long. Next to the arbor lay a little cement patio with a small, intricately designed, white caste iron table and two matching chairs. That little corner was one of my most favorite places as a child. I held all my best tea parties at that little table, surrounded by my favorite dolls dressed in their finest attire. I felt like a princess dining in her castle garden. It was a dreamy time in a magical place. To this day, when I read the stories of fairytales and princesses, I think of those days in Cowansville.

Aunt Helen's house was often full of people and always full of love. Little things like the candy jars filled with peppermint lozenges and the sweet sound of gospel music playing on the old pump organ made everyone who entered feel welcome and at home. I remember sitting at the foot of that organ at many family gatherings as Aunt Helen played old hymns surrounded by family members

singing in harmony—"Rock of Ages," "How Great Thou Art," "The Old Rugged Cross." I learned all the old greats at the foot of that organ. Aunt Helen was a fan of country music too—especially Kenny Rogers. I was only seven years old when I had memorized "Lucille" and could sing every word by heart without skipping a beat. I had no idea what I was singing, but I was sure proud to be singing with the grown-ups.

There was always a buzz that went through the family when a distant cousin would come to town and everyone knew they would be stopping at Aunt Helen's house to catch up on family news and share the stories of their lives. Most of those stories were shared on Aunt Helen's front porch. Stretching the entire length of the front of the house, the porch was a relaxing haven filled with cozy chairs and two porch swings that hung from either end.

The whole porch just seemed to be a big welcome, sign and I guess I wasn't the only one who thought so because the entire town seemed to accept the invitation at one time or another. You never knew who would pass by and stop in, but almost everyone did. I loved to sit on the steps and listen to the stories of everyone's lives and all the news of the day. I didn't always understand what they were saying, but I sure loved hearing them talk. I can still hear the creaking of the swing, the chattering of voices, the rumble of cars going up and down the road in front of the house, and the occasional hum of a distant lawn mower filling the air with the smell of fresh cut grass.

Soon after my husband Derek and I were married, we had an opportunity to visit Cowansville. I wanted to share my most treasured memories with the man I loved, and I wanted to share him with the people I spent so much time with, so of course, we went to Aunt Helen's house.

The town had changed a lot by then. Grandma Jesse had passed away when I was twelve, and the old parson's house where she had lived for so many years, and where I had spent all those summers, had been torn down. The grass had completely grown over, and there was no sign there was ever a house there.

Uncle George retired and sold his store shortly before Grandma passed away. The postal service purchased it and converted it into a mail warehouse and post office. The rest of the town seemed pretty much the same as we came to Aunt Helen's front porch, which hadn't changed a bit.

Aunt Helen had grown late in years, her husband had passed on, and her eyesight was dwindling, but she looked as wonderful to me as she always did. My husband and I spent hours on that old porch talking to my aunt Helen that day. We shared the story of how we met, the places where we'd been, and she caught us up on all the family news. Visits to Aunt Helen's had grown fewer and fewer over the years, but Aunt Helen still seemed to have all the news. Though the days of parties and reunions were over and people stopped visiting, they all stayed connected through Aunt Helen's letters—a virtual gathering place through her pen and paper.

Just a few years after that visit, Aunt Helen passed away, and I was so glad Derek and I had a chance to make that last trip to the Gathering Place. I wondered who would keep the family connected now that Aunt Helen was gone.

In the summer of 2002, my children and I were driving through Pennsylvania on the way to visit family, and I decided to take the children to see our ancestral home. I was so excited to share all the memories of one of the happiest places of my childhood with them.

As we reached the bend that led into town my heart ached at the sight of so much change. The row of houses that once led up to the big white church was now just a big empty field of grass. Many of the houses had either been torn down or were in serious disrepair and needed to be. We drove by the old family homestead—the place that held so many years of memories as the original Gathering Place. As we passed by, I counted the pine trees in front of the house. Grandma Jesse had carefully planted one for each child—eleven in all. There were only five now. The house had been sold years earlier, and the

Pine trees in front of the homestead

new owners had no knowledge or understanding for the purpose of the trees. They didn't see the value; all they saw was an obstructed view that needed cleared. I told the children about the trees, but they just said, "That's great, Mom."

We drove down the main road and stopped at Uncle George's store. The outside looked the same, but when the children and I stepped inside, there was not even a hint of the place it used to be. The store had been completely gutted, and the only thing left was a small white room with tile floors, a large glass pass-through window, and walls lined with mailboxes. I closed my eyes, and for a moment, I could smell the old wood that once lined the floors and heard the bell that chimed when someone entered the store. Familiar sights and sounds echoed through my mind—the rattle of the old manual cash register, the chattering of neighbors shopping and collecting their mail, the smell of pipe smoke. "Mommy," my young son pulled me from my memories, "Mommy, I'm hungry."

Suddenly, the room felt cold again. All the warmth that made it a special place was gone, and I realized all my children could see were boring white walls lined with mailboxes. I gave the kids a snack, and we drove over to the cemetery where I had walked so many times with Grandma Jesse to place fresh cut flowers on family graves. As we walked through the cemetery past names of people I never met but came to know, the children became more and more restless. "Mom, this is boring," they moaned. "Can we go now?" It was apparent they weren't seeing what I could see. While I saw the history and heritage in the lives of those laid to rest in this place, all my children saw were a bunch of names of dead people who didn't matter. It was heart wrenching.

Place after place we stopped, memory after memory I shared, but their reaction was the same. They were tired; they were hungry; they were bored. "Can we go now?"

I just couldn't understand why they didn't appreciate what I was sharing with them. Why didn't they respect the places and people whose lives were immortalized in my memory? Why didn't they understand the importance of this place?

And then I realized—it was because I didn't share it with them. The reason I had such a love and respect for all those things is because Grandma Jesse allowed me to experience them. She took the time to take me to a cemetery to visit family members and tell me the stories of our family and the place we called home for two centuries.

Me and Grandma Jesse at Aunt Helen's house, 1972.

I sent the children back to the car and we headed out of town. I had one place left to show them—the

Gathering Place. I knew Aunt Helen had passed away, but I could at least show them the house and the front porch that welcomed so many guests and was the focal point for generations of family gatherings. As we crested the hill I pointed to the place where Aunt Helen lived for so many years, but to my utter shock, there was nothing there. The house was gone!

Devastated and stunned, I pulled over and called my mother to ask what had happened. She said that after Aunt Helen passed away her grandchildren put the house up for sell and auctioned off all her things. A few years later, the house caught fire and burned to the ground. The place our family had gathered for half a century was now nothing but a vacant lot!

With aching heart and tear-filled eyes, I drove out of town that day. Everything I knew was gone. The town that was once the picture-perfect backdrop for a Norman Rockwall painting was now just a shell of what it once was. I couldn't help the regret I felt at not sharing the stories of this place and the people who had lived there with my children. I felt such loss as I realized that, because of my neglect, the memory of this place that lived and breathed through our family for two hundred years…would die with me.

As I contemplated my experience in Cowansville that summer, I started to think about all the things I hadn't shared with my children. What else was dear to me that I should have shared with them and didn't? It wasn't long before I had my answer.

We were reading a book about the Founding Fathers and the Declaration of Independence one day after the children came home from school when my daughter, fourteen at the time, made a comment that left me utterly speechless. I was in the process of reading, "We hold these truths to be self-evident: That all men are created equal…" when my daughter interrupted me to explain that "What they really meant was that these rights were for wealthy, white, landing owning men with a secondary education. They believed that equality was only for this exclusive group."

> *Freedom is never more than one generation away from extinction. We didn't pass it to our children in the bloodstream. It must be fought for, protected, and handed on for them to do the same, or one day we will spend our sunset years telling our children and our children's children what it was once like in the United States where men were free.*
>
> –Ronald Reagan

I was stunned. And the question I had asked over and over again since 9-11 "how did we get here" was answered. Our history was being rewritten. Our people were being stripped of their heritage. The Founding Families who had sacrificed so much were being denigrated. Our founding documents were being disregarded and distorted. All the things I counted on our children learning in school—because I learned them—were no longer being taught. Our legacy was being stolen, and we had to reclaim it!

Suddenly, I realized just how vital I was, not only to my children, but to the preservation of America. How can future generations ever understand and embrace the history, heritage, and legacy of liberty that is uniquely American if we don't share it with our children? My heart ached at the thought of my children seeing the United States Constitution as just words on paper or looking at the images of our Founding Fathers and seeing nothing but a bunch of dead people who didn't matter. Would they stand in front of the Statue of Liberty, the Lincoln Memorial, or Constitution Hall like they did our family homestead and say "That's great, Mom" with complete disinterest? The answer was up to me. Would I be the bridge crossing the liberty gap that would link generations in freedom or would it die with me? I knew, for everything I hold dear, I had to be the bridge. I had to reclaim the American Legacy, and I had to start with me.

Sonya Carson: The Mother Who Influenced the Man

Learn to do your best. God will do the rest. **-Sonya Carson**

Dr. Benjamin Carson, the famous neurosurgeon from John Hopkins University, Baltimore, Maryland, attributes his mother, Sonya Carson, as the reason for his success in life. "I not only saw and felt the difference my mother made in my life, I am still living out that difference as a man."

But the story of this remarkable women goes even deeper than what you see in the film.

Sonya Carson was one of 24 siblings—half of whom she never even knew. Sonya grew up in foster homes until the age of thirteen when she married a man who called her his

"china doll." Some years later they had two sons—Curtis and Ben. When the boys were just 10 and 8, Sonya found out her husband was a bigamist, and she made the difficult decision to leave him.

Sonya only had a third grade education, and she did not know how to read. But neither that nor trials or difficult circumstances she faced kept her down. In spite of everything, she rose above the challenges of her life and made every effort to be the

best she could be and do the best she could to provide for her little family on her own.

Sonya found herself in a desperate situation. What could she, an illiterate mother who had married at 13, was now divorced, and struggled off and on with serious depression, do to help her growing boys? She worked such long hours cleaning houses that she wasn't even there during the kids' after-school time—often not arriving home until they were in bed.

Sonya knew she had to do something to help her boys begin to live up to their potential. She had no idea what to do, but she knew God did. So she prayed and asked God for wisdom and guidance. And he blessed her with it. Sonya began to pay attention to the things the people she worked for did. She recognized they were high achievers, and she wanted that for her

sons. She noticed that these people read a lot of books, so Sonya decided her sons need to read if they were to live up to their potential. She told her sons they were to choose and read two library books per week and she limited them to two pre-selected TV shows a week, which they could only watch when their homework was done. As if that weren't enough to frustrate these young boys, they were also required to write book reports on each book they read and turn them into their mother. And somehow, Sonya was able to hide from them the fact that she couldn't read the reports they turned in.

Ben was beside himself when his mother told them of her expectations. He had never read a book in his life. And how would he live with almost no TV? To top it off, Ben had a terrible temper that even he realized would land him in jail one day if he didn't learn to control it. But his mother continued to believe in him.

Sonya repeatedly told her sons that they could do anything anybody else could do, and do it better, if they would only work hard at it. She always had faith in them, and she never accepted excuses. She made none for herself, and would accept none from them—for their own good.

Sonya Carson's life motto is: "Learn to do your best, and God will do the rest." She put this motto into practice, and it served her well as she struggled in raising her two sons, cope with anxiety and depression, and tried to make ends meet. Sonya, having no friends, said she turned to God because she had no one else. "God," she said, "you're going to have to be my friend, my best friend. And, you're going to have to tell me how to do things and give me wisdom, because I don't know what to do." (*Gifted Hands: The Ben Carson Story*, by Ben Carson)

Sonya's relationship with God gave her the wisdom to put boundaries around Curtis and Ben, helped them overcome their weaknesses, and gave her the strength to persevere despite the insurmountable odds. Sonya's perseverance in her sons' educations paid off. Ben Carson's grades began to improve during the second half of fifth grade. He went on to succeed in school. He graduated from high school and later from Yale University.

Today, Dr. Carson is world renowned neurosurgeon who became famous with the groundbreaking surgery to separate conjoined twins who were joined at the head. Dr. Carson has co-authored three books about his life called—*Gifted Hands; Think Big: Unleashing Your Potential for Excellence; and The Big Picture*. But to this day he attributes his success, and the man he has become, to the mother who raised him.

Sonya Carson is a remarkable woman who overcame hardship, poverty, single- motherhood, and depression to work hard to raise two sons in the inner city. Today she is witness to the fruits of her labors. Both her sons grew up to be successful men—Ben as a neurosurgeon and Curtis as an aeronautical engineer—as she believed they would, and because she held true to her motto, and instilled it in the lives of her children: "Learn to do your best. God will do the rest."

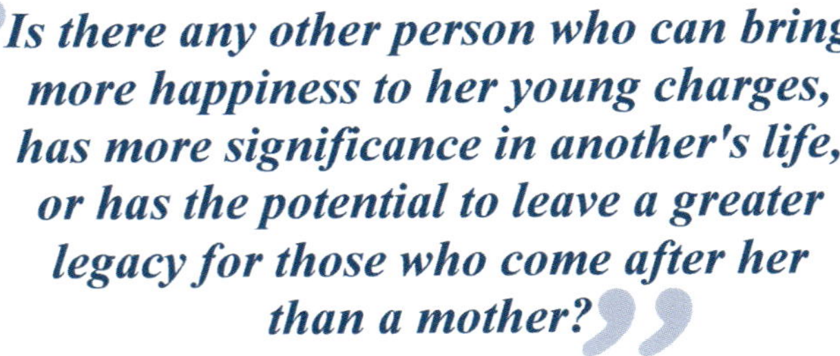

RELATED QUOTES

"On every mother's bosom there rests a bud of promise, and whether or not that promise shall be fulfilled depends upon her. Whether that bud shall blossom into a pure and fragrant rose or into the flower of the deadly nightshade is at the option of the guardian."

-C.E. Sargent, Our Home

"To a great extent, the level of any civilization is the level of its womanhood. When a man loves a woman, he has to become worthy of her. The higher her virtue, the more noble her character, the more devoted she is to truth, justice, and goodness, the more a man has to aspire to be worthy of her. The history of civilization could actually be written in terms of the level of its women."

-Archbishop Fulton Sheen

"Motherhood is the greatest potential influence either for good or ill in human life. The mother's image is the first that stamps itself on the unwritten page of the young child's mind. It is her caress that first awakens a sense of security, her kiss, the first realization of affection; her sympathy and tenderness, the first assurance that there is love in the world."

-David McKay

"Saruman believes it is only great power that can hold evil in check, but that is not what I have found. I've found it is the small, everyday deeds of ordinary folk that keep the darkness at bay. Small acts of kindness and love."

-J.R.R. Tolkien, The Hobbit

"We fancy that God can only manage his world with battalions, when all the while he is doing it by beautiful babies. When a wrong wants righting, or a truth needs preaching or a continent wants opening, God sends a baby into the world, perhaps in a simple home and of some obscure mother. And then God puts the idea into the mother's heart, and she puts it into the baby's mind. And then God waits. The greatest forces in the world are not the earthquakes and thunderbolts. The greatest forces in the world are babies."

-E.T. Sullivan

"Some mothers in today's world feel "cumbered" by home duties and are thus attracted by other more "romantic" challenges. Such women could make the same error of perspective that Martha made. The woman, for instance, who deserts the cradle in order to help defend civilization against the barbarians may well later meet, among the barbarians, her own neglected child."

-Neal Maxwell

"Educate the women, and the men will be educated. Let the ladies understand the great doctrine of seeking the greatest good, of loving their neighbors as themselves; let them indoctrinate their children in this fundamental truth, and we shall have wise legislators."

-Mary Lyon

"The world has enough women who are tough; we need women who are tender. There are enough women who are coarse; we need women who are kind. There are enough women who are rude; we need women who are refined. We have enough women of fame and fortune; we need more women of faith. We have enough greed; we need more goodness. We have enough vanity; we need more virtue. We have enough popularity; we need more purity."
-Margaret Nadauld

"A sufficient measure of civilization is the influence of good women."
-Ralph Waldo Emerson

"How do we get women to stop saying, 'I'm just a mother.' Or, 'I used to be such and such but now I'm just a mother?' We need to market motherhood. So I came up with a saying: 'Motherhood: 24/7 on the frontlines of humanity. Are you man enough to try it?"
-Maria Shriver

"When Matthew Vassar gave a million dollars to found Vassar College (a woman's college), he said, "I considered that the mothers of a country mold its citizens, determine its institutions, and shape its destiny."
-Matthew Vassar

"Oh, if the world could only stop long enough for one generation of mothers to be all right, what a Millennium could be begun in thirty years!"
-Helen Hunt Jackson

FROM THE FOUNDERS

"If we mean to have heroes, statesmen and philosophers, we should have learned women."
-Abigail Adams

"My mother was the most beautiful woman I ever saw. All I am I owe to my mother. I attribute my success in life to the moral, intellectual and physical education I received from her."
-George Washington

"My mother was the daughter of a Christian clergyman, and therefore bred in the faith of deliberate detestation of War...Yet, in that same spring and summer of 1775, she taught me to repeat daily, after the Lord's Prayer, and before rising from bed, the Ode of Collins on the patriot warriors... I well recollect going into the kitchen and seeing some of the men engaged in running [pewter] spoons into bullets for the use of the troops! Do you wonder that a boy of seven years of age, who witnessed this scene, should be a patriot?"
-John Quincy Adams

"The women of America have at last become principals in the glorious American controversy. Their opinions alone and their transcendent influence in society and families must lead us on to success and victory."
-Benjamin Rush

Journal

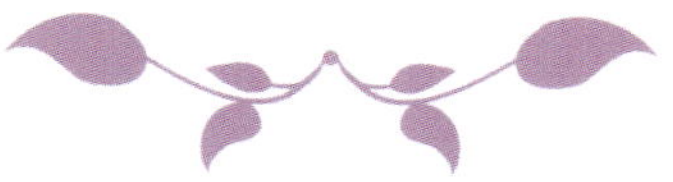

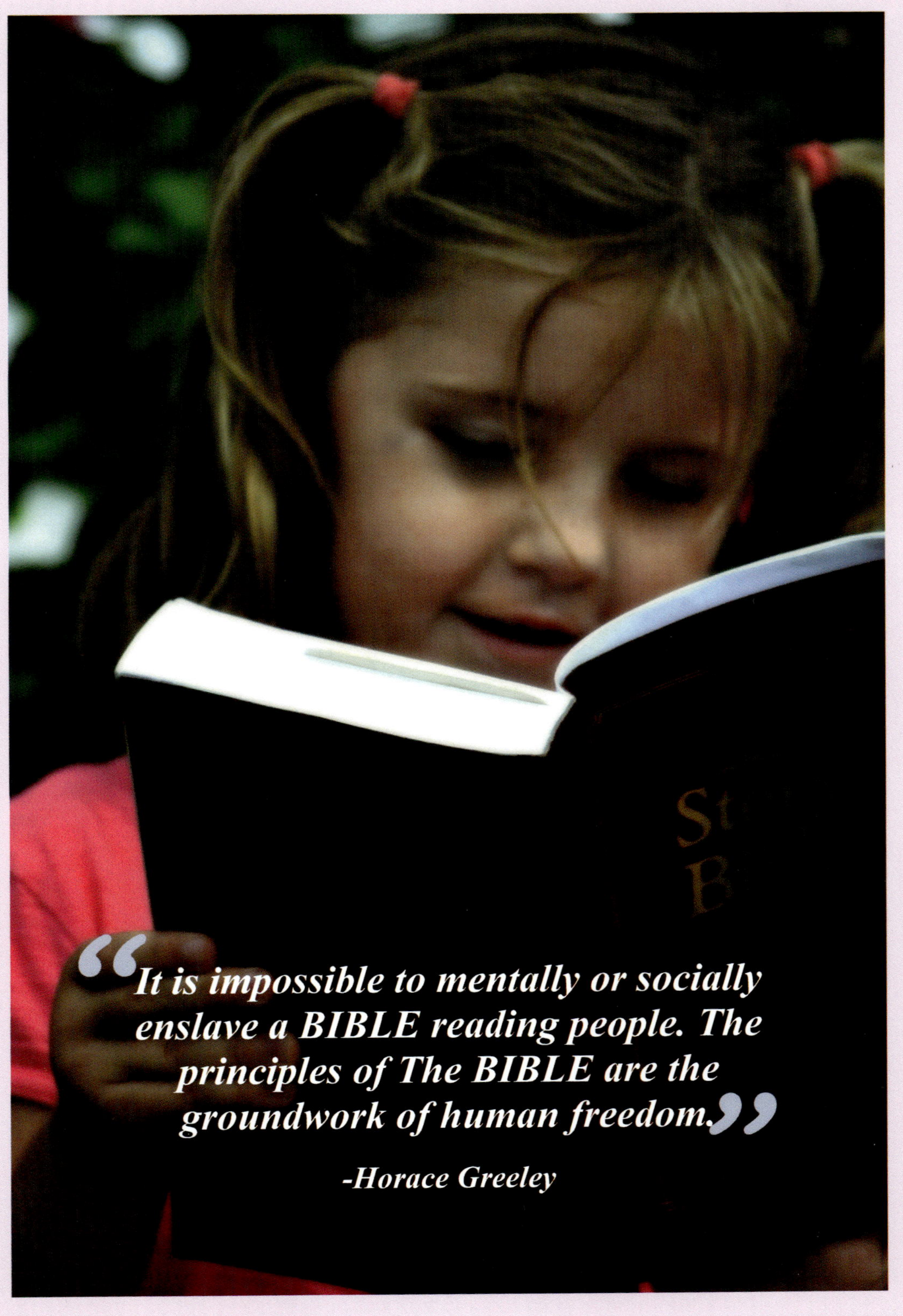

It is impossible to mentally or socially enslave a BIBLE reading people. The principles of The BIBLE are the groundwork of human freedom.
-Horace Greeley

Foundation of Faith

"Without God, there could be no American form of Government, nor an American way of life. Recognition of the Supreme Being is the first, the most basic, expression of Americanism."

~President Dwight Eisenhower

PREPARATION

To prepare yourself to lead this presentation please review and consider the following material:

- Read "A Time for Remembering" and "Born Free" found in the supplemental materials of this presentation

- View the video series *Fires of Faith* provided in the Hostess Resource Center on the Moms for America® website www.MomsforAmerica.us

- Send the Video link for *Fires of Faith* to the members of your group and encourage them to watch it before your meeting

- View the video *Pillar of Faith* provided in the Hostess Resource Center on the Moms for America® website www.MomsforAmerica.us

- Review Principles 5 in the *5000 Year Leap*

- Review the quotes found in the Supplemental Materials of this presentation

PURPOSE

The purpose of this presentation is to illustrate how God and faith were instrumental in the founding of America; Faith is the Pillar of Liberty that allows liberty to grow and prosper.

KEY POINTS

- The hand of God is evident in the establishment of freedom in America and the development of the United States Constitution

- All things were created by God; therefore, upon Him, all mankind are equally dependent, and to Him, they are equally responsible

- Without religion, the government of a free people cannot be maintained

Home Assignment

As a family, read a story from *The Story Bible* each day until the next meeting.

Personal Study

Watch the video series *"Fires of Faith"* available on the in Cottage Meeting Resources on the MFA website.

Family Enrichment

Read "The Light & the Glory for Children" together with your children. There is also an adult version.

Pray together as a family for the leaders of our country—that they may make wise decisions and seek God's guidance.

In this presentation, we introduce the first of the three Pillars of Liberty—Faith. An excellent resource to use in this presentation is *Fires of Faith*, a three-part video series we highly recommend that can be downloaded from the Cottage Meeting Resource Center.

Our Founding Families came to America with deep faith. These first families were the beneficiaries of the work of the great reformers, and as such, had been blessed with the actual written text of the Bible in their own language. It was this book that laid the groundwork and provided a firm foundation of liberty in the hearts and minds of our first families. Our Founding Fathers declared the Bible to be the rock upon which our nation was founded. Abraham Lincoln heralded the Bible as God's greatest gift to mankind. George Washington Carver attributed it as the secret to his success. And Robert E Lee credited it as his unfailing source of light and strength in his darkest hours.

Horace Greeley, an America newspaper editor in the 19th century, stated that "it is impossible to enslave mentally or socially a Bible-reading people," and further declared, "The principles of the Bible are the groundwork of human freedom." If we are to promote liberty and sustain the Republic, we must bring the Bible back into our homes and hearts. Without this Pillar, the other two Pillars will not be enough to sustain liberty. Just like the legs on a three-legged stool, no Pillar is more important than the other. It takes all three standing together to provide the stabilization needed to sustain liberty and support the stress and trials that may be inflicted upon our Republic.

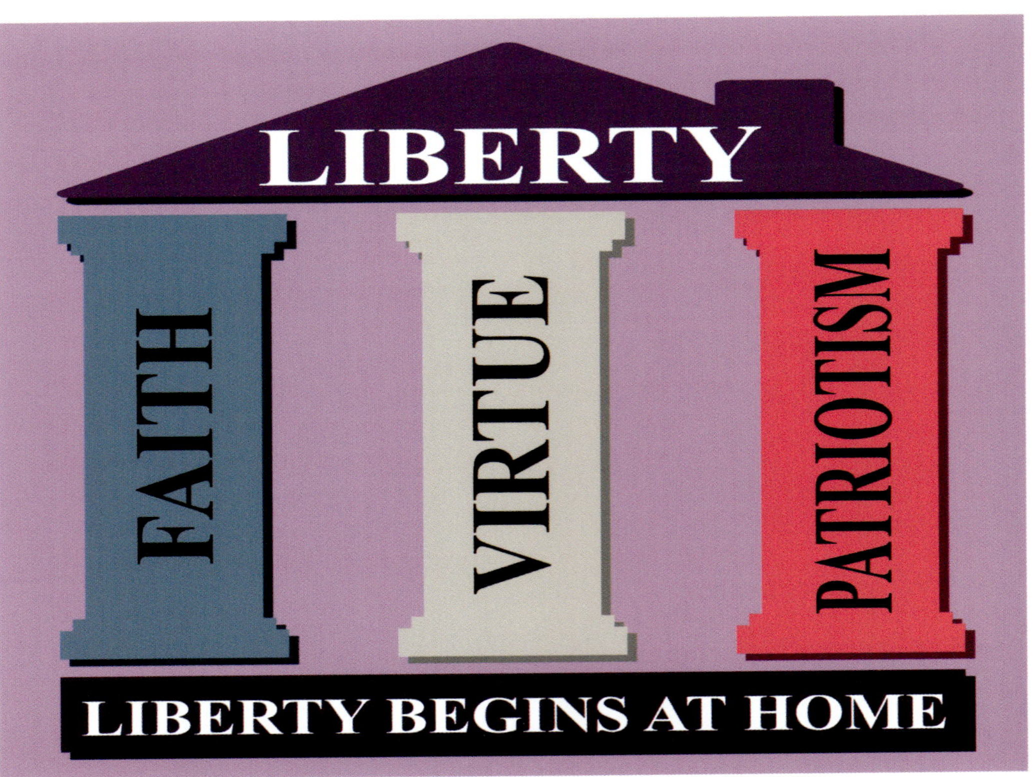

MEETING OUTLINE

Welcome & Gathering

We recommend starting your meeting with a prayer and the Pledge of Allegiance.

Show Video: *Pillar of Faith* (available in Hostess Resource Center). Ask participants to share their thoughts about the film *Fires of Faith*.

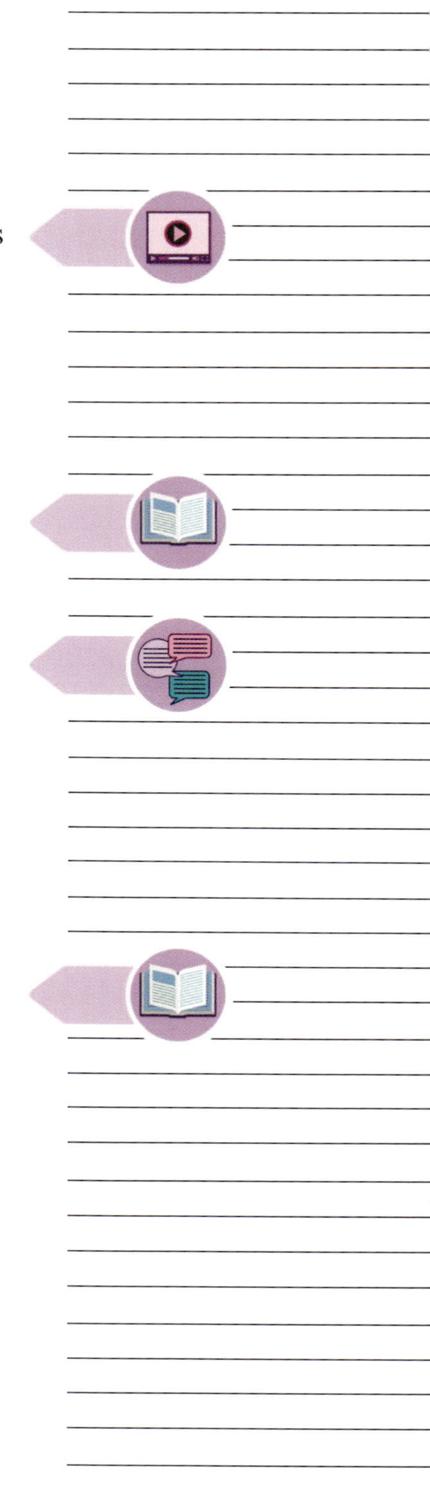

> *What role did faith play in the founding of America?*
>
> *Why is faith in God important for maintaining our freedoms today? (See Bible References Isaiah 54:13, 2 Chronicles 7:14, 2 Chronicles 3:17)*

Group Reading:

Read or have someone read "Born Free" found in the Supplemental Materials of this presentation.

Group Discussion

Faith may come naturally to some, but for many people, it must be cultivated and nourished before it can grow.

> *What tools did early Americans use to develop faith?*
>
> *What resources can we use today to develop greater faith in God? (See Bible Reference Joshua 24:14)*

Read or Summarize: "A Time for Remembering" found in the Supplemental Materials of this presentation.

Summarize: Specific points from Principle 5 of the *5000 Year Leap*.

Summary

Summarize your thoughts on the material covered in this presentation.

- Give the Home Assignment for the next meeting

- Announce date, time, and location for next meeting

ADDITIONAL PRESENTATION IDEAS

Here are some ideas for additional presentations, personal study and discussions on "A Foundation of Faith."

God's Hand in the Making of America

There is an abundance of evidence that shows the hand of God in the establishment of freedom in America. Read "God Is Too Controversial" found in the Hostess Resource Section of the Moms for America® website. Identify and record some of your favorite accounts that show the miraculous intervention of God in the colonization of America and the battle for liberty.

Read and Discuss the following short articles found in the Supplemental Materials of this presentation.

- "Message from Darrell Scott: A Columbine Father"

- "Acceptance of the Declaration of Independence is Acceptance of God as Our King"

- "God Governs in the Affairs of Men"

Show Movie: *Fires of Faith*

Read and Discuss the following quotes, additional materials, and questions"

- *"No nation is better than its sacred book. In that book are expressed its highest ideals of life, and no nation rises above those ideals. No nation has a sacred book to be compared with ours. This American nation from its first settlement at Jamestown to the present hour is based upon and permeated by the principles of the Bible. The more this Bible enters into our national life the grander and purer and better will that life become."*
  -David Josiah Brewer

- *"It is impossible to mentally or socially enslave a BIBLE reading people. The principles of The BIBLE are the groundwork of human freedom."*
  -Horace Greeley

- *"So great is my veneration for the BIBLE that the earlier my children begin to read it, the more confident will be my hope that they will prove useful citizens to their country and respectable members of society."*
  -John Quincy Adams

- *"We must be free not because we claim freedom, but because we practice it."*
  -William Faulkner

- After life, religious freedom is our first constitutionally protected right. It is important to understand that rights do not from the Constitution. There is no such thing as a "constitutional right." Our rights come from God, and the

Constitution protects our God-given rights. Therefore, we have "Constitutionally Protected Rights." It is a significant distinction and one our Founding Families understood very well. Knowing this key principle, helps us better understand Government overreach of our rights and how we can effectively address grievances to protect those rights.

- Read and Discuss Principle 4 of *The 5000 Year Leap*. If available, read *Promises of the Constitution* Vignette 13.2

- If available, read *Promises of the Constitution* sections 2 and 4 and vignette 13.2

- The chapter "Step 1: Cultivate the Soil with Faith" of *Raising Patriots: Restoring Our Garden of Liberty*

- How did the Founders of the United States establish equality for all religions?

- What is the Northwest Ordinance, and what did it emphasize should be taught in public schools?

- What are the five fundamentals of sound religion according to Benjamin Franklin?

MINI COTTAGE IDEAS

Mini Cottages are designed especially for moms of preschoolers and moms who work full-time jobs. Moms simply read and/or watch the same materials at home, on their own, then meet together once a week in a playdate or over lunch during the workday to discuss what they read. The articles and videos are short and can usually be read and/or viewed in less than hour. Below are some suggestions to host mini cottage discussions under the "Foundation of Faith" theme.

- Read Principle 5 of the *5000 Year Leap* and meet as a group to discuss the principles presented

- Read Principle 4 of the *5000 Year Leap* and meet as a group to discuss the principles presented

- Read "Born Free" and meet to discuss as a group

- Read and meet to discuss as a group

Read and Review the Quotes in the supplemental materials of this presentation. View the video *Pillar of Faith* provided in the Hostess Resource section of the Moms for America® website
- Watch Fires of Faith and meet as a group to discuss the film.

COTTAGE MEETING BOOK CLUB

For those who like the book club format, we've compiled a list of great books to help you gain an appreciation and foundational understanding of the concepts presented in "Foundation of Faith."

The 5000 Year Leap: A Miracle That Changed the World

Review Principles 4 and 5

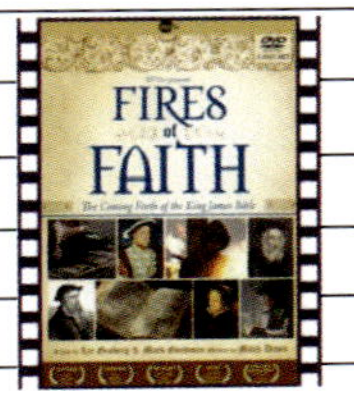

Promises of the Constitution

Review sections 1 and 2 and Vignette: 13.2

Fires of Faith

If the martyrs who brought the King James Bible into existence could still talk to us today, they would most certainly tell the tales of international politics, intrigue, subversion, bloodshed, fire, and the runaway libido of King Henry VIII that were the backdrop of its creation. These stories—along with a modern, scholarly perspective of the 16th century—are presented in *Fires of Faith: The Coming Forth of the King James Bible,* a series of films which celebrate the 400th anniversary of one of the most enduring pieces of writing in the history of humanity. An excellent film that captures the essence of the commitment, sacrifice, and blessings of the King James version of the Bible. All three episodes of this three-part series are available to view free on-line through the Cottage Meeting Resource Center. It is also available for purchase on DVD.

The Story Bible

Our Founding Fathers declared the Bible to be the rock upon which our nation was founded. American newspaper editor Horace Greeley said, "It is impossible to enslave mentally or socially a Bible-reading people. The principles of the Bible are the groundwork of human freedom."

The Story Bible, published by Libraries of Hope, lays a firm foundation in liberty. The Story Bible is a great way to introduce the beautiful stories of the Bible into the hearts of our children. The Story Bible is a unique treasure, presenting the simple stories of the Bible in Chronological order while retaining the beautiful language of the King James Version of the Bible. Available through Libraries of Hope and included in the Hostess Kit.

The Light and the Glory & The Light and the Glory for Children by Peter Marshall & David Manuel

The Light and the Glory Series and *The Light and the Glory for Children* are both exceptional works of non-fiction literature. The providential hand of God in America is clearly apparent as you read the stories of the people who founded America and hear how they felt about their experiences in their own words. The books have the same stories, they are just more detailed in the adult set. Great for reading aloud as a family.

COTTAGE MEETING FOR KIDS

Cottage Meeting for Kids is a liberty promoting program for the entire family and focused on children from preschool to teens. It is full of great stories and fun activities to help children gain a love of liberty. Families can join together each month for an Activity Day to share the concepts they've learned and enhance them through group activities. Here are some ideas to promote the concepts presented in "Foundation of Faith." You can find additional ideas, outlines, and activities on the Moms for America® website under "Cottage Meetings for Kids."

- View the film *Fires of Faith* as a family

- Read *Bulletproof George Washington* with your children.

Choose your favorite stories from the books *Miracles in American History* and *Miracle of America: Birth of A Nation* (Note: *Miracle of America* also comes with a coloring book and both are available in the Moms for America® online store.)

- Discuss 'what is a miracle' and compare the miracles from the Bible with those in the stories of America. Who creates these miracles? How can we be instruments in God's Hands to bring about miracles?

- Have the children create a script and present a mini play or puppet show of their favorite stories. Kids of all ages can participate in making puppets and presenting the show. Puppets can be simple or elaborate, from paper bags to paper mâché.

Suggested books and readings for children all ages to nurture a love of liberty in the home:

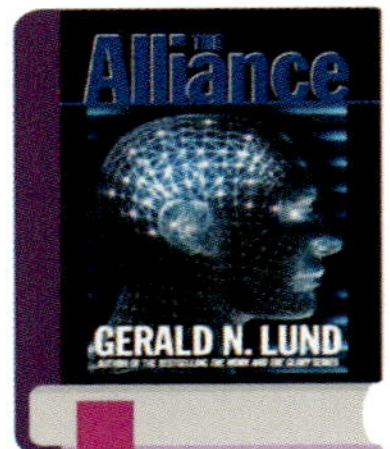

Miracles in American History
by Susan Federer

Miracle of America: Birth of A Nation y
by Bill Norton and Brian P. Trotter

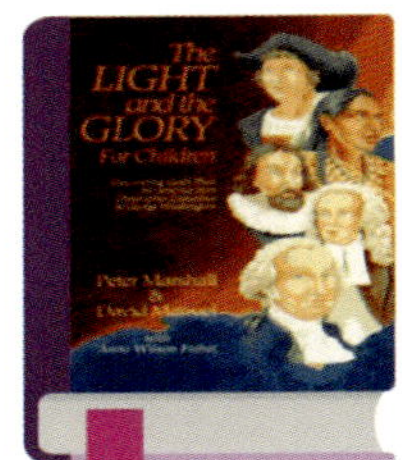

Light and the Glory for Children
by Peter Marshall and David Manuel

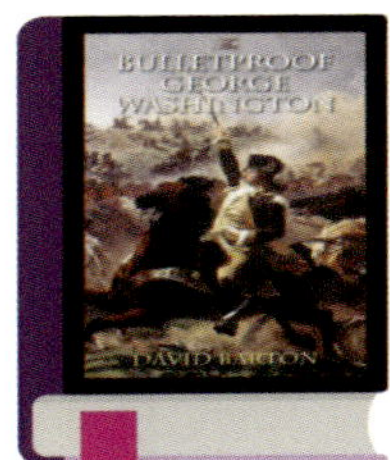

Bulletproof George Washington
by David Barton

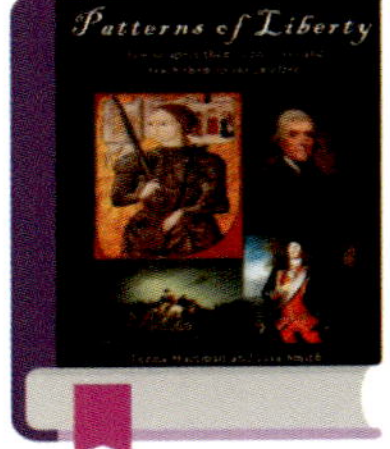

Patterns of Liberty
by Tenna Hartman

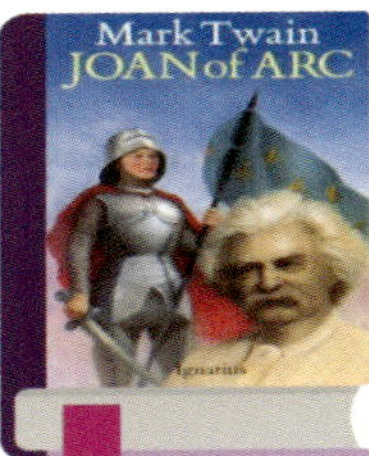

Joan of Arc
by Mark Twain

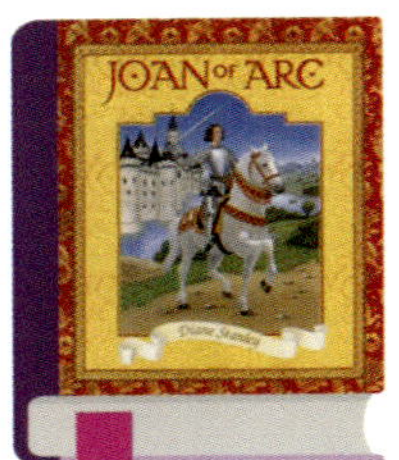

Joan of Arc
by Diane Stanley

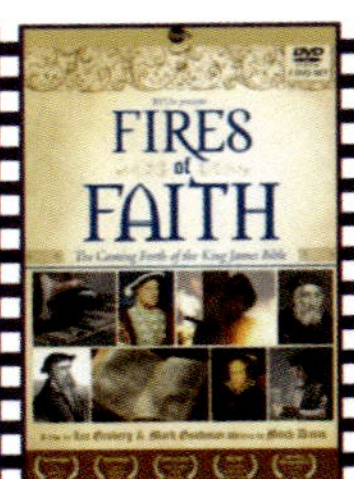

Fires of Faith
2012

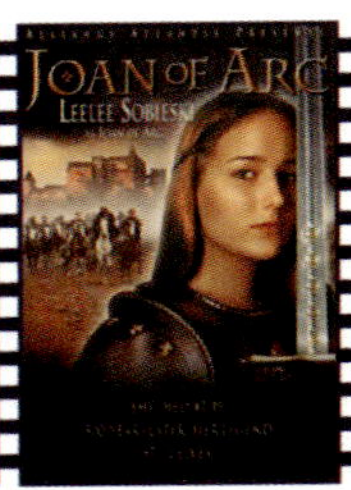

Joan of Arc
1999 miniseries

The Messenger: The Story of Joan of Arc
1999

Joan of Arc
1948

Born Free!

BY KIMBERLY FLETCHER

For five thousand years, people lived in grass houses, plowed fields with their bare hands, and lived every day just to survive. In a little over two hundred years, we have gone from grass houses to Victorian mansions, from wagons to motor cars, from the Pony Express to Federal Express, and it all began with the simple knowledge that men are free. Our Founding Fathers didn't just come up with an idea and thought they'd try it out. They had studied centuries of history repeating itself. They witnessed tyranny and oppression first hand. They knew that power corrupts and that absolute power corrupts absolutely, and they knew there must be a better way.

They found that better way at their mother's knee as she read to them the stories of the Bible.

Each night, families would gather together and read the stories that gave them hope, direction, guidance, and understanding. They read about the deep faith and unwavering obedience of Abraham, the courage of Stephen, the steadfastness of Job, and the charity of Ruth. They read of Daniel, who was willing to give his own life for what he knew to be right and true; David, who stood against Goliath; and Esther, who sacrificed her own well-being to save her people.

They read about Joseph, who mastered his own passions and later prepared Pharaoh for the coming famine by storing food for seven years—an act that made Egypt the richest nation in the world for centuries. They read the Sermon on the Mount where Jesus taught of all the attributes a person needs to govern himself. And when they read those powerful words of Paul as he stood before King Agrippa stating, "I was born free," they came to understand, for the first time in centuries, that their rights came from God and not from man.

With tear filled eyes, they read of the Israelites who knew they were free but begged for a King and traded their freedom for a monarchy because freedom was too much work. How it must have made our Founders ache to read those words. To them—being living witnesses to the evil and oppression of a monarchy—it was the same as trading a divine birthright for a bowl of soup.

> *We must be free not because we claim freedom, but because we practice it.*
>
> —William Faulkner

The Bible was the foundation that cultivated the soil of liberty, and America was the venue God chose to house it. Our Founding Families knew what freedom was long before it was openly declared in the Declaration of Independence. Because of that simple, consistent act of reading the bible together as families, the knowledge that man's rights came from God and not government was infused into their very souls. And when they saw that knowledge manifested in the United States Constitution, they embraced it as the banner of freedom that would secure their liberties not only for themselves but for their posterity for generations to come.

Our Founding Families learned all the key ingredients to a free society in those well-worn pages of the Bible—self-mastery, self-reliance, self-sacrifice, and self-governance. With this knowledge, they found the better way, and they thoroughly believed that with these key ingredients, and the divine intervention of a loving God, man could, in fact, govern himself. They believed it with all their heart and formed our entire government on that belief.

Our Founding Fathers learned what freedom was from the Bible. When they signed the Declaration of Independence, they knew they were going against Goliath. When they

pledged their lives, fortunes, and sacred honor they, like Daniel and Esther, sacrificed their own lives and well-being for what they knew to be right and true.

For over a hundred and fifty years, families read together, ate together, worked together, and served together. And in 1776, we saw the fruits of their labors as fifty-six men—raised with an understanding of these principles—pledged their lives, their fortunes, and their sacred honor for the greatest exhibition of freedom ever made on this earth. And when they penned the words "We hold these truths to be self-evident," they did so with the words of Paul echoing in their ears because they knew they were "born free!"

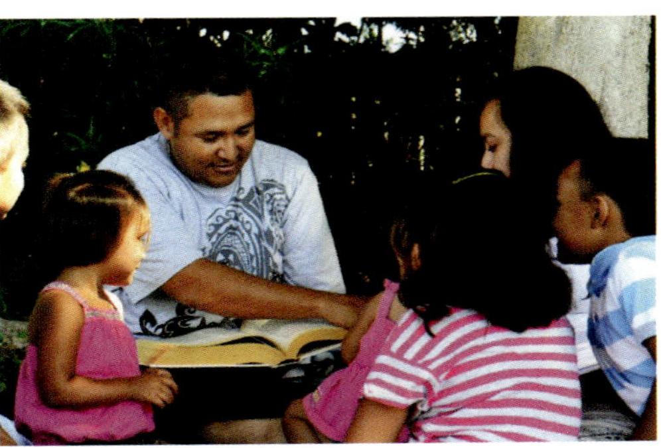

–Horace Greeley

For over a century, Americans learned what freedom meant. For the next two centuries, they lived it, and now, in this century, we are in danger of losing it. There are troubling times ahead for our nation.

Now, more than ever, we need those timeless stories of faith, courage, and freedom from the Bible in our lives. They are the stories that touched the hearts of our Founding Families; they are the stories that laid the foundation of freedom; they are the stories that will revive the spirit of liberty in the hearts of this generation and leave their imprint on generations to come.

"Perhaps," as Kriss Anne Halls has suggested, "our job is not necessarily to win this fight but to prepare the ground; to make the soil fertile and sow the seeds so that Liberty may thrive when the battle is done." When we lay that foundation as our Founders did—firmly rooted in the Bible—then the foundation will be sure, and we will be evidenced in the hearts and actions of our children.

When our sons and daughters raise their hands to defend the Constitution of the United States, to pledge their lives, their fortunes, and their sacred honor for the cause of freedom, then we will know liberty is secure, because we will know our children know what it means. They will know because they will remember the stories we read to them. They will know because they will remember the love of liberty we shared with them. They will know, because they will remember that story they once heard us tell about a man named Paul, and they will know they were born free!

Message from Darrell Scott

A COLUMBINE FATHER

Darrell Scott's daughter Rachel was killed April 20, 1999 at Columbine High School when two teenage boys shot 12 of their fellow students and one teacher, then took their own lives. The event has become known at the Columbine Massacre. Following the shooting, Mr. Scott was invited to speak before the House Judiciary Committee in Washington D.C. Following is a partial transcript of what he said:

"Since the dawn of creation, there has been both good & evil in the hearts of men and women. We all contain the

seeds of kindness or the seeds of violence. The death of my wonderful daughter, Rachel Joy Scott, and the deaths of that heroic teacher, and the other eleven children who died, must not be in vain. Their blood cries out for answers. The first recorded act of violence was when Cain slew his brother Abel out in the field.

The villain was not the club he used. Neither was it the NCA, the National Club Association. The true killer was Cain, and the reason for the murder could only be found in Cain's heart. In the days that followed the Columbine tragedy, I was amazed at how quickly fingers began to be pointed at groups such as the NRA.

I am not a member of the NRA. I am not a hunter. I do not even own a gun. I am not here to represent or defend the NRA—because I don't believe that they are responsible for my daughter's death. Therefore, I do not believe that they need to be defended. If I believed they had anything to do with Rachel's murder, I would be their strongest opponent.

I am here today to declare that Columbine was not just a tragedy—it was a spiritual event that should be forcing us to look at where the real blame lies! Much of the blame lies here in this room.

Much of the blame lies behind the pointing fingers of the accusers themselves. I wrote a poem that expresses my feelings best. This was written way before I knew I would be speaking here today:

> *Your laws ignore our deepest needs, Your words are empty air.*
>
> *You've stripped away our heritage, You've outlawed simple prayer.*
>
> *Now gunshots fill our classrooms, And precious children die.*
>
> *You seek for answers everywhere, And ask the question "Why?"*
>
> *You regulate restrictive laws, Through legislative creed.*
>
> *And yet you fail to understand, That God is what we need!*

Men and women are three-part beings. We all consist of body, soul, and spirit. When we refuse to acknowledge a third part of our make-up, we create a void that allows evil, prejudice, and hatred to rush in and reek havoc. Spiritual influences were present within our educational systems for most of our nation's history. Many of our major colleges began as theological seminaries. This is a historical fact.

What has happened to us as a nation? We have refused to honor God, and in so doing, we open the doors to hatred and violence. And when something as terrible as Columbine's tragedy occurs, politicians immediately look for a scapegoat, such as the NRA. They immediately seek to pass more restrictive laws that contribute to erode away our personal and private liberties.

We do not need more restrictive laws. Eric and Dylan would not have been stopped by metal detectors. No amount of gun laws can stop someone who spends months planning this type of massacre. The real villain lies within our own hearts.

Political posturing and restrictive legislation are not the answers. The young people of our nation hold the key. There is a spiritual awakening taking place that will not be squelched! We do not need more religion. We do not need more gaudy television evangelists spewing out verbal religious garbage. We do not need more million dollar church buildings built while people with basic needs are being ignored.

We do need a change of heart and a humble acknowledgment that this nation was founded on the principle of simple trust in God! As my son Craig lay under that table in the school library and saw his two friends murdered before his very eyes, he did not hesitate to pray in school. I defy any law or politician to deny him that right!

I challenge every young person in America, and around the world, to realize that on April 20, 1999, at Columbine High School, prayer was brought back to our schools. Do not let the many prayers offered by those students be in vain. Dare to move into the new millennium with a sacred disregard for legislation that violates your God-given right to communicate with Him. To those of you who would point your finger at the NRA—I give to you a sincere challenge:

Dare to examine your own heart before casting the first stone! My daughter's death will not be in vain! The young people of this country will not allow that to happen!"

Acceptance of the Declaration of Independence Is Acceptance of God as Our King

EXCERPT FROM EARL TAYLOR, PRESIDENT, NATIONAL CENTER FOR CONSTITUTIONAL STUDIES

The true spirit of the Declaration is the spirit of liberty. It severs all ties to any earthly authority, except those whom the people choose for the protection of their unalienable rights. The Declaration of Independence is a declaration of individual liberty. It is a declaration of our individual belief that God is our one and only King.

When we reject the Declaration or let it fall into oblivion by our ignorance of it, it seems we are putting ourselves into the same position ancient Israel did when the people asked for a king. Samuel was the last great judge of Israel. The Israelites seemed to fall for the one-world philosophy and began to ask for a king so they could be like their neighbors. Samuel pleaded with them to stay free and independent of the rest of the world and of a king, but they refused to listen. When he went to the Lord, Samuel was told, "they have not rejected thee, but they have rejected me, that I should not reign over them." (1 Samuel 8:7)

Benjamin Franklin described the plight of ancient Israel, which is the fate America seems to be experiencing as we reject the freedom saving-principles of our precious Declaration of Independence. Said he: "Only a virtuous people are capable of freedom. As nations become corrupt and vicious, they have more need of masters."

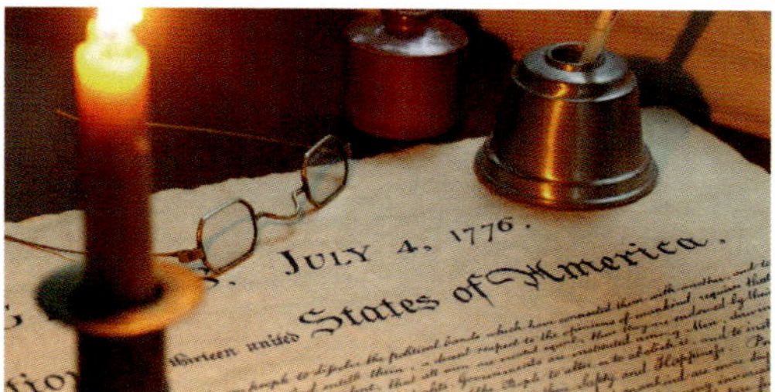

A Time for Remembering

BY TAMMY HULSE

It was early autumn in Boston, Massachusetts. The year was 1746. The entire community of Boston was in turmoil. The most powerful fleet of the time was sailing from France under the command of French Duke d'Anville. There were 70 ships carrying over 10,000 troops with a mission to burn Boston to her very foundations.

The men of Massachusetts, some of whom were veterans of the earlier French war, with their old outdated weapons, gathered at Boston Common in preparation for the coming attack. The following account of the event was shared on William J. Federer's American Minute.

"The fleet was at their doorstep when reverend Thomas Prince, from the pulpit of the Old South Meetinghouse prayed before his congregation.   The morning was clear and calm. 'Deliver us from our enemy!' the minister implored. 'Send thy tempest, Lord, upon the waters to the eastward! Raise Thy right hand. Scatter the ship of our tormentors and drive them hence., Sink their proud frigates beneath the power of Thy winds!' He had scarcely pronounced the words when the sun was gone and the morning darkened. All the church was in shadow. A wind shrieked so hard that the great church bell struck twice. Thomas Prince paused in his prayer, both arms raised. 'We hear thy voice, O Lord! We hear it! Thy breath is upon the waters of the eastward, even upon the deep, The bell tolls for the death of our enemies!' He bowed his head; when he looked up, tears streamed down his face.

'thine be the glory, Lord. Amen and amen!'

Historian Catherine Drinker Bowen related that as he finished praying, the sky darkened, winds shrieked and church bells rang 'a wild, uneven sound…though no man was in the steeple.' A hurricane subsequently sank and scattered the entire French fleet. With 4,000 sick and 2,000 dead, including d'Anville, Vice-Admiral Cornelle's threw himself on his sword. The French attack never came. A week later details were provided by other vessels entering Boston from the northeastward. The French fleet was nearly lost. All who survived the sudden storm suffered from a pestilential fever. The great Admiral Duke d'Anville was dead. The few remaining ships, half manned, were limping off to the south invasion of America!"

The following week would bring news that a miracle had occurred-a virtual hurricane had risen out of the Atlantic and sunk nearly all of those French frigates. The remaining ships were observed sailing, broken and battered, from whence they came.

Boston wasn't burned! Charleston wasn't burned! New York wasn't burned! God had once again preserved the colonists from utter destruction."

Henry Wadsworth Longfellow wrote the following Ballad of the French Fleet:

> *Admiral d'Anville had sworn by cross and crown,*
>
> *to ravage with fire and steel our helpless Boston Town...*
>
> *From mouth to mouth spread tidings of dismay,*
>
> *I stood in the Old South saying humbly: 'Let us pray!'*
>
> *Like a potter's vessel broke, the great ships of the line,*
>
> *were carried away as smoke or sank in the brine.*

This story is just one of many accounts of divine intervention on behalf of the United States of America. Our heritage is rich with accounts of faith, sacrifice, devotion, and the miraculous hand of God in the building and establishment of the United States and its Constitution. The challenges and threats to freedom for the early colonists were great, yet brave men and women rose to the challenge of their day, exercised faith in the God who brought them to this land, and participated in the miracle and making of America.

Enemies of freedom have always been present from the beginning of time. And thus, a free America will always have her enemies. But there is a difference in the threats we experience today in comparison to the challenges we have faced before. This difference is found in the memory of the American people. Unfortunately, the memory of the faith, the character, and the patriotism of our Founding Fathers is waning. Too many of the rising generation are unfamiliar with the great patriots of the past. Karl Marx stated that "a people without a heritage are easily persuaded." We can see evidence all around us of the vulnerability of Americans who are unfamiliar with her heritage and legacy.

How do 21st century Americans rise to the challenge of their day with the strength and power of our Fathers before us? Has the day of miracles ceased in regards to America? Or can we, as Americans today, dare to believe that God will come to our aid? I believe He will. Hope is on the horizon as modern-day patriots connect with the faith, character, and patriotism of the past.

The connection that modern-day Americans have with the faith and power of their forefathers can be found in one word: remember. Remember the courage and the sacrifice. Remember the perseverance and faith. Remember the virtue and morality. Remember the heroes. Remember those who were lost.

The word "remember" carries great power because it maintains a link to the lessons of history and the inspiration of the past. The richness of American heritage will infuse life, purpose, and meaning into her future. The power of the past begins to flow within the veins of modern-day patriots the moment they participate in a story, memorial service, event, or activity that causes them to re-visit an episode in America's dynamic history. Furthermore, when "remembering" experiences are repeated frequently, they will create a propelling force that will move America towards a promising future.

God Governs in the Affairs of Men

The Constitutional Convention had reached a tipping point. Arguments had become heated, and several members of the convention threatened to leave; the work of writing the Constitution would have been abandoned—most probably forever.

At this crucial moment in history, a lone voice spoke out from the back of the room. Quietly, Benjamin Franklin, the respected elder statesmen then 81 years of age, stood and addressed the convention.

"In the beginning of the contest with Britain, when we were sensible of danger, we had daily prayers in this room for Divine protection. Our prayers, Sir, were heard, and they were graciously

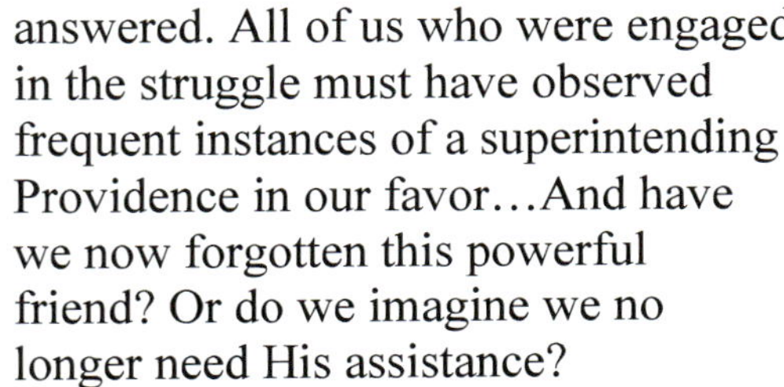

answered. All of us who were engaged in the struggle must have observed frequent instances of a superintending Providence in our favor…And have we now forgotten this powerful friend? Or do we imagine we no longer need His assistance?

I have lived, Sir, a long time, and the longer I live, the more convincing proofs I see of this truth: that God governs in the affairs of man. And if a sparrow cannot fall to the ground without His notice, is it probable that an empire can rise without His aid?

We have been assured, Sir, in the Sacred Writings that except the Lord build the house, they labor in vain that build it. I firmly believe this. I also believe that, without His concurring aid, we shall succeed in this political building no better than the builders of Babel…and what is worse, mankind may hereafter, from this unfortunate instance, despair of establishing government by human wisdom and leave it to chance, war, or conquest.

I therefore beg leave to move that, henceforth, prayers imploring the assistance of Heaven and its blessings on our deliberations be held in this assembly every morning before we proceed to business."

RELATED QUOTES

"If we ever forget that we're one nation under God, then we will be one nation gone under."
-Ronald Reagan

"No nation is better than its sacred book. In that book are expressed its highest ideals of life, and no nation rises above those ideals. No nation has a sacred book to be compared with ours. This American nation, from its first settlement at Jamestown to the present hour, is based upon and permeated by the principles of the Bible. The more this Bible enters into our national life the grander and purer and better will that life become."
-David Josiah Brewer

"It is impossible to mentally or socially enslave a BIBLE reading people. The principles of The BIBLE are the groundwork of human freedom"
-Horace Greeley

"So great is my veneration for the BIBLE that the earlier my children begin to read it, the more confident will be my hope that they will prove useful citizens to their country and respectable members of society."
-John Quincy Adams

"Those people who will not be governed by God will be ruled by tyrants."
-William Penn

"It is when people forget God that tyrants forge their chains."
-Patrick Henry

"We on this continent should never forget that men first crossed the Atlantic not to find soil for their ploughs but to secure liberty for their souls."
-Robert J. McCracken

"Living by faith includes the call to something greater than cowardly self-preservation."
-J.R.R. Tolkien, The Hobbit

FROM THE FOUNDERS

"Suppose a nation in some distant Region should take the BIBLE for their only law Book, and every member should regulate his conduct by the precepts there exhibited! Every member would be obliged in conscience, to temperance, frugality, and industry; to justice, kindness, and charity towards his fellow men; and to piety, love, and reverence toward ...What a Utopia, what a Paradise would this region be."
-John Adams

"We have staked the whole future of American civilization not upon the power of the government—far from it. We have staked the future of all of our political institutions upon the capacity of each and all of us to govern ourselves according to the Ten Commandments of God."
-James Madison

"Of all the dispositions and habits which lead to political prosperity, religion and morality are indispensable supports. It is impossible to rightly govern the world without God and the Bible."
-George Washington

"Should not the Bible regain the place it once held as a schoolbook? Its morals are pure, its examples are captivating and noble....In no Book is there so good English, so pure and so elegant, and by teaching all the same they will speak alike, and the Bible will justly remain the standard of language as well as of faith." **-Fisher Ames**

Journal

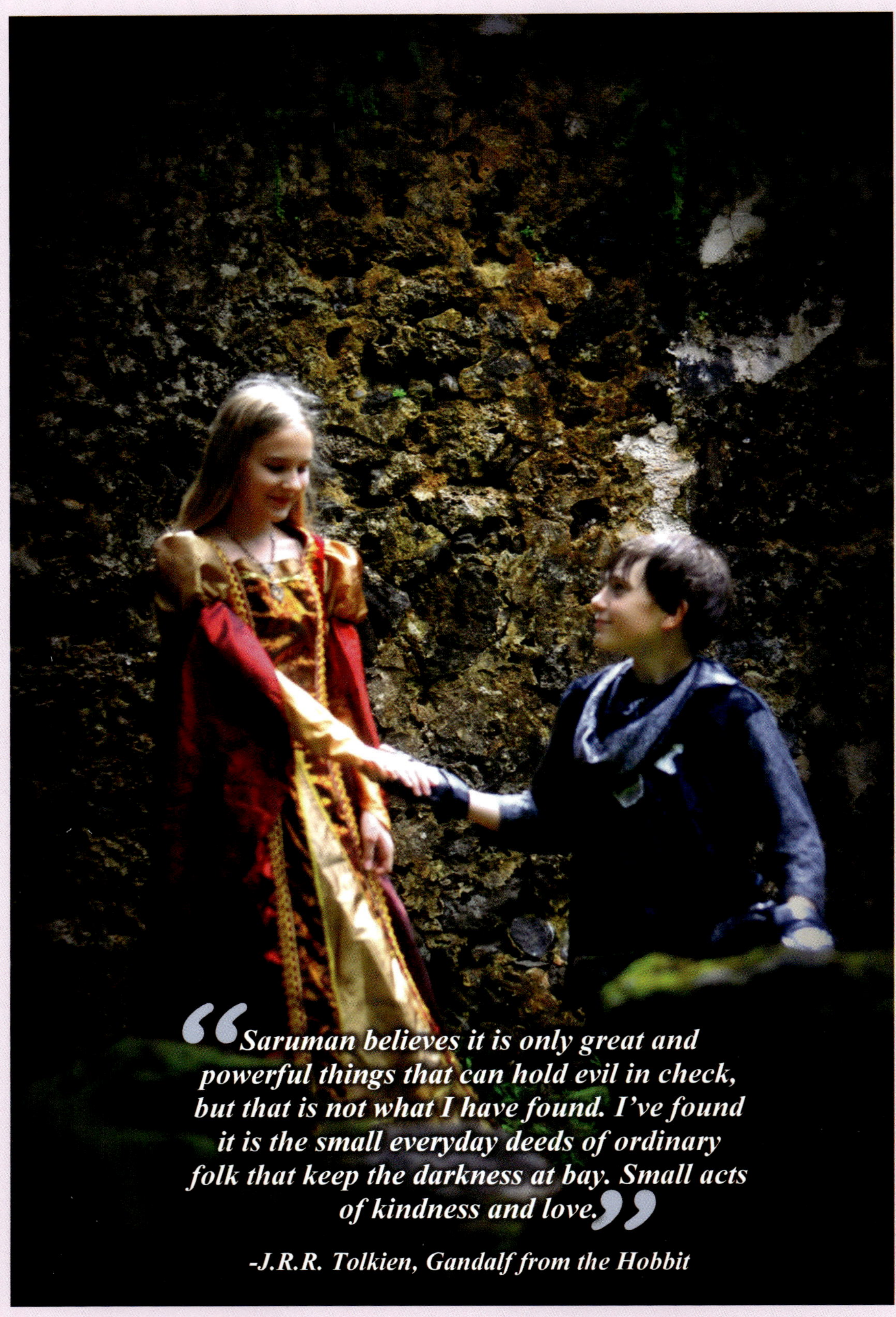

"Saruman believes it is only great and powerful things that can hold evil in check, but that is not what I have found. I've found it is the small everyday deeds of ordinary folk that keep the darkness at bay. Small acts of kindness and love."

-J.R.R. Tolkien, Gandalf from the Hobbit

Valor of Virtue

"Educate the women, and the men will be educated. Let the ladies understand the great doctrine of seeking the greatest good, of loving their neighbors as themselves; let them indoctrinate their children in this fundamental truth, and we shall have wise legislators."　**-Mary Lyon**

PREPARATION

To prepare yourself to lead this presentation, please review and consider the following material. There are a wealth of great books that promote virtue and open the door for great discussions. We highly encourage reading good books with your children. It is not just the story or the things they internalize from the stories that make the experience so valuable, but also the time parents spend with their children sharing those stories. If you get a chance to do so, visit the library and borrow a copy of *The Whipping Boy* to read to your children prior to your meeting. You can share your experiences with the group as part of your meeting presentation.

- Read "The Heart of Education" and "Nobility of a Boy" found in the Supplemental Materials of this presentation

- Read "Liber and Public Virtue" making notes and highlighting areas you want to use when leading the discussion

- View the video *Pillar of Virtue* provided in the Hostess Resource Center on the Moms for America® website www.MomsforAmerica.us

- Read Principle 1 of the *5000 Year Leap*

- Optional: if available, read *Promises of the Constitution* Vignettes 1.7, 3.6, 7.7, 12.1, 12.12

- Bible References on this topic—Philippians 4:8, Isaiah 5:20, Proverbs 31:10-31, Isaiah 5:20

- Review the Quotes provided in the Supplemental Materials of this presentation

PURPOSE

The purpose of this presentation is to introduce the second Pillar of Liberty—Virtue—and illustrate how and why a virtuous citizenry is vital to sustaining liberty; introduce the concept of "public virtue."

Home Assignment

– Read "Liber" in the Supplemental Material of this presentation and chapter excerpt "Rise Up Ye Women" available in Cottage Meeting Resources on MFA website.

Personal Study

Read the book "Alliance" by Gerald N. Lund.

Read chapter excerpt "White Wigs and Fat Cats" available in the Cottage Meeting.

Family Enrichment

Plan a family Service Project. As a family choose a project of act of service you can do for a neighbor, the elderly, your church or community. Some ideas are park beautification, neighborhood clean-up, humanitarian service, yard work for neighbor, etc.

- The only reliable basis for sound government and just human relations is natural law

- A free people cannot survive under a republican constitution unless they remain virtuous and morally strong

- The most promising method of securing a virtuous and morally stable people is to elect virtuous leaders

MEETING OUTLINE

Welcome & Gathering

We recommend starting your meeting with a prayer and the Pledge of Allegiance.

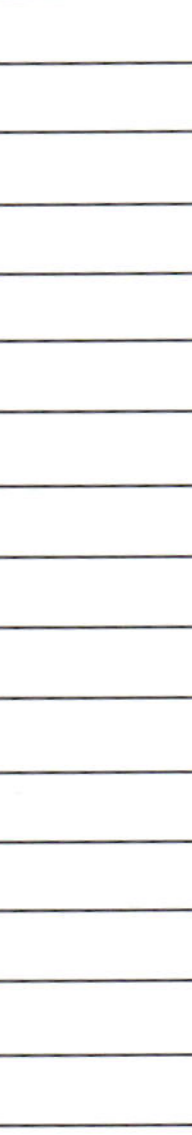

Show Video: *Pillar of Virtue* (available in Hostess Resource Center)

> *Why is virtue an essential pillar in the Founder's Freedom Formula?*

Read "Heart of Education" provided in the Supplemental Materials of this presentation.

> *How can we teach our children the principle of virtue?*

Stories are a powerful way to teach children virtues. Telling children to be good doesn't work as well as showing them what good looks like.

Read the story "Nobility of a Boy" with your group. Encourage those in your group to share the story with their children prior to the next meeting.

Group Discussion

Lead a discussion on Principle 1 from the *5000 Year Leap* using the notes and highlighted sections you marked during preparation.

Summarize the article "Liber and Public Virtue" by Oliver DeMille

- According to Cicero, a model society needs to be built on natural law. How do you define "natural law?"

- How does Cicero suggest we teach virtue to members of society?

Bible Reference Isaiah 5:20

Summary

Summarize your thoughts on the material covered in this presentation

- Give the Home Assignment for the next meeting

- Announce date, time and location for next meeting

ADDITIONAL PRESENTATION IDEAS

Here are some ideas for additional presentations, personal study and discussions on "Valor of Virtue."

A Free and Virtuous Society

Virtue is not hereditary; it has to be earned and learned. Neither is virtue a permanent quality in human nature. It has to be cultivated continually.

- Read and Discuss the *5000 Year Leap* Principle 2 and pages 72-73 of Principle 3.

- Consider the following questions when leading the discussion: What is an effective method to educate the rising generation in virtue today? Why is it important to maintain "public virtue" in a free country?

- Read "Nathan Hale: One Life to Give" provided in the Supplemental Materials section of this presentation.

- Read and Discuss Philippians 4:8

- Optional: If available, read *Promises of the Constitution* Vignettes 1.7, 7.7, 12.1, 12.12

- Review the quotes provided in the Supplemental Materials section of this presentation

Seeking Virtuous Leaders

> *"It's easier to build strong children than repair broken men."*
> *-Frederick Douglas*

- Read and Discuss Principle 3 of the *5000 Year Leap.* Consider the following questions when leading the discussion.: What is the difference between a "natural aristocracy" and an "artificial aristocracy" as described by Thomas Jefferson? Why is it important to seek out virtuous leaders?

- Read "A Perfect Gentleman" provided in the Supplemental Materials section of this presentation

- Read & Discuss "Fulfilling Our Civic Duty" provided in the Supplemental Materials section of this presentation

How can we identify Statesman? How can we raise statesmen in our homes?

- Read "Benjamin Franklin: Pursuit of a Virtuous Life" provided in the Supplemental Materials section of this presentation.

MINI COTTAGE IDEAS

Mini Cottages are designed especially for moms of preschoolers and moms who work full-time jobs. Moms simply read and/or watch the same materials at home, on their own, then meet together once a week in a playdate or over lunch during the workday to discuss what they read. The articles and videos are short and can usually be read and/or viewed in less than hour. Below are some suggestions to host mini cottage discussions under the "Valor of Virtue" theme.

- Read and Discuss "Liber and Public Virtue" provided in the Supplemental Materials section of this presentation

- Read "The Heart of Education." Share the story "The Nobility of a Boy" with your children

- Read and Discuss Principle 1 of the *5000 Year Leap*

- Read and Discuss Principle 2 of the *5000 Year Leap*

- Read and Discuss Principle 3 of the *5000 Year Leap*

- Read and Discuss "Ben Franklin: Pursuit of a Virtuous Life" and "Reflecting the Light of Virtue" provided in the Supplemental Materials section of this presentation

- Review the quotes provided in the Supplemental Materials section of this presentation

COTTAGE MEETING BOOK CLUB

For those who like the book club format, we've compiled a list of great books to help you gain an appreciation and foundational understanding of the concepts presented in "Valor of Virtue."

The 5000 Year Leap: A Miracle That Changed the World

- Review Principles 1, 2, and 3.

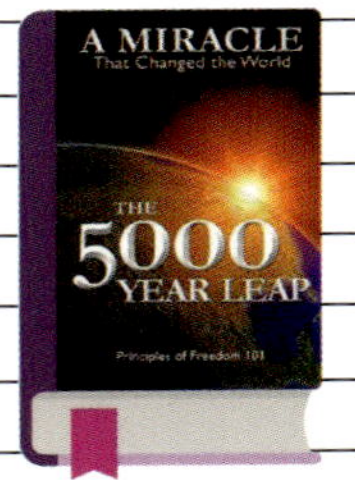

Promises of the Constitution

- Review the following vignettes: 1.7, 3.6, 7.7, 12.1, 12.12

The Alliance by Gerald N. Lund

It's eighteen years after the end of civilization as we know it. In the aftermath of a nuclear holocaust, survivors are being relocated to a new society known as the Alliance. For Eric Lloyd and the members of his village, the Alliance seems like a dream come true. There is work and safety and food enough to spare. But the utopia is not what it seems. Though crime, anger, and prejudice appear to have been eliminated, under the mask of perfection is a society chafing with discontent. Eric vows to destroy the Alliance, but is there any hope of withstanding the Alliance's power structure and its computerized control of its citizens? And what of Eric's growing attachment to Nicole, a Guardian of the Alliance? Author Gerald N. Lund invites you into a futuristic setting where he explores the principle of moral agency through a gripping tale of good and evil, danger and escapes, and the power of one person to change the world.

The Alliance is an excellent book that helps us understand the principle of virtue in a deeper and more meaningful way than ever before. It is an easy read; a captivating, attention-grabbing story richly woven together with exceptionally well-developed characters—an excellent read! Highly recommended!

The Chronicles of Narnia by C.S. Lewis

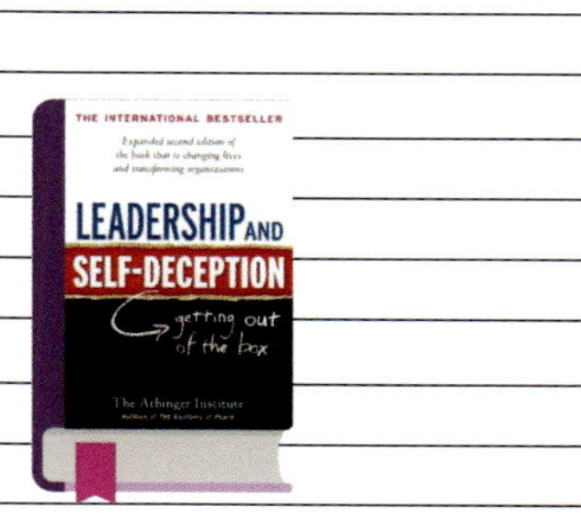

Few books introduce virtuous principles in a story like *the Chronicles of Narnia*. Through the characters and concepts shared in this fiction classic, readers of all ages will come to recognize and appreciate the importance of virtue and strong moral character. Once you read through the series, *the Last Battle* is a riveting conclusion that leaves us spellbound. *The Chronicles of Narnia* is a classic worth reading with your children over and over again. They did an excellent job with the films as well. Not many films can capture the true essence of a book, but the *Narnia* films come very close. They are great films to have in your library, but we highly recommend reading the books. Not only is the story beautifully enriching, the time you share and the experiences you have while reading with your children is absolutely priceless.

Leadership and Self-Deception

Since its original publication in 2000, Leadership and Self-Deception has become a word-of-mouth phenomenon. Its sales continue to increase year after year, and the book's popularity has gone global, with editions now available in over twenty languages. Through a story everyone can relate to about a man facing challenges on the job and in his family, the authors expose the fascinating ways that we can blind ourselves to our true motivations and unwittingly sabotage the effectiveness of our own efforts to achieve success and increased happiness.

The Screwtape Letters by C.S. Lewis

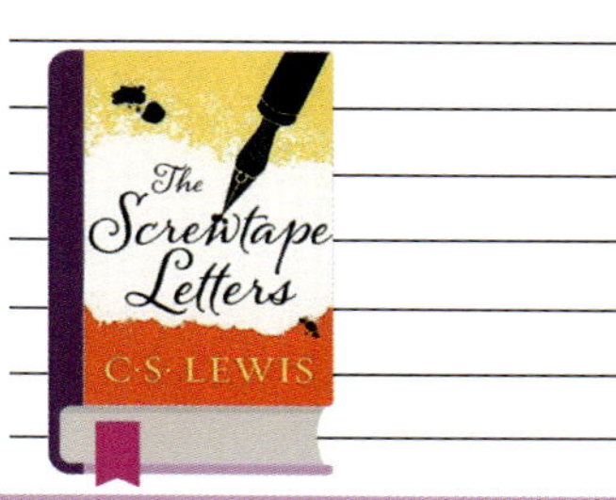

This is an absolute classic masterpiece and must-read for anyone seeking answers on why things go so wrong when we're trying to be so right. It is written as a religious satire that entertains readers with its sly and ironic portrayal of human life and weaknesses from the vantage point of Screwtape, a highly placed assistant to "Our Father Below" AKA the devil. It is wildly comic, deadly serious, and strikingly original—all at the same time. C.S. Lewis's *The Screwtape Letters* is the most engaging account of temptation—and triumph over it—ever written.

The Whipping Boy by Sid Fleischman (Read-aloud)

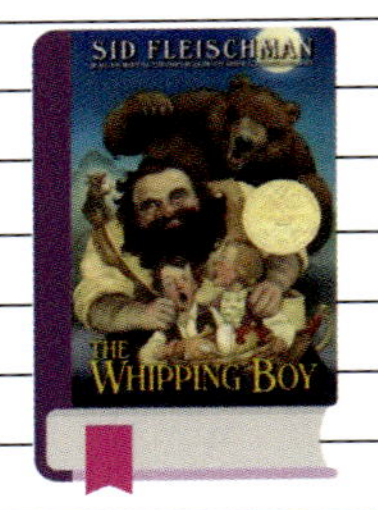

If you're looking for a book that will immediately spark an understanding of the importance of virtue in the hearts of your children and show them what "good" looks like, this is it! The plot involves the orphan Jemmy, who must take the whippings for the royal heir, Prince Brat—for it is forbidden to spank, thrash, or whack the heir to the throne. The two boys have nothing in common and even less reason to like one another. But when they find themselves taken hostage after running away, they are left with no choice but to trust each other as the book turns to a surprising close. You will loving reading this book to your children. A great to story to spark all kinds of amazing conversations.

Stories that Teach Values

This book is full of wonderful stories that teach children values by showing them what good looks like. Your children and grandchildren will learn of the great heroes of American history and how ordinary people did extraordinary things in difficult times. They will learn the values and virtues that sustain a free society by reading of those who lived them, and they will gain an appreciation for those who came before us, the sacrifices they made, and the character they developed. Great as bedtime stories or for morning devotional reading. (Available through the Moms for America® online store and at Libraries of Hope www.LibrariesOfHope.com)

Animal Farm by George Orwell

As ferociously fresh as it was more than a half century ago, this remarkable allegory of a downtrodden society of overworked, mistreated animals and their quest to create a paradise of progress, justice, and equality is one of the most scathing satires ever published. As readers witness the rise and bloody fall of the revolutionary animals, they begin to recognize the seeds of totalitarianism in the most idealistic organization—and in the most charismatic leaders.

Animal Farm is a nearly perfect piece of writing, both an engaging story and an allegory that actually works. When the downtrodden beasts of Manor Farm oust their drunken human master and take over management of the land, all are awash in collectivist zeal. Everyone willingly works overtime, productivity soars, and for one brief, glorious season, every belly is full. The animals' Seven Commandment credo is painted in big white letters on the barn. All animals are equal. Too soon, however, the pigs, who have styled themselves leaders by virtue of their intelligence, succumb to the temptations of privilege and power. Satire *Animal Farm* may be, but it's a stony reader who remains unmoved when the stalwart workhorse, Boxer, having given his all to his comrades, is sold to the glue factory to buy booze for the pigs.

COTTAGE MEETING FOR KIDS

Cottage Meeting for Kids is a liberty promoting program for the entire family and focused on children from preschool to teens. It is full of great stories and fun activities to help children gain a love of liberty. Families can join together each month for an Activity Day to share the concepts they've learned and enhance them through group activities. Here are some ideas to promote the concepts presented in "Valor in Virtue." You can find additional ideas, outlines and activities on the Moms for America® website under "Cottage Meetings for Kids."

- This presentation is a great opportunity to introduce Benjamin Franklin and his significant contributions to our society. We've listed some books you can share with your children to learn more about him. You can read the articles and stories of Benjamin Franklin provided in the Supplemental Materials section of this presentation. The story of Ben and the lantern in "Reflecting the Light of Virtue" is a great opportunity to focus on "light" as opposed to darkness. Some suggested activities:

- Do a Bible Treasure Hunt, searching for scripture passages with "light" in them

- Read and Discuss "Reflecting the Light of Virtue" with your children

- Make lanterns; there is a video and instructions on how to make three different kinds of lanterns in the Cottage Meeting Resources under "Valor of Virtue" on the Moms for America® website

- Read "Ben Franklin: Pursuit of a Virtuous Life." Review the virtues he lists and compare them to the attributes Jesus espoused and lived by. You can create your own family chart to do a daily or weekly assessment on your progress. A sample chart is provided in the Supplemental Materials section of this presentation. It is also available for download in the Cottage Meeting Resources and Hostess Resource Center on the Moms for America® website

- Writing Activity: Have your children and teens read "A Story of George Washington." As a fun activity, have them rewrite the story using different characters, time periods, and settings but with the same subject, theme, and conclusion. The worksheet with the story and story boarding exercise are included in the Supplemental Materials section of this presentation.

Book & Movie List

Suggested books and readings for children all ages to nurture a love of liberty in the home:

The Alliance
by Gerald N. Lund

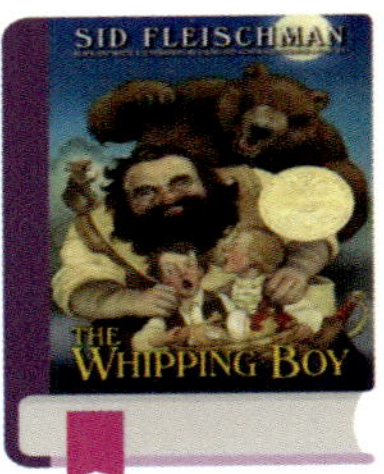

The Whipping Boy
by Sid Fleischman

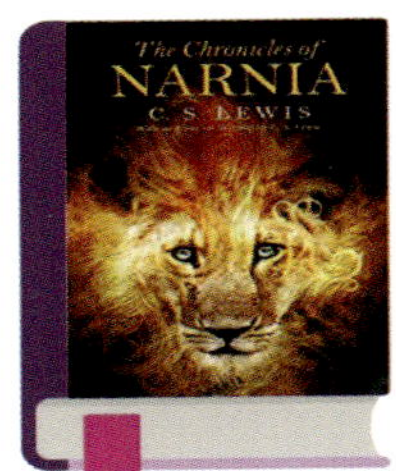

Chronicles of Narnia
by C.S. Lewis

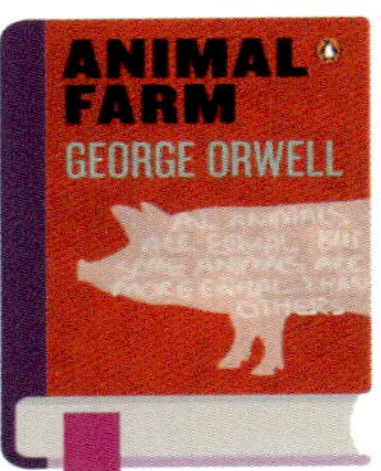

Animal Farm
by George Orwell

Childhood of Famous Americans: Ben Franklin
by Augusta Stevenson

Benjamin Franklin
by Ingri &
Edgar Parin d'Aulaire

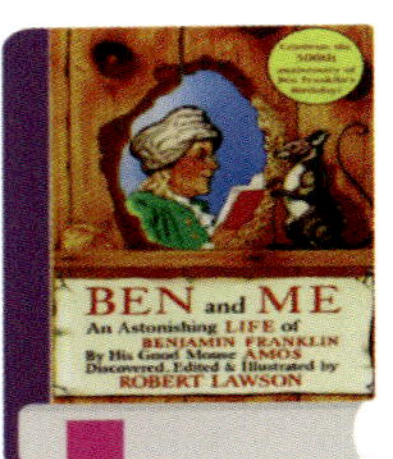

Ben and Me
by Robert Lawson

Cinderella
2015

Grace Unplugged
2013

Soul Surfer
2011

Up
2009

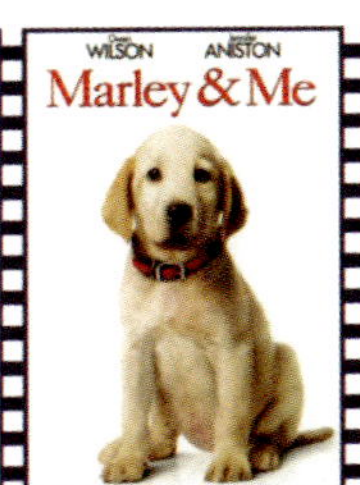

Marly and Me
2009

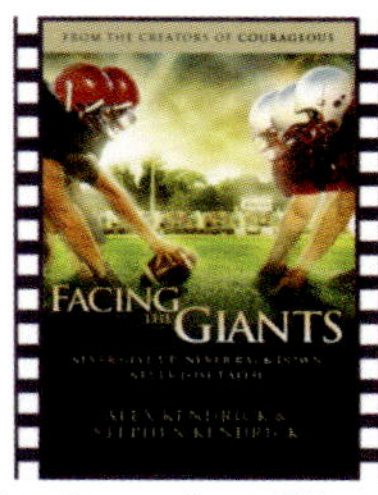

Facing the Giants
2006

Nanny McPhee
2005

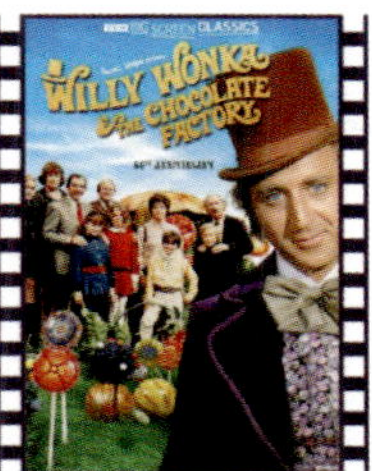

**Willy Wonka and
the Chocolate Factory**
1971

The Secret of Nimh
1981

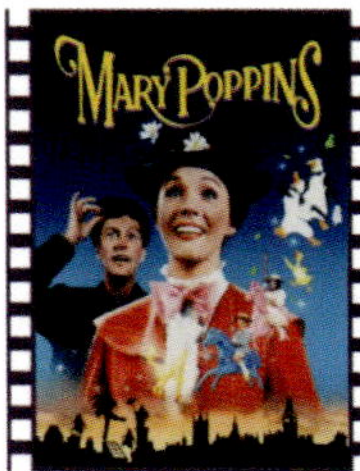

Mary Poppins
1964

The Blind Side
2009

Ben and Me
1953

**The Pursuit of
Happiness**
2006

The Heart of Education

BY KIMBERLY FLETCHER

There is a lot of focus in our nation right now on educating the minds of our youth. While I agree that education is a vital component to a free society, I am deeply concerned that all the discussions on "reform" or proposals to "fix" the problems of education focus on the mind and completely neglect the heart. It is our hearts that guide our actions, not our brains, so if all we focus on is the brain, the result is a nation of highly intelligent people with no moral foundation, and that is a very dangerous thing.

Oliver DeMille, former president of George Wythe University, addresses this very concern in his book *TJED for Teens*. He states:

"As Allan Bloom pointed out in his classic bestseller, The Closing of the American Mind, the last society to be as highly trained and as poorly educated as the current U.S. was Germany in the 1930s. A significant number of German engineers were highly enough trained to build cutting-edge weaponry, submarines, missiles, airplanes and so on, but not well-read enough in history to vote against Hitler or refuse to do his bidding.

Same with German scientists, who understood chemicals and genetics enough to experiment on their neighbors when they were thrown immorally into prison camps, but not learned enough in ethics, morals, history, psychology or basic politics to not elect Hitler or refuse to torture their countrymen.

Critics could say that by the time submarines were being launched and people were being tortured, it was too late to do anything. But only the combination of top technical training and poor Leadership Education could have allowed this all to happen. A less highly-trained people could not have done it, and a truly educated people would not have done it. This may seem extreme to some, but seriously, what is education all about? If it is not to teach us what is good, ideal, and right, then it isn't really education."

We are all deeply concerned for the moral decay in our society and the violence that has erupted because of it. Strengthening the mind will not cure what ails us. As J.K. Rowling so poignantly states, "It is our choices....that show who we really are, far more than our abilities."

It's not what's in our minds that inspires greatness; it's what is in our hearts. A moral nation of free, intelligent, loyal citizens must start there.

> *To educate a person in the mind but not in morals is to educate a menace to society.*
>
> –Theodore Roosevelt

Liber and Public Virtue

BY OLIVER DEMILLE

A speech delivered by Dr. Oliver DeMille at America's Freedom Festival on June 30, 2000. Dr. DeMille is the author of several books including *Thomas Jefferson Education* and *Leadershift.* He is also the cofounder of TJED, a leadership education philosophy that teaches parents to nurture a love liberty in the hearts of their children and raise great leaders. Visit www.TJED.org to learn more.

The Liber

On July 4, 1776, John Hancock, as head of the Continental Congress, signed his name at the bottom of the newly written Declaration of Independence and sent it to the world. The rest of the signers didn't sign until Congress reconvened on August 2. So for a month, John Hancock's name stood alone declaring independence from the greatest power on the face of the earth.

What motivates a man to voluntarily sacrifice his own safety, jeopardizing his family and all his earthly possessions, on the lean hope that his neighbors and nation will support him, and even if they do, that his side has any chance of winning? What motivates a man to voluntarily submit himself to the legal and violent reaction that he knew would come, and which surely did come?

There are two phrases which have been forgotten today, but which help explain why a man like John Hancock, and so many others in his generation, would choose what they did at such high cost. These two phrases were the foundation of freedom on July 4, 1776.

In those days, the average farmer or housewife understood both of these phrases, and based on the response to the Federalist Papers, could have debated and discussed them openly. Unfortunately, in the year 2000, neither phrase is widely understood. The first phrase is public virtue, the second is Liber.

I have submitted these two phrases to thousands of people in seminars around the nation, and I have often stopped at this point in my presentation and asked how many people could give me a definition of Public Virtue or Liber. A few people have known Liber, and in most seminars several people raise their hand and try to define Public Virtue. A few have even come close.

So, what do these phrases mean?

Liber is the Latin word for tree or tree bark, and since tree bark was used to write on and make contracts with and processed to make paper for more writing and contracts, the word Liber can be associated with those who can read, write and engage in contract. With this definition, in the classical world of Greece and Rome, there were two classes of people: slaves and Liber.

There were varying levels and types of slaves and peasants, and likewise different types of Liber: from citizens to merchants to the aristocracy and royalty. But the fundamental difference between slaves and Liber was freedom, and Liber is the root word of Liberty. It is also the root of book, libro, and library.

Liberty is the state of being Liber. Liberty is not just the absence of bondage, but the fitness of the individual to act as a citizen.

Liber is also the root of the phrase "liberal arts," such as in liberal arts colleges; the arts in a Bachelor of Arts or B.A. degree comes from the liberal arts. The liberal arts are the knowledge and skills necessary to remain free. As Robert M. Hutchins, former president of the University of Chicago, put it: ". . . liberal education . . . is the education that prepares us to be free men. You have to have this education if you . . . are going to be an effective citizen of a democracy; for citizenship requires that . . . you do not leave your duties to be performed by others . . . . A free society is composed of freemen. To be free you have to be educated for freedom."

What are those arts? Well, for the founders they were the arts of reading the classics and thinking clearly and independently.

The Founding generation was a generation of Liber, of men and women and children who could read the law and government bills and resolutions in detail and understand and debate them. These regular farmers and housewives read and hotly debated the Federalist Papers in New York in 1789.

History has proven that Freedom is not free. It must be earned. And one of the ways the Founding generation earned it was in becoming Liber: getting the kind of education required to remain free. And by education they didn't mean diplomas or degrees, but knowledge gained from reading the classics of history, law, government, and the arts.

It is true that hardly any schools in our day focus on training people to be Liber, but the classics are still available and all we must do is take them off the shelf, dust them off, and get to work earning our freedom. If our generation loses the understanding necessary to remain free, we will lose our freedom. No society in all of history has avoided this inevitable consequence. Over and over in history, when the people of a nation stop being Liber and just become focused on getting jobs and making a living, freedom wanes and finally is sold.

Unless we pay the price to be a nation of Liber, we will not maintain the freedoms we so cherish and celebrate.

That is the first great word that we have forgotten since July 4, 1776— Liber, which means the body of citizens reading the classics and history and knowing what is required to remain free.

Public Virtue

The other forgotten key to maintaining our liberty and prosperity and ability to worship and choose freely is public virtue.

Benjamin Franklin said: "Only a virtuous people are capable of freedom. As nations become more corrupt . . . they have more need of masters.

Samuel Adams said: "I thank God that I have lived to see my country independent and free. She may enjoy her . . . freedom if she will. It depends on her virtue."

The founding generation spoke of two types of virtue: private virtue and public virtue. Private virtue is morality, obedience to the commandments, doing what is right. And private virtue is essential to freedom: immorality leads inevitably to loss of freedom—personal and eventually national.

Public virtue, on the other hand, is a totally distinct concept from private virtue, though equally vital to liberty. Most of the people in our seminars who try to define public virtue say something like: public virtue is where government officials are moral in their personal lives, or public virtue is when leaders pass moral laws. But public virtue is even more fundamental than these things—it is one of the things which makes them possible.

In 1776, the term public virtue meant voluntarily sacrificing personal benefit for the good of society. Consider the signers of the Declaration of Independence and their closest associates, their wives. The signers and their wives epitomized both Liber and Public Virtue. Like Robert Morris of Pennsylvania.

Robert and Mary Morris

Robert Morris was at a holiday celebration dinner when news came of the Battle of Lexington. The group was astonished and most people soon left for home, but Robert and a ". . . few remained and discussed the great question of American freedom: and there, within that festive hall, did Robert Morris and a few others, by solemn vow, dedicate their lives, their fortunes, and their honor, to the sacred cause of the Revolution."[i]

Robert Morris was self-educated and guided by a mentor, Mr. Thomas Willing, and became Liber through studying the classics. He started in business at age 21 and became extremely wealthy. In fact, he was known as the Financier of the Revolution. When the Tea Act was passed, Robert Morris openly supported it though he lost thousands of dollars in his business.

When Congress went bankrupt in 1776, Robert Morris loaned $10,000 of his own money to feed and cloth Washington's "handful of half-naked, half-famished militia." In their day, this was a fortune. One historian wrote: "When Congress fled to Baltimore, on the approach of the British across New Jersey, Mr. Morris, after [fleeing with] his family into the country, returned to, and remained in Philadelphia. Almost in despair, Washington wrote to him, and informed him that to make any successful movement whatever, a considerable sum of money must be had. It was a requirement that seemed almost impossible to meet.

Mr. Morris left his counting-room for his lodgings in utter despondency. On his way he met a wealthy Quaker, and made known his wants. "What security can'st thou give me?" asked he. "My note and my honor," promptly replied Mr. Morris. The Quaker replied:

"Robert, thou shalt have it."—It was sent to Washington, the Delaware was crossed [remember the picture with Washington at the helm?], and victory was won!"

On another occasion, when Washington was preparing for his attack at Yorktown, which turned the tide of the war to America's side, he approached Robert Morris and Judge Peters. "'What can you do for me?' said Washington to Mr. Peters. 'With money, everything, without it, nothing,' he replied, at the same time turning an anxious look toward Mr. Morris. 'Let me know the sum you desire,' said Mr. Morris; and before noon Washington's plan and estimates were complete. Mr. Morris promised him the amount, and raised it upon his own responsibility."

Time after time, Robert Morris gave his own resources and raised money on his own credit to keep Washington and his men going. One record remarked: "If it were not [proven] by official records, posterity would hardly be made to believe that the campaign . . . which . . . closed the Revolutionary War, was sustained wholly on the credit of an individual merchant."

When the War ended, this self-made millionaire spent 3 ½ years in debtors prison after he lost everything. His

wife, Mary Morris, who was born to a wealthy family and educated in the classics, watched possession after possession disappear during the War. When Robert went to prison after giving so much to the cause of freedom, she tended a borrowed little farm and walked each day to the prison with her daughter Maria to visit her husband. Robert left prison a broken down old man and died shortly thereafter. The financier of the Revolution, and his family, understood public virtue—voluntarily sacrificing personal benefit for the good of society.

Thomas and Lucy Nelson

So did Thomas Nelson, Jr. a signer of the Declaration of Independence from Virginia. He was Liber educated in the classics under the tutelage of his father and was later individually mentored by the celebrated Dr. Proteus at Cambridge. When the Revolutionary War started, he was called as the head of the military of the state of Virginia. "The sudden call of the militia from their homes left many families [destitute], for a great part of the agricultural operations were suspended."

General Nelson used his own money and resources to support many of his poorest soldiers, "and thus more than a hundred families were kept from absolute want."[ii]

The biographer of the Signers, B.J. Lossing, wrote: "Mr. Nelson made many and great [financial] sacrifices for his country. When, in 1780, the French fleet was hourly expected, Congress felt it highly necessary that provision should be made for them. But its credit was prostrate, and its calls upon the States were [ignored]. Virginia proposed to raise two million . . . dollars, and Mr. Nelson at once" set out to raise the money. "But many wealthy men told Mr. Nelson that they would not contribute a penny on the security of [Congress], but they would lend him all he wanted. He at once added his personal security."

I have wondered which type of person I would be in similar circumstances—the men who made sure their bank accounts grew during the War, or the Thomas Nelson and Robert Morris type who gave their all. At one point in the War, Washington was losing and his men starving while the British were well supplied from American merchants. I have wondered whether in the same circumstances I would keep selling to the British, or do like so many American Farmers and Merchants did and burn down my own business, crop or livelihood. Can you imagine voluntarily pouring the kerosene on your shop, and hand in hand with your spouse lighting the match and walking away to bankruptcy—all because your side was so close to losing the war?

Thomas Nelson was elected Governor of Virginia when Thomas Jefferson's term expired, and during the Battle of Yorktown, the one which Robert Morris funded and which turned the tide of the War to the Americans, Governor Nelson noticed that the American troops were firing at every home in town except his own personal home. The British had stationed a number of their officers in his home, perhaps believing that as the home of the governor and head of the state military it was safe. Governor Nelson positioned himself at the head of his troops and begged them to open fire on his home—and it was shelled by canon fire.

Within a month of this battle, his health broke and he shortly passed away. Thomas Nelson's biographer wrote that "he descended into the grave honored and beloved, and alas! of his once vast estates, that honor and love was almost all that he left behind him. He had spent a princely fortune in his Country's service; his horses had been taken from the plough and sent to drag the munitions of war; his granaries had been thrown open to a starving soldiery and his ample purse had been drained to its last dollar, when the credit of Virginia could not bring a sixpence into her treasury. Yet it was the widow of this man who . . . had yet to learn whether republics can be grateful."

Lucy Nelson had been born wealthy and had helped Thomas make his fortune and rise to the Governor's mansion. When he died early, broke and destitute, she was left to raise eleven children and eke out a living for three decades alone. When she died at eighty years of age she was "blind, infirm" and still poor, and she willed her only earthly possession, $20, to her minister. The Nelson family understood both Liber and Public Virtue.

Samuel and Eliza Adams

Another man, whose name is more familiar, also personified these forgotten virtues. Samuel Adams was educated by his father in the liberal arts through the classics.[iii] He attempted to go into business several times but he spent so much time studying the classics and reading about government and politics that he nearly went bankrupt in every business endeavor. He finally got a job as a tax collector through one of his political contacts. However, he had a hard time with this job also. As a biographer tells it: "Times were hard, money was scarce, and the collections fell [way behind]. Adams's enemies raised the cry of [mismanagement].

"Then it came out that Sam Adams had refused to sell out the last cow or pig or the last sack of potatoes or corn meal or the scant furniture of a poor man to secure his taxes. He had told his superiors in authority that the town did not need the taxes as badly as most of these poor people needed their belongings and that he would rather lose his office than force such collections." This job fell through like his other financial endeavors.

Another biographer wrote: "For years now, Samuel Adams had laid aside all pretense of private business and was devoted simply and solely to public affairs .. His wife, like himself, was contented with poverty; through good management, in spite of their narrow means, a comfortable home life was maintained in which the children grew up happy and in every way well trained and cared for."

Sam Adams and his wife, Elizabeth Wells Adams (she went by the name Eliza), and all of their children sacrificed and suffered for the cause of freedom, including a son who was imprisoned. Even the family dog, a big Newfoundland named Queue, got involved in the War. In fact, Queue was "cut and shot in several places" by British soldiers, because every time a red uniform passed by the Adams farm Queue viciously attacked. Perhaps this dog understood the issues or at least the views of his master. As Eliza Adams's biographer wrote: "[Queue] had a vast antipathy for the British uniform . . . and bore to his grave honorable scars from his fierce encounters."

In 1763, Sam Adams gave the first public speech in the Americas against the British and the first call for Independence. He was so successful in stirring up support for the Revolution, that when the British later offered clemency to all the signers of the Declaration who would recant, Samuel Adams and John Hancock were purposely left of the list. He was an instigator of the Boston Tea Party and was involved in almost every major event of the Revolution. He served in the Continental Congress and the records show that he was involved in almost every significant committee and spoke on nearly every important issue.

Once, in response to a suggestion to try to compromise with the British, Samuel Adams obtained the floor and said to the General Council of the States: "I should advise persisting in our struggle for liberty, though it were revealed from Heaven that nine hundred and ninety-nine were to perish and only one of a thousand were to survive and retain his liberty! One such freeman must possess more virtue, and enjoy more happiness than a thousand slaves . . ."

In a time when many people spoke against slavery but owned slaves, Samuel and Eliza Adams urged everyone to free any and all slaves, and then set the example by promptly freeing all slaves the moment they came into possession of them.

In 1774, when Samuel Adams was elected to Congress, he had no money for the necessary expenses, and his absence would likely have left his family destitute. A private letter, written on August 11, 1774, tells the story: some of his neighbors, their names kept anonymous, "asked his permission to build him a new barn . . . which was executed in a few days."

A second benefactor repaired his house; a third invited him to a tailor's shop and then had him measured for and purchased him a new suit of cloths which was later delivered to his home. A fourth presented him with a new wig and a fifth bought him a new hat. Three others purchased him six articles of clothing, including a new pair of shoes. Another community member slipped him a purse of money; when he searched it, it contained adequate gold to cover his expenses.

His kinsman John Adams wrote: ". . . Samuel Adams . . . never planned, laid a scheme or formed a design of laying up anything for himself . . . .The case of Samuel Adams is almost without a parallel as an instance of enthusiastic, unswerving devotion to public service throughout a long life."

Francis and Elizabeth Lewis

Another family that epitomized Liber and Public Virtue was the Francis and Elizabeth Lewis family.[iv] Francis was a signer of the Declaration from New York, was educated in the classics and built a successful business from scratch with the help of Elizabeth. They both gave their wealth and health for our freedom.

"Like Floyd, Livingst one, and Robert Morris, the other New York signers, Francis Lewis was

[outlawed] by the British and a price set on his head. The enemy did not stop there. Very soon after they were in possession of Long Island, Captain Birtch was sent with a troop . . . 'to seize the lady and destroy the property.' As the soldiers advanced on one side, a ship of war from the other fired upon the house . . . . Mrs. Lewis looked calmly on. A shot from the vessel struck the board on which she stood. One of her servants cried: 'Run, Mistress, run.' She replied: 'Another shot is not likely to strike the same spot," and did not change her place. The soldiers entered the house and . . . destroyed books, papers, and pictures, ruthlessly broke up the furniture, and then, after pillaging the house, departed taking Mrs. Lewis with them."

"She was carried to New York and thrown into prison. She was not allowed a bed or change of clothing and only the coarse and scanty food that was doled out to the other prisoners." She soon died from the treatment and illnesses she sustained in prison. Francis lived without her for twenty-four more years; he never remarried, but lived to know the lonely price of public virtue.

The Teachers of Liberty

Consider the contribution of four great teachers of the Founding generation, three of whom were signers of the Declaration: George Wythe, John Witherspoon, Benjamin Rush and a man who is remembered simply as Mr. Lovell. Among them they mentored almost an entire generation of leaders in Liber and Public Virtue. Their students include John Adams, Jefferson, Madison, Monroe, Henry Clay, John Marshall, Hancock, Paine, four future U.S. Presidents, many future Supreme Court Justices, over sixty future governors, senators, representatives and judges, and as Professor Forrest McDonald put it, "enough other Founding Fathers to populate a small standing army."

Biographer Robert Peterson said that George Wythe's school alone "produced a generation of lawyers, judges, ministers, teachers and statesmen who helped fill the need for leadership in the young nation." This was, in fact, George Wythe's explicit agenda. The curriculum and message of these teachers, both on paper and through example, was Liber, private virtue and public virtue.

Roger and Rebecca Sherman

Or consider Roger and Rebecca Sherman.[v] Roger Sherman, was apprenticed as a shoemaker and gained a Liber education reading the classics he placed on his bench in front of him while he worked on shoes. He started with mathematics classics and became a leading mathematician; for example, he did the astronomical calculations for an almanac that was published in New York when he was twenty-seven. He went from mathematics to a study of the law, and became a leading jurist in Rhode Island and later the only man to participate in the creation of and sign all four of the founding documents of

the United States—all springing from the books on his cobbler bench.

His wife Rebecca was similarly self-educated in the classics, and when she married Roger she was twenty years old and took over the raising of Roger's seven children from his first wife Elizabeth. She educated the seven children, plus the eight additional children she and Roger had, and she taught them Liber, private virtue and public virtue.

Other Examples

So many other stories could be told: Like Honest John Hart, who was "hounded and hunted as a criminal" while his wife lay dying."[vi]Or, Richard Stockton, who was thrown in prison, his lands were destroyed, and he ended up literally begging for food and money to keep his family alive.[vii]

Or, Martha Jefferson, who fled with her two-month old baby in her arms to escape the invading British. The baby died soon after, and within two years she herself passed on from illnesses incurred during the conflict.[Viii]

Abraham and Sarah Clark

But consider the Public Virtue of one more family, who more than self their country loved: Abraham and Sarah Clark.[ix] Self-educated in the classics, Abraham become known as "the poor man's lawyer" because of his habit of service without pay. A poor farmer, his reading and study made him prominent and he was elected to Congress and signed the Declaration of Independence with the New Jersey delegation.

The British gave this simple man and his wife perhaps the cruelest punishment of all. They captured two of his sons who were serving under Washington, 25-year-old Thomas and young teenage Isaac, and threw them into the prison ship in the harbor. Then they informed Abraham Clark that his sons would be not be given food until he publicly recanted his signature on the Declaration of Independence.

He gladly offered his life, his freedom and all his possessions, but they weren't accepted. The British demanded that he recant or his sons would slowly starve.

Abraham and Sarah determined that they could give up their life. They could give up their fortune. But they simply could not give away their sacred honor, even to save the lives of their dear sons. They never signed the recantation. Imagine, on a 4th of July in 1780, Abraham and Sarah Clark sitting at home meditating on the price of Public Virtue.

What of the Future?

On the 4th of July in 1776, John Hancock, man of Liber and public virtue, signed the Declaration of Independence and sent it to the world with his name alone.

On the 4th of July in 1826, as if by divine mandate, both John Adams and Thomas Jefferson passed away—on the same special day, only a few hours apart.

On the 4th of July in 1862, a bloody Civil War tested whether this union would survive.

On the 4th of July in 1943, Americans gave their lives in Europe and around the Pacific to keep the flag of freedom waving.

In this 4th of July in the year 2000, consider this question: How many Liber are there today in the United States?

And secondly, how many acts of public virtue fill the courthouses, congressional chambers or governors mansions across this land?

The answer tells us what the future of our freedoms will be. But more importantly, how many homes are training young men and women to be Liber, to spend their lives in public virtue? I know that we are busy going to school, making a living, enjoying the leisure our freedom gives us. But if we are too busy to read the classics and become Liber, to sacrifice our time and resources to protect our freedoms and build our communities, to stand for something, then we are too busy to remain free. Too busy to secure the blessings of liberty to ourselves and our posterity.

Think ahead to the 4th of July in the year 2032.

What will America be like then?

The answer depends on three things: how many Liber there are, how many people dedicate their lives to private virtue, and how much public virtue we choose between now and then. The future of America depends on whether we are willing to stand for something. To become Liber, men and women of public virtue. I believe that we will still be free on the 4th of July, 2032. If we are, it will be because someone, somewhere, pays the price.

Some of you have tonight felt the call to become men and women of Liber and public virtue. Do not ignore that call.

[i] The idea of using the signers of the Declaration of Independence as examples of public virtue came from a speech I read by Rush Limbaugh's father, and I appreciate his speech and the fact that his son has published and distributed it. None of the stories in this speech are taken directly from that speech; most of the stories hereafter, including all of the stories and quotes about Robert and Mary Morris come from two excellent books: B.J. Lossing. 1848. Lives of the Signers of the Declaration of Independence (hereafter Signers). Reprinted in 1998 by Wallbuilders in Aledo, Texas, 93-98; and Wives of the Signers, The Women Behind the Declaration of Independence (hereafter Wives), also published by Wallbuilders, 155-168. I have not done independent research to verify the stories in these books. I highly recommend both of these books to students who choose to study further. [ii] Stories and quotes about Thomas and Lucy Nelson come from in Signers, 188-193 and Wives, 250-254. [iii] Stories and quotes about Samuel and Eliza Adams come from Signers, 33-36 and Wives, 62-80. [iv] Stories and quotes about Francis and Elizabeth Lewis come from Signers, 71-73 and Wives, 119-126. [v] Stories and quotes about Roger and Rebecca Sherman come from Signers, 50-52 and Wives, 92-98. [vi] See Wives, 144-147. [vii] See Wives, 132-139. [viii] See Wives, 240-247. [ix] Stories and quotes about Abraham and Sarah Clark come from Signers, 90-92 and Wives, 147-149.

Nobility of a Boy

ADAPTED FROM A STORY TOLD BY MARGARET EGGLESTON IN HER BOOK
"THE USE OF THE STORY IN RELIGIOUS EDUCATION"

There was once a young boy named David who lived in New York City in the early 1900's. He worked as an errand boy at a bank near his home. His job was very important to the family for his father had recently passed away and he had a mother and sister at home who were ill and could not walk. David was the only one left to care for his mother and sister and he was the sole support for them. It took every cent he could possibly earn to take care of their little family.

A few weeks after David's father's funeral, the doctor came to the house to check in on David's mother and sister. The doctor told David that unless he could get his mother to the country where there was plenty of fresh air that she would grow increasingly worse and may very well be gone by winter. David tried everything he could to find a way to send his mother and sister to the country but there was no way. He made barely enough money to provide their basic needs; there was no money to pay for them to stay in the country and no one to house them. David was broken hearted, and he felt helpless as he watched, day after day, as his mother grew less and less strong.

One day, while working at the bank, David was sweeping under a table when he found a roll of bills—a big

roll—and he could see that some of them were yellow-backs. Now at that time, yellow-backs were a type of paper currency that was redeemable for gold coin. These were issued until the early 1900's and thought very valuable as they were able to be exchanged into precious metal on demand.

David scooped up the bills and started to head for the office of the bank president when he suddenly hesitated, realizing what this money would mean. "Just think," he thought, "of what these bills will do. They can send mother and Millie away for the whole summer and then they will be well. No one knows I have them, and they don't belong to the bank. They were on the floor with trash paper. I'm going to keep them. Finding is keeping, and they are mine."

So David dropped the wad of bills into his front pocket, then his back pocket, then shifted them into his coat pocket. He felt sure that everyone could see them as he left the bank, but no one stopped him. All the way home, he fingered the bills in his pocket, taking his hand in and out of the pocket and shifting the bills inside. When he arrived home he checked on his mother and sister and then walked to the cupboard in the hallway, opened the front drawer and dropped the bills inside, closing the drawer with a hard thud.

An hour later, David walked back into the bank and shuffled quickly through the front room, making his way to the office of the bank president. Entering the office, he threw the bills on the desk and whispered, "I found these when I swept." Then, with a cry of pain, he fled from the bank.

The next morning David was back at the bank to do his work when he was called into the bank president's office. When David entered the room, the bank president looked up from his desk and spoke.

"David," he said, "I wish you would tell me why you brought those bills back last night. I know why you wanted them and what they would have done for you and your family. No one knew you had them. Why did you bring them back?"

David leaned far over the desk and looked right in the eyes of the president of the bank. "Sir," he said, "as long as I live, I have to live with myself, and I don't want to live with a thief."

A few days later the mother and Millie went to the country, but not alone. David went with them, and they spent the whole summer in the countryside—a gift from the bank to show their deep appreciation for the nobility of the boy.

Perfect Gentleman

EXCERPTED FROM THE BOOK *TEACHING THE CHILD PATRIOTISM*, 1918

During the last few years, magazines have published many helpful series on politics and a number of these deserve special credit for their work in this area. In one of these articles the writer reminds us that though the sins of our time are the same old sins which were denounced by Jeremiah and Ezekiel, they are likely now to be enameled with fine new exteriors and called by new names.

A dazzling outside may cover a black heart. Many public men of ancient and modern times afford striking examples of inconsistency. For instance, take William M. Tweed, whose gigantic thefts almost bankrupted a great city, yet who read a chapter in his Bible every day, and who possessed many kind and even noble qualities.

A certain excellent country gentleman, who did not realize the possible deceitfulness of the outside, went down to the capital of his state to see about some bills which vitally affected his business. He had written to the Senator from his district that he was coming and had asked for an appointment to meet him. He had never met this man, but the papers had criticized him severely, and our friend was prepared to encounter a mean and churlish creature.

"Instead," he reported upon his return to his home, "I found him a perfect gentleman. He met me at the train and took me to my hotel in his own automobile, and invited me to dine with him the next day. He lives in a beautiful home. I was surprised to see what kind of a man he really is. You would think the way the papers go on about him that he had horns and hoofs, but," he repeated, "he was a perfect gentleman." Yet he knew this man was one of the most dangerous 'practical politicians' in the state—one of those who believe that the Ten Commandments have no place in politics, and who scrupled at nothing which could benefit himself and his friends.

"Unlike the old-time villain," says Mr. E. A. Reed, "the latter-day malefactor does not wear a slouch-hat and a comforter, and breathe forth curses and an odor of gin. Fagin and Bill Sykes and Simon Legree are vanishing types."

Let us see that our children are taught the elementary ethics of politics—the duty of every voter to vote and do jury work, the need of looking at every question from both sides, and avoiding blind partisanship. And it is upon the mother that this patriotic duty must chiefly devolve….It must be emphasized that though school discipline should be of the best, yet the real education of your child depends more upon his home than on his school. You can bring very near your boy and your girl the responsibility of us all for good home government by mentioning often to them the burning issues of their own home town.

Explain to your children how the taxes are laid—how a town has to spend a good deal to keep itself up, so to speak, and how important it is that its tax-money should be carefully spent.

Particularly should we impress it upon our children that if a town is a slipshod, ugly or unhealthy place, it is not the fault of a vague, formless thing called "the town" or "the city" or "the state," but of each and every one of us—and especially of every separate voter—who fails to be on hand at the town meetings or caucuses, and to try his best to get good men elected and good measures passed.

Children should early be taught to regard the neatness and beauty of their town. If they complain that these matters are too hard to remember and to do, give them to understand that patriotism in not easy. Few virtues are easy to practice, and perhaps unselfish patriotism is the hardest of all.

It is up to us whether our children grow to just look and seem like perfect gentleman, or if they will actually be such. Our town, our state, our nation will reflect our choice.

Nathan Hale: One Life to Give

"I only regret that I have but one life to lose for my country" were the last words of 21-year-old American patriot Nathan Hale, who was hanged by the British without a trial on SEPTEMBER 22, 1776.

A Yale graduate, 1773, he almost became a Christian minister, as his brother Enoch did, but instead became a teacher at Union Grammar School.

When the Revolutionary War began in 1775, Nathan Hale joined a Connecticut militia and served in the siege of Boston. On July 4, 1775, Hale received a letter from his Yale classmate, Benjamin Tallmadge, who was now General Washington's chief intelligence officer: "Was I in your condition...I think the more extensive service would be my choice. Our holy Religion, the honour of our God, a glorious country, & a happy constitution is what we have to defend."

Hale accepted a commission as first lieutenant in the 7th Connecticut Regiment under Colonel Charles Webb of Stamford. The following Spring, they joined the Continental Army's effort to prevent the British from taking New York City. According to tradition, Nathan Hale was part of a daring band of patriots who captured an English sloop filled with provisions from right under the guns of a British man-of-war.

General Washington, at this time, was desperate to know where the British planned to invade Manhattan Island, writing on September 6, 1776, "We have not been able to obtain the least information on the enemy's plans."

Washington sought a spy to penetrate the British lines at Long Island to get information, and Nathan Hale was the only volunteer.

Fellow officer Captain William Hull attempted to talk him out it, but Hale responded, "I wish to be useful, and every kind of service necessary to the public good becomes honorable by being necessary. If the exigencies of my country demand a peculiar service, its claim to perform that service are imperious."

On September 21, 1776, Hale was captured by the "Queen's Rangers" commanded by an American loyalist, Lieut. Col. Robert Rogers. General William Howe ordered him to be hanged the next morning. Hale wrote a letter to his mother and brother, but the British destroyed them, not wanting it known a man could die with such firmness. He asked for a Bible but was refused. Nathan Hale was marched out and hanged from an apple-tree in Rutgers's orchard, near the present streets of East Broadway and Market in New York City.

The Essex Journal stated of Nathan Hale, February 13, 1777, "At the gallows, he made a sensible and spirited speech; among other things, told them they were shedding the blood of the innocent, and that if he had ten thousand lives, he would lay them all down, if called to it, in defense of his injured, bleeding Country."

A fellow soldier of Nathan Hale, Lt. Elisha Bostwick said of him, "when any of the soldiers of his company were sick, he always visited them and usually prayed for and with them in their sickness."

American Heritage Magazine, "The Last Days and Valiant Death of Nathan Hale" (April 1964)

Nathan Hale's nephew, Massachusetts Governor Edward Everett, spoke at the dedication of the Battlefield right before Abraham Lincoln gave his Gettysburg Address, November 19, 1863. Nathan Hale's grandnephew was well-known author Edward Everett Hale, who wrote, "We are God's children, you and I, and we have our duties...Thank God I come from men who are not afraid in battle."

Capturing this patriotic spirit, American poet Ralph Waldo Emerson wrote in his poem "Voluntaries" (1863):

"So nigh is grandeur to our dust,

So near is God to man,

When Duty whispers low, 'Thou must'

The youth replies, 'I can'"

Reflecting the Light of Virtue

ADAPTED FROM WINGS OF FLAME BY JOSEPH B. EGAN, 1929

One night, long before street lighting was heard of, as Benjamin Franklin sat cooling himself by an open window, he heard a man stumble and fall on the uneven cobblestones in front of his door. The man obviously hurt himself judging by the words he growled while picking himself back up.

Franklin made note of what had happened and said to himself, "It is evident that I am, in a sense, the cause

of this man's fall. Had there been a light in my window it would have shone on the street and so prevented his misfortune."

The next morning, he hurried to the lantern maker's shop. The shopkeeper asked if he was looking for a small lantern to light his way as he walked in the night. "Oh, no," was Franklin's reply. "My friend, I want a huge lantern with wide light spaces on four sides and I want a good strong rack to hang it from." Mr. Franklin then pointed to the largest lanterns in the shop.

The keeper laughed. "There's not a room big enough in all Philadelphia for that lantern."

Franklin replied, "It's not too big for the out-of-doors. Please prepare the rack and hang it over my front door before nightfall. Make sure it carries out well onto the street, but high above every passing head. I shall personally tend to lighting it each evening."

The keeper was puzzled but agreed to do just as he was told.

Soon, people came from far and near to see the light Franklin had swung out in front of his own door.

"What an idea," said one.

"I shall do the same," said another.

"Why stumble over these cobbles when a little light over each man's door makes the dark way plain?"

"Why didn't someone think of this before?"

"Trust Old Ben to think up a scheme like this to get the citizens of this town busy on street lighting. Any other person would have talked and argued, but Old Ben—well—he just went ahead and hung up a light."*

As confusion and contention increases in our nation and world, *Moms for America* offers a simple solution: Don't underestimate the power and influence that one home reflecting the light of virtue can have on an increasingly dark world.

Ben Franklin's Pursuit of a Virtuous Life

Benjamin Franklin became an incredibly respected man, despite his humble beginnings. It was because of his life-long pursuit of virtue that he garnered so much respect. Mr. Franklin made it his life's mission to maintain high moral standards, and his dedication allowed him to accomplish unimaginable things in his life. He realized early in life the critical need of a virtuous society to sustain a free one. "Only a virtuous people are capable of freedom," he lamented. "As nations become more corrupt and vicious, they have more need of masters."

Benjamin Franklin's influence on our society and culture has been profound. His words have been immortalized with timeless treasures of truth; the University of Pennsylvania adopted Ben's declaration, "Laws without morals are in vain" as their school motto. From his short quips to his world-changing inventions, he has left a mark on our nation that continues to this day.

Throughout his life and career, Ben worked to be the best self he could be. He didn't wait for a prestigious position to invest his time, cultivate his talents, or engage in things that were important to him.

At the young age of 12, he began to publish his witty and insightful newspaper articles under the pseudonym "Silence Dogood" while still bound as a printer's apprentice under his half-brother James. After working for several printers in New England and beyond, he eventually set up his own print shop, along with Hugh Meridith, at the age of 22, buying out his partner a year later. He also began printing "Poor Richard's Almanack" at the age of 26, a publication that continued for more than 20 years.

Ben's path for a virtuous life led him to create good relationships, which was essential in his small print business and, later, his political career. Because of his strength of character, he easily won the trust of others. He

The virtues Benjamin Franklin strove to personify are very similar to the attributes that Jesus Christ taught and lived by.

Ben Franklin's
Pursuit of a Virtuous Life

Silence

Speak not but what may benefit others or yourself; avoid trifling conversation

Temperance

Eat not to dullness: drink not to elevation.

Order

Let all your things have their places; let each part of your business have its resolve.

Resolution

Resolve to perform what you ought; perform without fail what you resolve.

Frugality

Make no expense but to do good to others or yourself; ie, waste nothing.

Lose no time; be always employed in something useful; cut off all accordingly.

Industry

Use no hurtful deceit; think innocently and justly, and, if you speak, speak accordingly.

Sincerity

Wrong none by doing injuries, or omitting the benefits that are your duty

Justice

Moderation

.Avoid extremes; forbear resenting injuries so much as you think they deserve

Cleanliness

Tolerate no uncleanliness in body, clothes, or habitation.

Tranquility

Be not disturbed at trifles, or at accidents common or unavoidable

Chasity

Rarely use venery but for health or offspring, never to dullness, weakness, or the injury of your own or another's peace or reputation

Humility

Imitate Jesus and Socrates

We stand at the crossroads, each minute, each hour, each day, making choices. We choose the thoughts we allow ourselves to think, the passions we allow ourselves to feel, and the actions we allow ourselves to perform. Each choice is made in the context of whatever value system we have selected to govern our lives. In selecting that value system, we are, in a very real way, making the most important choice we will ever make.

~Ben Franklin,
The Art of Virtue

was entrusted with numerous positions of leadership and responsibility. He served as a commander of militia forces and supervisor of construction while building stockades for defense against the Indians during the French and Indian War. He was appointed as a diplomat during the Revolutionary War and held multiple elected offices throughout his life. He negotiated treaties with France and England over the course of 30 years. And in 1790, he founded the Pennsylvania Abolition Society, calling for the end of slavery—the greatest evil of his day.

While working on the newspaper when he was 12 years old, Ben came upon a book entitled *Essays to do Good*. In a letter to Samuel Mather, he said of the book "[it] gave me such a turn of thinking, as to have an influence on my conduct through life; … and if I have been, as you seem to think, a useful citizen, the public owes the advantage of it to that book."

The book had such a profound impact on Ben Franklin that he decided to use the principles to do a daily assessment of his character. He created a small chart, and each day, he would make a mark on next to the areas he neglected to reflect on, making notes of where he needed to do better or where he did well. Over the years, his improvement was visible as he kept these virtues in mind from day to day. When you read through the list of virtues Benjamin Franklin strove to personify, it is interesting note they closely mirror the attributes that Jesus Christ taught and lived by. The culmination of his list concludes with "Imitate Jesus and Socrates."

Because of what Mr. Franklin learned, he desired to share with the youth what he considered principles that could be applied, with reward, to anyone willing to work for it. He introduced twelve foundational principles of virtue, which became the guiding principles of his life. Ben wrote a book titled the *The Art of Virtue* to share these principles. In this classic memoir he writes, "We stand at the crossroads, each minute, each hour, each day, making choices. We choose the thoughts we allow ourselves to think, the passions we allow ourselves to feel, and the actions we allow ourselves to perform. Each choice is made in the context of whatever value system we have selected to govern our lives. In selecting that value system, we are, in a very real way, making the most important choice we will ever make."

We encourage families to acquire a copy of Benjamin Franklin's *The Art of Virtue*, which details Franklin's thoughts on each of these virtues and leads to great family discussions.

Living a virtuous life in times such as we are living now can influence the world for good. It can raise our hope, give us power, and lesson our fear. It will stretch and extend us to become better, and behave better, in our family relationships and our interactions with others. When families across America adopt these principles, liberty will be that much closer to being secured.

Fulfilling Our Civic Duty

BY KIMBERLY FLETCHER
PRESIDENT/FOUNDER, MOMS FOR AMERICA

Over the Years, I have heard a lot of people say things like "I don't get involved in politics." I completely understand why you wouldn't want to; after all, politics is not a pleasant thing. In fact, it is all those things your mother told you to stay away from when you were growing up. But it is important that we understand the difference between politics and civic responsibility, because they are *not* the same thing. Our nation is in the terrible state it is—where freedom hangs in the balance—because we have not fulfilled our civic responsibility. The harsh reality is, if

we don't like what is happening in America, then we only have ourselves to blame.

We have heard a great deal about what the government can do for the people but hear very little about "by the people" and "of the people". In America, the people rule. We are the defenders of liberty, we are the keepers of freedom, and we are the creators and overseers of our government. So, what happens when we stop watching over that government? What happens when we are no longer willing to serve in elected office? What happens when We the People walk away? The answer is POLITICS.

Defending liberty is not politics. Sharing the light of liberty with our children is not politics. Respecting the law, honoring God, and defending the Constitution are not politics. All of these things are our civic duty. Politics is simply a word people hide behind when they don't have any principles and lack the courage to stand up for what is right. We can't talk about life because "it is political." We can't talk about God because "it is political." We can't talk about right and wrong and the Ten Commandments because "it is political." Just look at all the things that have been politicized today—life, religion, God, healthcare, income, work, freedom; even America itself has become a political issue. It is absurd!

We need to rise above the scum line of politics and realize that being proud to be an American and willing to defend freedom and the Constitution is not political—it is our civic duty. To better explain and emphasize just what that means, we have provided some definitions for you.

Politics is a product of pride, worldliness, and a lust for power.

Civic responsibility is that duty which every American has as a citizen of this country to respect the law, be involved in our communities, preserve the Constitution, safeguard the Republic, watch over our government, and seek out and elect good leaders to represent us. Politics is what happens when not enough of us fulfill that duty.

A Politician is a person who lusts for power, is obsessed with self-importance, and motivated by greed. Politicians have been groomed in politics. They learn the artful craftiness of deceit, the clever tactics of scheming to get gain and win votes, and the cunning methods of distraction, distortion, denial, and blame shifting. Politicians will say and do whatever it takes to keep and add to their power. They are motivated by self-preservation and personal gain and put their own interests above the people they serve. Politicians will vote for anything they feel benefits them regardless of how their constituents feel or whether or not it is in the best interest of the country. Politicians are self-serving individuals who hold little regard for God or country and feel no loyalty or affection for the people they serve.

A statesman, on the other hand, is a person of integrity and high moral character who possesses a strong desire to serve others, recognizes his/her imperfections, and strives to overcome them to be the best person he/she can be. Statesmen have been trained in humanity. They learn the moral code of right and wrong, the positive attributes of honesty, humility, patriotism, accepting responsibility, and the selfless standards of love thy neighbor, the golden rule, and country before self.

Statesmen are people of faith who believe in a supreme being and a future state of rewards and punishments. They research issues carefully and do their best to vote in the best interest of the Republic and the people they represent—even if it means losing votes.

Statesmen cherish freedom and liberty, have a deep affection and concern for those they serve, and feel a profound sense of duty and loyalty to their Country. They live their faith, reverence God, and respect the faith of others.

Perhaps you feel I am oversimplifying my definitions. Perhaps you think I'm being too harsh on politicians. That is possible. I am sure there are politicians who possess some of the characteristics of a statesmen, and I know there are statesmen who fall prey to politics, but we must ask ourselves, are we willing to settle with mediocre? Is 80% statesman good enough? How do you feel about your husband or wife being 80% faithful? I want a husband who is 100% faithful, and I want my elected officials to be 100% faithful to the Constitution and the Republic. We may disagree on policy, but we must be unified on those core principles because they are the principles that unite us and protect our God-given rights.

It is important that we clearly understand the difference between civic responsibility and politics because politics is what is tearing this country down, and we need a major infusion of civic responsibility to save it.

Part of civic responsibility is to find and elect good people to office to represent us, but "We the People" must first be statesmen ourselves because we need statesmen filling all aspects of society to maintain and advance freedom. We need to ask ourselves: do we want politicians serving in Congress or Statesmen? Do we want Politicians serving in city councils and school boards or Statesmen? Do we want Politicians or Statesman in media, entertainment, business and sports? And who do we want teaching our children: a Statesman or a Politician?

Corruption doesn't begin in Washington, and it doesn't end there either. We need Statesmen in our schools teaching our children, in the media presenting the news, in our elected offices serving the people. And we need to be statesmen ourselves.

We're losing our country because we have been fighting principle with policy. We need to fight principle with principle because when we do, freedom wins!

What we need is a mighty change of heart in America, and we need to begin with our own hearts. We live in the greatest, freest country on earth. America is not our enemy; she is our home. Liberty is not the problem, the lack of it is.

It is easy for us to blame Congress, the president, and government at large for all our "problems" but the fact is, none of these are the problem. They are only symptoms of the it. The real problem is that We the People have abdicated our Civic Responsibility, and the solution is to rise up and fulfill that vital role.

There are no easy answers to the 'big government' problem. But there are simple solutions. Term limits, third parties, and endorsements are duplications of a failed system. The only way to truly preserve liberty is to take our government back in our own hands where it belongs, and where it was always meant to be.

It won't be easy. Benjamin Franklin knew this when he said they left us a Republic if we could keep it. We are the only ones who can keep it. It will take hard work, dedication and a long-term commitment. We did not get here overnight, and we are not going to fix it overnight. There is no easy way out, and no one is coming to save us. There is only We the People, and it is We the People who will have to save ourselves. If ever there was a people who could do it, it is us. And Liberty is worth the cost.

A Story of George Washington

FROM THE FREEDOM SERIES, AMERICAN HISTORY STORIES VOLUME 1 BY
MARA L. PRATT

During the Revolution, George Washington was one day riding by a group of soldiers who did not know him. They were busily engaged in raising a beam to the top of some military works. It was a difficult task, and often, the corporal's voice could be heard shouting, "Now you have it!" and "All ready! Pull!"

Washington quietly asked the corporal why he didn't help them. "Sir," the corporal angrily replied, "do you not realize that I am a corporal?"

Washington politely raised his hat saying, "I did not realize it. Beg your pardon, Mr. Corporal."

Then, dismounting his horse, General Washington himself fell to work and helped the men until the beam was raised. Before leaving, he turned to the corporal and wiping the perspiration from his face said, "If ever you need assistance like this again, call upon Washington, your commander-in-chief, and I will come."

The confused corporal turned red and then white as he realized that this was Washington himself to whom he had been so pompous, and we hope he learned a lesson of true greatness.

Rewrite the story using different characters, time period, and setting but staying with the same theme and storyline. The story can take place anywhere in time. It can be science fiction, historical, fantasy, etc. The characters can be people, animals, mythical creatures, even inanimate objects. Use the story board below to launch your story and let your creative juices flow!

Characters	Time Period	Setting

STORY SKETCH

Beginning	Middle	End

PURSUIT OF A VIRTUOUS LIFE

THIS WEEK FOCUS ____ **DATE** __________

Temperance						
Silence						
Order						
Resolution						
Frugality						
Industry						
Sincerity						
Justice						
Moderation						
Cleanliness						
Tranquility						
Chastity						
Humility						

MY PERSONAL PROGRESS:

____
____
____
____
____
____
____

> *Patriotism is not short, frenzied outbursts of emotion, but the tranquil and steady dedication of a lifetime.*
>
> -Adlai Stevenson

Power of Patriotism

PREPARATION

Patriotism includes celebrations, service, and sacrifice. This presentation contains stories of patriotism from the past and explores methods of experiencing patriotism today in the form of celebrations, Liberty Trips, service opportunities, and examples of former patriots. We are infused with patriotism when we have a knowledge of who we are, what it means to be American, and what the dream of America is all about. This knowledge transforms into sacrifice, devotion, and service. What the heart knows, the heart yearns to do. And when the heart is touched, the seeds of patriotism are planted firmly in our souls and we will witness firsthand the Power of Patriotism!

To prepare yourself to lead the presentation, please review and consider the following material:

NOTE: Video links and additional resources are available on the Hostess Resource Center at MomsforAmerica.us

- Watch the Videos: *America Why I Love Her, The Story Behind the National Anthem* and *Great American Treasure Hunt.* The videos are provided in the Hostess Resource Center of the Moms for America® website

- Read: "Nothing to Love About America" and "A Place Called Liberty"

- Review Principle 9 pages 137-138 and Principle 10 of *The 5000 Year Leap* and mark any sections you would like to share in your meeting

- Quote: "Patriotism is not short, frenzied outbursts of emotion, but the tranquil and steady dedication of a lifetime." -Adlai Stevenson

- Read the National Anthem (all four verses) provided in the Supplemental Materials section of this presentation. If possible, print copies of the Anthem with all 4 verses to pass out to your group members at the meeting

- Review the Quotes provided in the Supplemental Materials section of this presentation

- Bible References—Joshua 4:4-9, 21-24, Genesis 34:16

- Optional: If available, Review *Promises of the Constitution* vignettes 3.1, 3.3, 3.8, 3.10, 3.11, 3.12

Home Assignment

With your family, visit a monument, history landmark, history event or hands-on history location. Red and share the stories about the location prior to your visit.

Personal Study

Read chapter excerpt *"Lest Forget"* available in Cottage Meeting Resources on the MFA website.

Read *"7 Miracles that Saved America"* as a family.

Family Enrichment

View the video *"Story Behind the National Anthem"* and other patriotic videos available in Cottage Meeting Resources on the MFA website. Discuss as a family how you can show patriotism through your actions.

The purpose of this presentation is to introduce the Pillar of Patriotism as a matter of the heart and manifested through devotion to a cause higher than oneself—not for what the Patriot knows in his mind, but for what he understands in his heart. This is leads to lasting dedication to living and promoting the principles of liberty.

KEY POINTS

- American Heritage is rich with accounts of great patriots

- Instilling love of country in the hearts of our children is accomplished through stories, experiences, and by example

- The God-given right to govern is vested in the sovereign authority of the whole people

MEETING OUTLINE

Welcome & Gathering

We recommend starting your meeting with prayer and the Pledge of Allegiance. Have members of the group share their thoughts and experiences from your last meeting's take home assignment.

Show Video: *America Why I Love Her* by John Wayne

Read & Discuss: "Nothing to Love About America"

George William Custis said:

> *"A man's country is not a certain area of land, of mountains, rivers, and woods, but it is a principle; and patriotism is loyalty to that principle."*

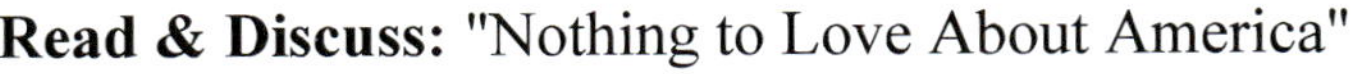

What principle or principles is American patriotism founded on?

How can we instill these principles in the hearts of our children? (suggested ideas are reading stories of heroes and patriots, visiting memorials, monuments, and historic sites, and participating in celebrations)

Show Video: *The Story Behind the National Anthem* provided in the Hostess Resource Center

Do you know there is more than one verse to the national Anthem? (Read through the other verses. Pass out copies of the words as you reach through them as a group) Show the video Man Sings

National Anthem *provided in the Hostess Resource Center on the Moms for America® website.*

The United States flag is a symbol of liberty earned by great sacrifice. How can we teach and show our children to take proper care of and and offer respect for the flag? (Optional video "Red Skelton Pledge Allegiance. Link provided in Hostess Resource Center)

Read (or have someone read): "A Place Called Liberty" provided in the Supplemental Materials section of this presentation

Group Discussion

Lead a discussion on Principle 9 (pages 137-138) and Principle 10 from the *5000 Year Leap* using the notes and highlighted sections you marked during preparation. Consider the following questions when leading the discussion:

What is the Supreme Law of the Land? How did the Anglo-Saxons and Israelites look upon law? What is Natural Law? Who decides the law?

Who can alter government? What is meant by 'majority rule'?

Show Video: *Great American Treasure Hunt*

Summary

Summarize your thoughts on the material covered in this presentation

- Give the Home Assignment for the next meeting

- Announce date, time and location for next meeting

ADDITIONAL PRESENTATION IDEAS

Here are some ideas for additional presentations, personal study, and discussions on "Power of Patriotism."

A Dream Called America

There are those, I know, who will say that the liberation of humanity, the freedom of man and mind, is nothing but a dream. They are right. It is the American dream. -Archibald MacLeish

The American Dream is the uniquely American idea that anyone, regardless of where they were born or what class they were born into, can attain their own version of success in a society where upward mobility is possible for everyone. The American Dream isn't something that is just handed to you; it is achieved through sacrifice, risk-taking, and hard work.

- Read "A Dream Called America" provided in the Supplemental Materials section of this presentation

- Read and Discuss Principle 15 of the *5000 Year Leap*. Consider the following questions when leading the discussion:

  - *What is a Free Market economy? What is the best economic system to facilitate the American Dream of individual success? What is the role of government?*

- To aid your discussion, review the "American Dream" quotes provided in the Supplemental Materials section of this presentation

American Exceptionalism

America is an exceptional nation. What makes it exceptional? What makes the United States different in all the world?

- Show Video: Bono *The American Idea*—Speaking at Georgetown University (video link available in the Hostess Resource Center on the Moms for America® website.)

- Read and Discuss Principle 9 of the *5000 Year Leap*. Consider the following questions when leading your discussion:

  - *What is the relationship between obedience to God's law and the protection of man's unalienable rights? What is the difference between private duty and public duty? How does a true patriot perform his public duty?*

- Show Video: Dennis Prager *American Exceptionalism* (video link available in the Hostess Resource Center on the Moms for America® website.)

- Read and Discuss Principle 10 of the *5000 Year Leap*. Consider the following questions when leading your discussion:

  - *What is the difference between the Divine Right of Kings and the Divine Right of People to govern themselves? What responsibility rests upon the individual to maintain a Republican form of government?*

Symbols of Freedom

The Principles of Freedom are represented in many of American symbols.

- Read, Review, and Discuss "Symbols of Freedom" proved in the Hostess Resource Center on the Moms for America® website

- Read and Discuss Principle 28 of the *5000 Year Leap*. Consider the following questions when leading your discussion:

- *What is manifest destiny? What did the founders believe about the providence of America?*

- Review the Quotes provided in the Supplemental Materials section of this presentation.

MINI COTTAGE IDEAS

Mini Cottages are designed especially for moms of preschoolers and moms who work full-time jobs. Moms simply read and/or watch the same materials at home, on their own, then meet together once a week in a playdate or over lunch during the workday to discuss what they read. The articles and videos are short and can usually be read and/or viewed in less than hour. Below are some suggestions to host mini cottage discussions under the "Power of Patriotism" theme.

- Read and Discuss "Nothing to Love About America" and "A Place Called Liberty" provided in the supplemental materials section of this presentation.

- Read "The Heart of Education" Share the story "The Nobility of a Boy" with your children

- Read and Discuss Principle 9 of the *5000 Year Leap*

- Read and Discuss Principle 10 of the *5000 Year Leap*

- Read and Discuss Principle 15 of the *5000 Year Leap*

- To enhance your discussions, review the quotes provided in the Supplemental Materials section of this presentation

- Read "Abigail Adams Patriot Mother" provided in the Supplemental Resources section of this presentation. View the videos *Red Skelton Pledge of Allegiance* and *America Why I Love Her* provided in the Hostess Resource Center on the MFA website

- Watch the video *The Story Behind the National Anthem*. Read through the verses of The National Anthem provided in the Supplemental Resources section of this presentation. View the video *Man Sings National Anthem* provided in Hostess Resource Center of the MFA website

COTTAGE MEETING BOOK CLUB

For those who like the book club format, we've compiled a list of great books to help you gain an appreciation and foundational understanding of the concepts presented in "There's No Place Like Home."

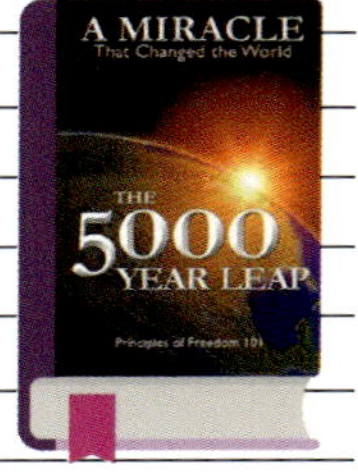

The 5000 Year Leap: A Miracle That Changed the World

Review Principles 9, 10, 15

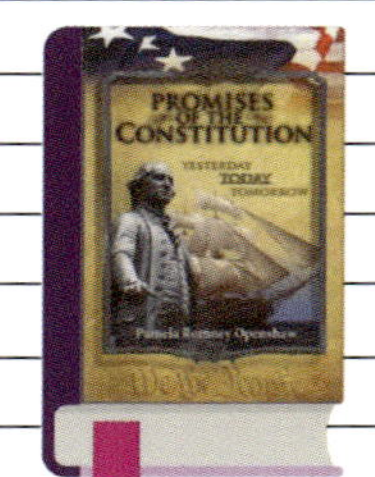

Promises of the Constitution

Review the following vignettes: 1.7, 3.6, 7.7, 12.1, 12.12

Freedom Factor by Gerald N. Lund

"Well," Gorham said slowly, "You are now in an America that has never had the Constitution." Nathaniel Gorham, an original Founding Father, visits young Bryce Sherwood, a rising aide to a Washington senator and a key player in an attempt to pass an amendment that would eliminate the checks and balances built into the Constitution. When Bryce refuses to change his position, Gorham transports him into a world where the Constitution was never ratified. His life-changing journey to an alternate universe helps him realize how precious our country's form of government is, and how much we take freedom for granted. This is also a great family read-a-loud for 10 and up. If you have little ones, they can color or play while you read or, if you read in the evening, you can read to the older children after the little ones go to bed.

COTTAGE MEETINGS FOR KIDS

Cottage Meeting for Kids is a liberty promoting program for the entire family and focused on children from preschool to teens. It is full of great stories and fun activities to help children gain a love of liberty. Families can join together each month for an Activity Day to share the concepts they've learned and enhance them through group activities. Here are some ideas to promote the concepts presented in "Power of Patriotism." You can find additional ideas, outlines, and activities on the Moms for America® website under "Cottage Meetings for Kids."

- Read the Quote by Archibald MacLeish with your children. *"There are those, I know, who will say that the liberation of humanity, the freedom of man and mind, is nothing but a dream. They are right. It is the American dream."* Discuss the following questions: What is the American Dream? What does the American mean to you? What is your dream and how to you plan to achieve it? Note: In America "What do you want to be when you grow up," means whatever it is, you can!

- Invite your teenagers into the story. Hillsdale College has produced a fantastic video series called *The Great American Story: Land of Hope*. It is great for middle and high school age kids as well as parents! You can sign up for the series through the Hostess Resource Center or Cottage Meeting Resources section of the MFA website.

- Read "A Dream Called America" as a family (provided in the Supplemental Materials section of this presentation). Watch the video *America: Why I Love Her* and *Red Skelton's Pledge of Allegiance* in Cottage Meeting Resource section of the MFA website. Review the symbols of liberty with your children. You can print off the cards and play a fun matching game. These resources and more are provided in the "Cottage Meetings for Kids" section of the MFA website.

- Watch the video *The Story Behind the National Anthem* provided in the Hostess Resource Center and "Cottage Meetings for Kids" section of the MFA website. Read through the words of the National Anthem provided in the Supplemental Materials section of this presentation. Watch the video *Man Sings National Anthem* with your children. (Video link provided in the Hostess Resource Center)

- Fun Patriotic Craft Ideas: Painting Fireworks, Making Liberty Bells, Patriotic Rice Crispy Treats. Videos and instructions for these and other projects are provided in "Cottage Meetings for Kids" section on the MFA website.

Book & Movie List

Suggested books and readings for children of all ages to nurture a love of liberty in the home.

Tuttle Twins Book Series
by Connor Boyack

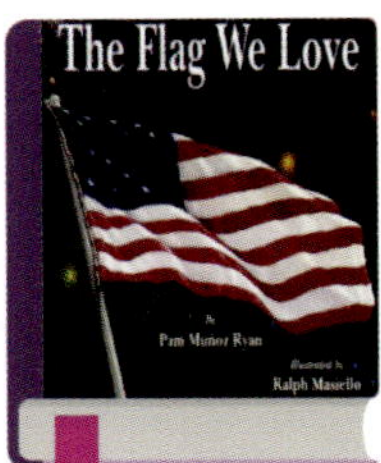

The Flag We Love
by Pam Munoz Ryan

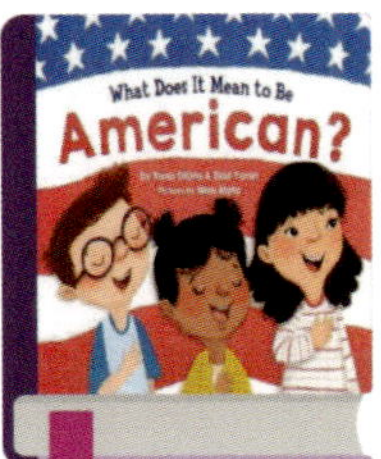

What Does It Mean to Be an American?
by Rana DiOrio and Elad Yoran

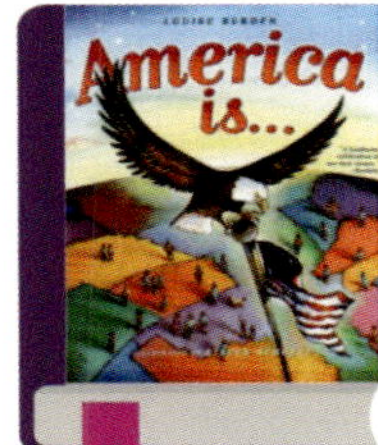

America Is
by Louise Borden

**The Night Before
the 4th of July**
by Natasha Wing

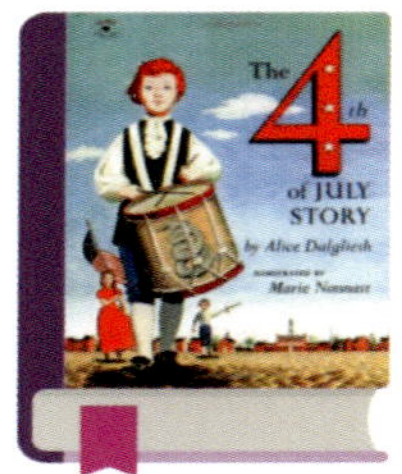

The 4th of July Story
by Alice Dalgliesh

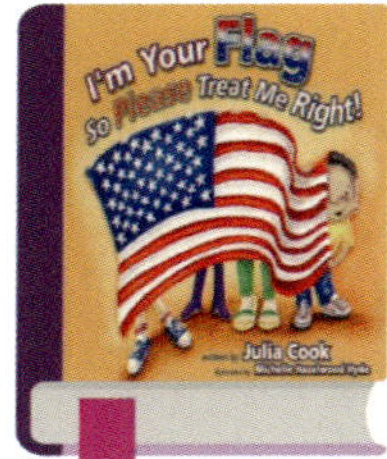

**I'm Your Flag,
Please Treat Me Right**
by Julia Cook

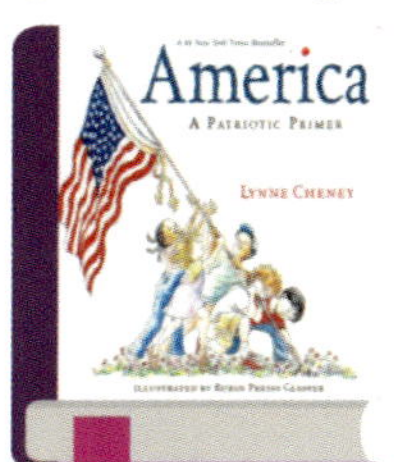

America, A Patriotic Primer
by Lynne Cheney

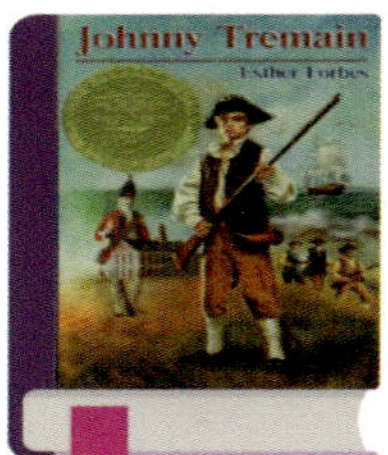

Johnny Tremain
by Esther Forbes Book

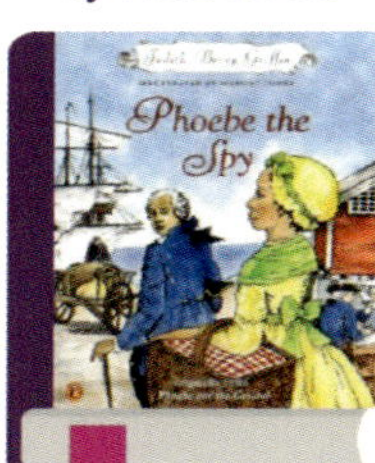

Phoebe the Spy
by Judith Griffin

Toliver's Secret
by Esther Brady

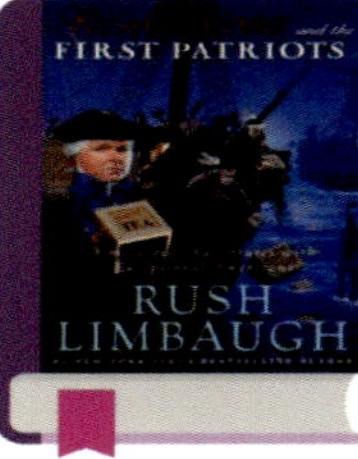

**Rush Revere
and the First Patriots**
by Rush Limbaugh

Johnny Tremain
1957

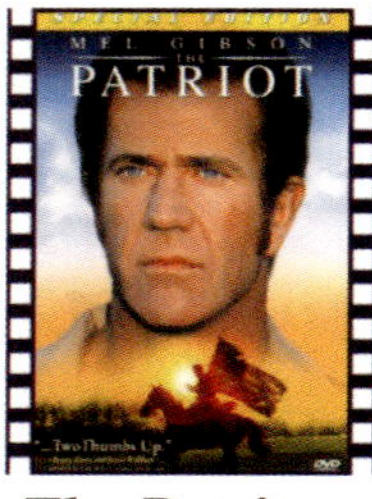

The Patriot
2000
(Parental guidance recommended)

National Treasure
2004

Battle of the Bulge
1965

The Longest Day
1962

Tora Tora Tora
1970

**Mr. Smith
Goes to Washington**
1939

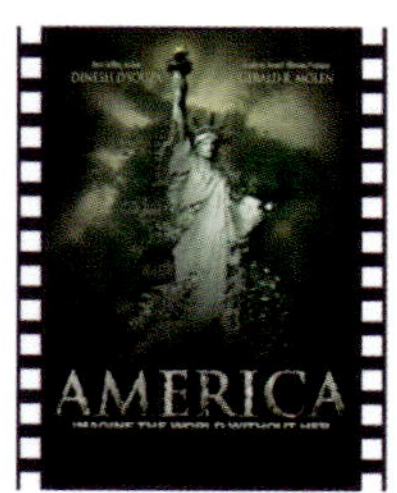

America: Imagine the World Without Her
2014

Yankee Doodle Dandy
1942

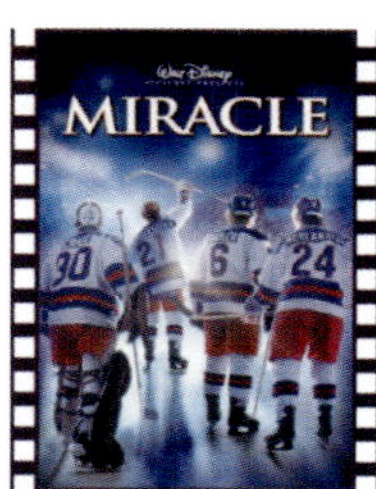

Miracle
2004

Take Your Hat Off When the Flag Goes by is a great way to teach your children about the Constitution and respect for the flag. It is a musical CD and book set that includes songs like "Take Your Hat Off When the Flag Goes By," "I Love America," and more. The CD comes with a large, full-color, 9x11 inch paperback picture book complete with all the lyrics to the songs. The book has a quiz section in the back to see how much the children really learned. You'll be surprised how much information sticks when you learn it to music. Suggested for ages 5-12, but it's a fun and easy way to learn for the whole family. (Available in the Moms for America® online store.)

Abigail Adams: A Mother Patriot

In 1775, as war raged around her Boston home, Abigail bravely cared for her young family alone while her husband was away serving his country.

Her son, John Quincy, later spoke of this time as "the space of twelve months (in which) my mother, with her infant children, dwelt, liable every hour of the day and the night, to be butchered in cold blood."[1]

Many of the women of the Revolutionary era were Quakers and Christians who were adamantly opposed to war. And yet, they supported the battle because they deeply believed in the dream of America. John Quincy spoke of his mother's influence. "My mother was the daughter of a Christian clergyman, and therefore bred in the faith of deliberate detestation of War…Yet, in that same spring and summer of 1775, she taught me to repeat daily, after the Lord's Prayer, and before rising from bed, the Ode of Collins on the patriot warriors."[2]

Abigail instilled a love of God and Country in her children. She stood courageously against the evils of her day and supported her husband all throughout his long life of public service. Abigail was a strong supporter of the battle for Independence. She frequently opened her home as a headquarters for the Minutemen. Her son, John Quincy, later spoke of this. There were "some dozen or two of pewter spoons," he said, "and I well recollect going into the kitchen and seeing some of the

men engaged in running those spoons into bullets for the use of the troops! Do you wonder that a boy of seven years of age, who witnessed this scene, should be a patriot?"[3]

This is where patriotism comes from. It comes from a young child seeing their mother put her hand over her heart, from seeing their father carefully fold the flag, from witnessing their grandfather remove his hat when the flag goes by. They feel it, they see it. And when we share with them why we do it, why we feel America is so great-—what the dream is all about—then we will be able to secure liberty because our children will know what it means to be American, and they will love Her too.

1.　Memoirs of John Quincy Adams 1795 to 1848, page 5
2.　Life of John Quincy Adams: the complete biography written in his lifetime, 1856, page 323
3.　Life of John Quincy Adams: the complete biography written in his lifetime, 1856, page 323

A Place Called Liberty

BY KIMBERLY FLETCHER

Several years ago, I was driving through Ohio with a friend when we came upon a town called Liberty. I was so fascinated by the discovery I pulled over and sat by the sign wondering what it would be like to live in a town called Liberty. Of course, I knew it was just a name but what if there really was a place called Liberty—a place that didn't just carry the name but lived up to it? My mind raced with all the marvelous possibilities, and as I drove out of town that day, I knew the idea was planted deep in my heart. If there ever was a place called Liberty, I wanted to live there.

Years later, a friend asked me how my children came to be so patriotic. I hadn't really thought about it until then. It was like asking how your children got so tall. It happens so gradually, you don't really recognize the dramatic changes. But looking at them, I could see my friend was right. It is more than apparent that our children have a deep love and respect for America and all She stands for. They automatically stand when the National Anthem plays, take their hats off when the flag goes by, proudly pledge allegiance to the flag, and graciously thank and honor all those who serve and protect our freedoms. So how did they come to be this way? Is it in their genes? Maybe. But I assure you, it isn't hereditary. Patriotism isn't something you are born with; it is something you develop with time and through experience. So, when my friend asked me how our children developed this deep love and devotion for their country, I told her the simple truth, "I share the story of America with them."

A few years ago, our family took a trip to Washington D.C. One of the things we wanted to make sure and do while there was visit Arlington Cemetery and the tomb of the Unknown Soldier. Our youngest boys, Ethan and Noah, were only four and seven-years-old at the time. And yet, when we neared the cemetery, they quieted to a whisper. As we reached the tomb of the Unknown Soldier, our teenage sons instinctively removed their hats, and our two daughters bowed their heads with tear-filled eyes. Where did that instinct and emotion come from? It came from stories!

For months before we took our trip, I read stories to our children of people who gave their lives for their country. We read books about Arlington Cemetery and specifically the tomb of the Unknown Soldier. We talked about what it was and what it represents. My husband shared his

"

feelings about that sacred place, and we told our children about all the people in our family who served in battle, some giving their lives, so that we could remain free.

By the time we arrived at the Cemetery, our children already knew it was a sacred place that held great honor and deserved the utmost respect. They knew because we took the time to tell them; we told them with love and reinforced it with stories. This is why our children have such a love for their country and cherish freedom—because their father and I have been faithfully devoted to tending and nurturing a love of liberty in their hearts. We instill this love and devotion in them, through the stories we read, the experiences we provide, and the examples we set. We love America because our parents shared the story of America with us. And our children love America because we share the story with them. It is a beautiful story well worth telling over and over again, and it is my deepest hope that you will share it with your children.

As my husband and I have shared these stories and experiences with our children, we have made an important discovery: there *is* a place called liberty, and that place is our hearts!

Nothing to Love About America?

BY MARLENE PETERSON

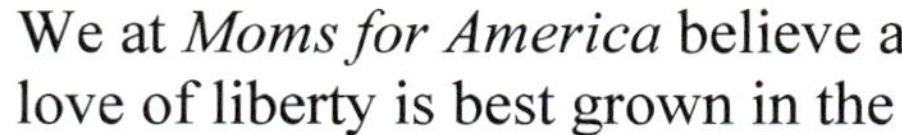

An assignment was given to a Jr. High school class in Virginia recently—the students were to write about why they loved America. After the papers were turned in and graded, the teacher regretfully shared with the class that not one of them had come up with a single reason.

What good is a balanced budget, fresh faces in Congress, and getting "back" to the Constitution if the next generation doesn't love America and value freedom?

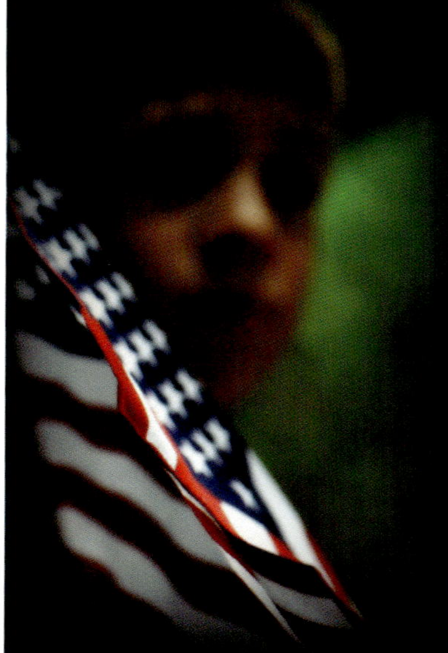

We at *Moms for America* believe a love of liberty is best grown in the home. We suggest a simple solution: starting tonight, put down the book, look your kids or grandkids in the eyes, and tell them a story from your heart about why YOU love America. Pajamas are recommended. It's a formula that has worked throughout history and around the globe.

However, if you plan on stopping by your public library to pick up some American History books to take your stories from, you may want to reconsider.

The story our children are being told about America is not the same story children were told a hundred years ago. There are three key elements that are missing from today's telling:

1.   An acknowledgment that our system of government is the best system of government the world has ever seen and that it demands our diligence in understanding and maintaining it.

2.   The belief that freedom is a rare gift that can only be held onto by a moral and religious people who comprehend liberty in law.

3.   The idea that our nation was raised up by the Hand of Divine Providence and that our inalienable rights come from Him.

> *A man's country is not a certain area of land, of mountains, rivers, and woods, but it is a principle; and patriotism is loyalty to that principle.*
>
> –George William Curtis

These three elements that are missing today are the very three pillars the school children of yesterday were taught our Republic rested upon—our patriotism, our character, and our faith. They were told they would be reminded of them every time they looked at our flag.

The red stripes reminded them of the blood that was sacrificed for them and was a call to patriotism in defending their Constitution and freedom.

The white stripes stood for virtue and purity. They understood a limited government only worked among a people who understood the personal responsibilities of freedom and were capable of self-governance.

The white stars on a blue background reminded them of Heaven's guiding and protective hand.

These wonderful writers of yesterday were so anxious to instill these principles in the hearts of the next generation that they filled their stories with examples and reminders.

From time to time, I plant myself on the floor of a public library in front of the American History shelf and look for these principles in our modern books. I'm not finding them. On my most recent visit, I finally found a reference to Columbus' faith. But his claim that he felt inspiration from heaven is attributed to his malarial delirium. Thomas Jefferson is portrayed as a hypocritical slaveholder, but, hey, we're all human, aren't we? And the story of the genocide of the Native American is paraded over and over again.

Not much to love.

It appears our three pillars are gradually being replaced with just one—money. Plymouth and its seekers of religious freedom is being replaced with Jamestown and its seekers of economic prosperity as the root of our nation. Most everyone seems to think that if the economy turns around, America will be just fine. But freedom is not the product of a strong economy. Rather, a strong economy is the product of freedom, and freedom rests on the three pillars that are being systematically removed.

What if that one replacement pillar—our economy—gives way? What will hold us up then?

Even Joseph Stalin recognized the secret of America's strength: "America is like a healthy body, and its resistance is threefold: its Patriotism, its Morality, and its Spiritualism."

How "healthy" is America's body today?

We call on the mothers and fathers and grandparents of America to rebuild these three pillars. And the way we rebuild them is through the stories we share heart-to-heart with our children and grandchildren. It is not in the classroom that we will restore America's liberty but in our homes.

We (Libraries of Hope) are gathering the stories of yesterday and reprinting them so they can be preserved in homes all across America. You can find them at librariesofhope.com

Nothing to love about America? We need to give our children reasons to love her every single day. We can restore the heart of America one story at a time. When the heart is strong, America will thrive.

One Mom on A Mission

BY VIVIAN D BROWN

As a mom, it has always been my belief that the most important job we have is to raise good citizens. So, when it came time to find a new school for my fourth-grade daughter, I choose a school where their mission is to prepare scholars "for success in college and citizenship."

When I received the call that my daughter was accepted, my husband and I were very excited.

A week or so later, I dropped off school supplies for teachers, and in the front office, something caught my eye that I just could not believe. It just was not possible…how could this happen?

In plain sight, sitting on top of a bookcase, were the United States and Texas flags haphazardly thrown on the top shelf. How could anyone do this to our flags? Patriots like our Founding Fathers sacrificed everything for our United States Flag. I was so shocked and upset that I could not even bring myself to say anything. I hoped this was a one-time thing…Sadly, it was not. I wondered how you can teach citizenship if you don't respect the flag?

Not only was this upsetting to me but also to my daughter. She would come home every day and say, "Mom, we didn't pledge to the flag." They did not even have a flag in the classroom. I have always taught my daughter to respect our heritage, be a proud American, and stand for the flag.

What kind of mother would I be if I did not act?

So, about the fourth time I went to the school and saw the bundle on the bookcase, I finally spoke up. I asked

the receptionist, "Who is in charge of the proper care and display of flags?" She told me the janitor was. Fortunately, (or not so fortunate for him) I was able to ask him directly about it.

"Sir, do you realize that men and women gave their blood and paid the ultimate sacrifice for our flag? Those flags are to be revered, respected. They are not pieces of cloth you just throw around. What kind of message are you sending students and families, when one of the first things they see is blatant disrespect for who we are as a nation?"

He told me, "Ma'am, I've served my country." I replied, "Then shame on you, sir; shame on you! You must understand firsthand the sacrifices and what it means. You should know better."

I knew my daughter and the other students needed to learn the values, meaning, and heroism the represents, but my messaged seemed to go on deaf ears. The flags continued to lay there, and no flag was even flown at the school. What was I going to do? I could not drop it. How could I?

One day, I was having lunch with Congressman Lamar Smith (TX21). I explained my story to him, and he was dismayed. He told me, "Vivian, call my office, and I will send the school a U.S. Flag flown over our Nation's

Capital." I was a bit hesitant and told him, "I do not know if that is a good idea; I do not want them to disrespect it." He said, "Well, maybe it will make an impression that they need to do something." So, I called his office, and they immediately dispatched a U.S. Flag to the school. Weeks went by, and still no flag.

I was not to be deterred. I thought there must be something I could do. I needed to look for help. I heard that my friend State Senator Donna Campbell had put forth a bill in the education committee that would give charter schools $1000 per student. I immediately thought that this is what I am looking for.

I went to the Capitol in Austin and met with her. I explained the situation and asked her if there was a way to tie funding to them respecting the flag. She told me that she likes to keep her bills clean and would not want to do that. Still, wanting to help, she told me she would also send a Texas Flag to the school.

Time went by, and still no flag. I was just so disappointed, and so was my daughter. She, too, decided to act. The students practicing for the mandatory state testing were given a writing prompt: "A day at the circus." When I picked her up from school that day, she told me , "Mom, who cares about the circus? I wanted to write about something important, like how they were disrespecting our Flag."

As a mother who prides herself on what it means to be an American Patriot and to respect our Nation's Heritage, I was beaming with pride. The school was not impressed. She did not receive a passing grade, but it did not matter to her or to me. She saw an injustice and chose to respond to it—no matter the consequences.

Isn't that what we want for our children, to raise them so they have the confidence to use their voice, be a good citizen, and be a positive influence on their peers and in the community?

Once again, I had to go to the school, which was something I began to dread. I was greeted by the janitor. He said, "Mrs. Brown, I have something to show you."

The school had purchased two display boxes to hold each flag along with the certificates from the Capitol Architect's that the flags were indeed flown over the United States and Texas Capitols. He then said, "The school decided to buy a brand new 6'x8' U.S. Flag to fly over the school." And that's just what they did. In fact, the school went on to install lights on the flag poles so both flags would be illuminated at night. I was later told that they adopted this policy across all their schools. I had done it!

Fast forward to the end of the Texas legislative session. I came across S.B. No. 1200, it was introduced by Senator Donna Campbell. The bill title was "Relating to guidelines for the proper care and display of the United States and Texas Flags by public schools." Was I reading that right? Was I responsible for getting a bill written?

I contacted her office to thank them; the Senator had written and filed the bill the week following our conversation, and although it did not make it out of committee (bills rarely do the first time), I learned it was one of her biggest disappointments when that bill was stalled. I, however, was not disappointed. On the contrary, I wanted the school to respect our Flag, and I wanted my daughter to see her mom make a stand. I wanted her to see what it meant to do everything within the realm of possibility to make a difference to right a wrong. I had succeeded!

As I pass by the school every day, it warms my heart to see our glorious "banner wave," symbolizing the land of the free. The home of the brave.

As I said at the beginning, the most important job I have as a mother is to raise a good citizen. It was my obligation to demonstrate what that means. Even when something is challenging, it is worth the fight. Never give up! Stand up for what you believe! Even if you are the only one. One person, one mom…can make all the difference.

The Dream Called America

BY KIMBERLY FLETCHER

There is a place in Hawaii called the Kualoa Ranch. The ranch rests on 4,000 acres of some of the most breathtaking scenery on the island of Oahu. Visions of God's handiwork can be seen in the dense rain forests, open valleys, beautiful white beaches, and majestic mountains that characterize the property. Though you wouldn't know it, you have most probably seen the ranch as it has been the backdrop of many television shows and films. If you have seen *Jurassic Park, Windtalkers, Pearl Harbor, Godzilla, Tears of the Sun,* or *50 First Dates* then you have—through moving pictures—been to the Kualoa Ranch.

While the beauty and grandeur of the ranch is breathtaking, it is actually the history of the ranch that I find most fascinating. Kualoa Ranch was established in 1850 when King Kamehameha III sold the land to a missionary doctor who had served as his personal advisor.

For over a hundred years, the ranch sustained itself in agriculture and cattle, but as time passed, the income from these sources was no longer sustainable, so the family diversified the ranch and entered the tourism industry. Now, people from all over the world come to see this beautiful land and visit the places where Kings were trained and where films are made. You can still see remnants of the many movies that have been filmed there, including the famous entrance gate to Jurassic Park.

You never know who you might see at the ranch. Just a few months ago, George Clooney was at the ranch scouting locations for a film he is working on. And all the while, the ranch continues to operate as a working cattle ranch.

You and I wouldn't see anything unusual or particularly unique about that. After all, businesses diversify all the time. If your business is no longer making money, diversification is automatically a consideration. However, a few months ago, a group of businessmen from Japan came to visit the ranch. After hearing the history of the ranch and how they had successfully diversified into the tourism and film industries, the men were astonished. They couldn't understand how you could just change the direction of your company like that. How do you go from being a cattle ranch to being a hub for tourism and movies?

Of course, the tour guide didn't understand why the whole thing shocked these businessmen so much. But that is because he, like so many Americans, didn't realize just how uniquely American something as simple as diversification is. In Japan, if you own a car industry, you always manufacture and sell cars. If business is slow, you give a big pep talk to your sales and manufacturing teams to try and pick up sales; you don't just decide to start selling infant car seats or build an amusement park. But people in America do it every day. Baseball players become car dealers, pharmacists become realtors, paper goods manufacturers add household cleaners to their product line. It's just another day in the life of an American. One day you're a car salesman, and the next day you're a nurse.

My son Jordan spent a couple years in Idaho, and while there, he met a man from Sweden who owned a bakery. Jordan said the man was completely perplexed at how people in America could just become whatever they wanted. "I studied and apprenticed for fifteen years before I could become a baker," the man said. "Here in America, people just wake up and say 'I'm going to be a baker today'. And then they do it."

There is a uniqueness about America that has become so commonplace to us that we don't even recognize just how unique we are. I have talked to many immigrants from other countries who have shared their feelings and impressions about America with me. I've heard them say everything from, "there is just no place like it on earth" to "you just don't know how good it is."

Kitty Werthmann, the current president of Eagle Forum in South Dakota, was born and raised in Austria. She spent seven years of her life under Hitler's rule and five years under Russian Communist rule. In 1950, Kitty came to America. The first thing she saw when the ship came into harbor was the Statue of Liberty—an image she has never forgotten.

Kitty spent her first night in America in a hotel. The next morning, she asked the concierge for directions to the nearest police station, which he told her was within walking distance. Kitty walked to the police station and told the desk sergeant she wanted to register. The desk sergeant asked what she was talking about. Kitty repeated herself and saying, "I want to register so you will know where I am. How will you find me," she asked, "if I break the law?"

"Don't worry Lady," the sergeant replied, "if you break the law we'll find you. Now get out of here!"

Kitty walked outside quite perplexed. She looked up at the clear blue sky and puzzled, "What kind of country is this?" And then she realized. "All of a sudden," she said, "it dawned on me. It's freedom!"

And that is the beauty of America. It is what people come from countries all over the world for. They know that America is the land of opportunity. They know it is a place of peace where they are free. And when they come and experience that freedom for the first time, it is something they treasure forever because they know it isn't just a dream. It's real!

God Save the Flag

BY OLIVER WENDELL HOLMES

Washed in the blood of the brave and the blooming,

Snatched from the altars of insolent foes,

Burning with star-fires, but never consuming,

Flash its broad ribbons of lily and rose.

Vainly the prophets of Baal would rend it,

Vainly his worshipers pray for its fall;

Thousands have died for it, millions defend it,

Emblem of justice and mercy to all;

Justice that reddens the sky with her terrors,

Mercy that comes with her white-handed train,

Soothing all passions, redeeming all errors,

Sheathing the sabre and breaking the chain.

Borne on the deluge of all usurpations,

Drifted our Ark o'er the desolate seas,

Bearing the rainbow of hope to the nations,

Torn from the storm-cloud and flung to the breeze!

God bless the Flag and its loyal defenders,

While its broad folds o'er the battle-field wave,

Till the dim star-wreath rekindle its splendors,

Washed from its stains in the blood of the brave!

The Star-Spangled Banner

In 1814, Francis Scott Key wrote the poem "Defense of Fort McHenry." The poem was later put to the tune of (John Stafford Smith's song) "The Anacreontic Song," modified somewhat, and retitled "The Star Spangled Banner." Congress proclaimed "The Star Spangled Banner" the U.S. National Anthem in 1931.

Oh, say, can you see, by the dawn's early light,

What so proudly we hail'd at the twilight's last gleaming?

Whose broad stripes and bright stars, thro' the perilous fight,

O'er the ramparts we watch'd, were so gallantly streaming?

And the rockets' red glare, the bombs bursting in air,

Gave proof thro' the night that our flag was still there.

O say, does that star-spangled banner yet wave

O'er the land of the free and the home of the brave?

On the shore dimly seen thro' the mists of the deep,

Where the foe's haughty host in dread silence reposes,

What is that which the breeze, o'er the towering steep,

As it fitfully blows, half conceals, half discloses?

Now it catches the gleam of the morning's first beam,

In full glory reflected, now shines on the stream:

'Tis the star-spangled banner: O, long may it wave

O'er the land of the free and the home of the brave!

And where is that band who so vauntingly swore

That the havoc of war and the battle's confusion

A home and a country should leave us no more?

Their blood has wash'd out their foul footsteps' pollution.

No refuge could save the hireling and slave

From the terror of flight or the gloom of the grave:

And the star-spangled banner in triumph doth wave

O'er the land of the free and the home of the brave.

O, thus be it ever when freemen shall stand,

Between their lov'd homes and the war's desolation;

Blest with vict'ry and peace, may the heav'n-rescued land

Praise the Pow'r that hath made and preserv'd us a nation!

Then conquer we must, when our cause is just,

And this be our motto: "In God is our trust"

And the star-spangled banner in triumph shall wave

O'er the land of the free and the home of the brave!

The America's Creed

BY WILLIAM TYLER PAGE
WRITTEN 1917,
ACCEPTED BY THE U. S. HOUSE OF REPRESENTATIVES ON APRIL 3, 1918

I believe in the United States of America as a government of the people, by the people, for the people; whose just powers are derived from the consent of the governed, a democracy in a republic, a sovereign Nation of many sovereign States; a perfect union, one and inseparable; established upon those principles of freedom, equality, justice, and humanity for which American patriots sacrificed their lives and fortunes.

I therefore believe it is my duty to my country to love it, to support its Constitution, to obey its laws, to respect its flag, and to defend it against all enemies.

Proper Care and Respect of the U.S. Flag

The Symbolism of the American Flag is of revolutionary significance. Beginning with 13, the now 50 stars displayed in the canton of the flag represent the current number of states in the union. This number has followed the growth of the United States since its infancy. Found from a book about the symbolism of the American Flag published in 1977 by the House of Representatives, we read:

"The star is a symbol of the heavens and the divine goal to which man has aspired from time immemorial; the stripe is symbolic of the rays of light emanating from the sun."

Alternating in red and white, the 13 stripes also represent the 13 original colonies that joined together to declare their independence from Britain in order to establish themselves as a sovereign nation.

Originally, the colors red, white, and blue had neither specific meaning nor representation when the flag was adopted in 1777. However, the colors in the Great Seal of the United States did have specific meanings.

Charles Thompson, Secretary of the Continental Congress, when reporting to Congress on the Seal stated: "The colors of the pales (the vertical stripes) are those used in the flag of the United States of America; White signifies purity and innocence, Red, hardiness & valour, and Blue, the color of the Chief (the broad band above the stripes) signifies vigilance, perseverance & justice."

Respecting the Flag

Flag respect is very important. The American Flag is a symbol of our nation's strength and unity. For over 200 years, it has been an inspiration for millions of citizens, and thus, we are to Respect the Flag.

The American flag has been a prominent icon in our national history. Many people have died to preserve our nation's freedom and way of life. Please be careful when handling the American flag.

Many rules and regulations can come into play when displaying our flag. We hope that some of these guidelines will help maintain the reverent respect and admiration for our country's national symbol.

Displaying the Flag

Flag Position - Manner of Flag Display - Do's:

Proper care should always be given to the flag

- Displaying it in a dignified and appropriate manner should always be considered before installing a flag pole, hanging it on the side of your home, or presenting it at a meeting or at other public places

- The flag should always be folded properly and stored in a safe place when not on display

Flag Position - Manner of Flag - Don'ts:

- Avoid flying the flag outdoors during periods of severe weather

- Damage to the flag should be avoided and proper cleaning of the flag should take place soon after it becomes dirty

- Flags should never be fastened to, displayed on, or draped over anything that would allow it to be easily torn, soiled, or damaged. Bunting should be considered for use in situations where harm may occur

Flying the Flag at Night

Using Flag Lights, the U.S. flag must be illuminated at nighttime. Other flags and banners may be illuminated for marketing purposes. Visibility is dependent on the position of the viewer and the flag as well as ambient light levels and contrast ratios with respect to other objects in the field of view. Although many variables are involved, the following rules of thumb should result in a satisfactory installation and proper Flag Lighting.

1. Always use multiple fixtures or flag lights; this will ensure that the flag is illuminated regardless of wind direction

2. Fixtures should be setback from the pole one-third to one-half the length of the flag

3. Three fixtures placed in a triangular configuration around a single pole produce the best overall effect

Flag Service - Storing Flags

Storing your flag properly is not only respectful but can also add life to your flag. It is important that you store your flag in a dry and dust-free environment. Also, avoid storing your flag in a garage or a basement next to chemicals that could damage your flag. Storing your flag in a proper case will protect your flag and also give you an attractive way to display it.

Retiring the Flag

Flag Retirement becomes necessary when the United States flag becomes worn, torn, repaired to the point that the flag makes a square, is faded, or badly soiled. It then is time to replace that flag with a new flag. The old flag should be "retired" with all the dignity and respect befitting our nation's flag.

Destroying A Worn Out Flag

A flag ceases to be a flag when it is cut into pieces. In addition, it is easier to completely incinerate the flag if it is cut into a lot of smaller pieces. A flag should never be torn up like an 'old bed sheet.' The flag should be cut up with scissors or shears in a methodical manner. The corners of the flag should be stretched out over a table top and someone should cut the flag in half, vertically (be careful not to cut up the blue star field (see the figure). Then, place the two halves together and cut them in half, horizontally. You will end up with four pieces of flag, one being the blue star field.

The reason we do not cut the blue star field is it represents the union of the fifty states, and one should never let the union be broken. Before accepting a flag for flag retirement, the recipient should obtain information about its history. For example: where has the flag flown? For how long did the flag fly ? Did any memorable events happen at that site? This information should be used in the flag retirement ceremony.

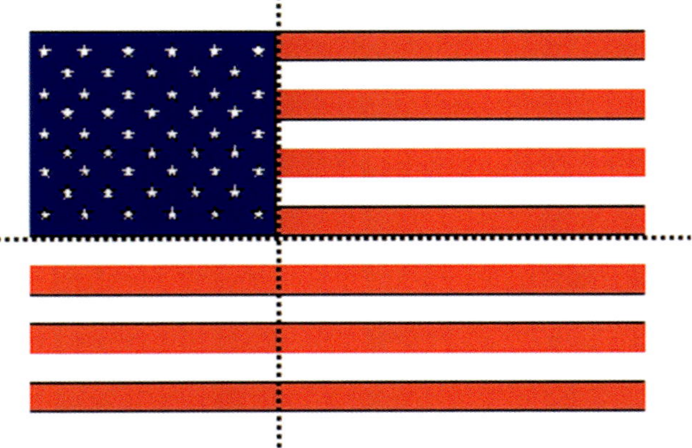

Folding an United States Flag

FLAG FOLDING - STEP 1

To properly fold the Flag, begin by holding it waist-high with another person so that its surface is parallel to the ground.

FLAG FOLDING - STEP 2

Fold the lower half of the stripe section lengthwise over the field of stars, holding the bottom and top edges securely.

FLAG FOLDING - STEP 3

Fold the flag again lengthwise with the blue field on the outside.

FLAG FOLDING - STEP 4

Make a triangular fold by bringing the striped corner of the folded edge to meet the open (top) edge of the flag.

FLAG FOLDING - STEP 5

Turn the outer (end) point inward, parallel to the open edge, to form a second triangle.

FLAG FOLDING - STEP 6

The triangular folding is continued until the entire length of the flag is folded in this manner. The loose end of the flag should be tucked in under the exposed layer of the flag.

FLAG FOLDING - STEP 7

When the flag is completely folded, only a triangular blue field of stars should be visible.

RELATED QUOTES

Patriotism

"The strength of this country isn't in buildings of brick and steel. It's in the hearts of those who have sworn to fight for its freedom." **-Captain America**

"The greatest act of patriotism a mother can perform will be within the walls of her own home!" **-Kimberly Fletcher**

"A man's country is not a certain area of land, of mountains, rivers, and woods, but it is a principle; and patriotism is loyalty to that principle." **-George William Curtis**

"No free government can stand without virtue in the people, and a lofty spirit of patriotism." **-Andrew Jackson**

Patriots

"No one really knows why they are alive until they know what they'd die for." **-Martin Luther King Jr.**

"Those who won our independence believed liberty to be the secret of happiness and courage to be the secret of liberty." **-Louis D. Brandeis**

"In the beginning of a change, the patriot is a scarce man, and brave, and hated, and scorned. When his cause succeeds, the timid join him, for then it costs nothing to be a patriot." **-Mark Twain**

"We must be free not because we claim freedom, but because we practice it." **-William Faulkner**

"Liberty lies in the hearts of men and women; when it dies there, no constitution, no court can save it." **-Learned Hand**

"Let us be sure that those who come after will say of us in our time, that in our time we did everything that could be done. We finished the race; we kept them free; we kept the faith." **-Ronald Reagan**

"...There can be no divided allegiance here. Any man who says he is an American, but something else also, isn't an American at all. We have room for but one flag, the American flag... We have room for but one language here, and that is the English language... and we have room for but one sole loyalty, and that is a loyalty to the American people." **-Theodore Roosevelt**

Freedom

"Liberty is not a means to a higher political end. It is itself the highest political end." **-Lord Acton**

"For what avail the plough or sail, or land or life, if freedom fail?" **-Ralph Waldo Emerson**

"The secret of happiness is freedom. And the secret of freedom is courage." **-Thucydides**

"What we once enjoyed and deeply loved we can never lose, for all that we love deeply becomes a part of us." **-Helen Keller**

"I would rather belong to a poor nation that was free than to a rich nation one that had ceased to be in love with liberty. But we shall not be poor if we love liberty, because the nation that loves liberty truly sets every man free to do his best and be his best, and that means the release of all the splendid energies of a great people who think for themselves." **-Woodrow Wilson**

"Voting is no substitute for the eternal vigilance that every friend of freedom must demonstrate towards government. If our freedom is to survive, Americans must become far better informed of the dangers from Washington—regardless of who wins the Presidency." **-James Bovard**

"Freedom is never an achieved state; like electricity, we've got to keep generating it or the lights go out." **-Wayne LaPierre**

"If a nation values anything more than freedom, it will lose its freedom; and the irony of it is that if it is comfort or money that it values more, it will lose that too." **-Somerset Maugham**

The American Dream

"There are those, I know, who will say that the liberation of humanity, the freedom of man and mind, is nothing but a dream. They are right. It is the American dream." **-Archibald MacLeish**

"May I never wake up from the American dream." **-Carrie Latet**

"The road to success is not easy to navigate, but with hard work, drive and passion, it's possible to achieve the American dream." **- Tommy Hilfiger**

"The American Dream is that any man or woman, despite of his or her background, can change their circumstances and rise as high as they are willing to work."   **- Fabrizio Moreira**

"The American Dream comes from opportunity. The opportunity comes from our founding principles, our core values that's held together and protected by the Constitution. Those ideas are neither Republican, Democrat, conservative, liberal, white, or black. Those are American ideologies."
- Ted Yoho

"The American Dream is a term that is often used but also often misunderstood. It isn't really about becoming rich or famous. It is about things much simpler and more fundamental than that."
- Marco Rubio

"To me, the American Dream is being able to follow your own personal calling. To be able to do what you want to do is incredible freedom."   **-Maya Lin**

"The American Dream is still alive out there, and hard work will get you there. You don't necessarily need to have an Ivy League education or to have millions of dollars startup money. It can be done with an idea, hard work and determination."
-Bill Rancic

"The American dream, to me, means having the opportunity to achieve, because I don't think you should be guaranteed anything other than opportunity."   **-Lenny Wilkens**

"The American Dream I believe in is one that provides anyone willing to work hard enough with the opportunity to succeed."
-Tammy Duckworth

"When it comes to the American dream, no one has a corner on the market. All of us have an equal chance to share in that dream."   **-J. C. Watts**

"Only in America can someone start with nothing and achieve the American Dream. That's the greatness of this country."
-Rafael Cruz

American Flag

"Off with your hat, as the flag goes by! And let the heart have its say; you're man enough for a tear in your eye that you will not wipe away."   **-Henry Cuyler Bunner**

"The American flag doesn't give her glory on a peaceful, calm day. It's when the winds pick up and become boisterous, do we see her strength. When she unfolds her hand, and shows her frayed fingers, where we see the stretch of red-blood lines of man that fought for this land. The purity of white stripes that strips our sins, and the stars of Abraham's covenant, broad in a midnight blue sky. The rights our forefathers established. As it waves high in the currents of freedom, where the Torch of Liberty shines over the sea, does she give meaning to unity. When we strive as one nation, or when it drops half-mast, to a fallen soldier."
-Anthony Liccione

"When I see the American flag rippling in the breeze against the majesty of Rocky Mountains, a thrill of patriotism runs through my soul. How I love America and all that she offers to her citizens and the world. We must protect her against all who would destroy her as an ensign to the world of freedom, liberty, and justice. May God bless America and the efforts of her citizens to restore her."
-Candace Salima

FROM THE FOUNDERS

"God grants liberty only to those who love it, and are always ready to guard and defend it."
-Daniel Webster

"Hold on, my friends, to the Constitution and to the Republic for which it stands. Miracles do not cluster and what has happened once in 6,000 years, may not happen again."
-Daniel Webster

"Freedom is not a gift bestowed upon us by other men, but a right that belongs to us by the laws of God and nature."
-Benjamin Franklin

"What we obtain too cheap, we esteem too lightly. Heaven knows how to put a proper price upon its goods; and it would be strange indeed, if so celestial an article as Freedom should not be highly rated."
-Thomas Paine

"Your love of liberty—your respect for the laws—your habits of industry—and your practice of the moral and religious obligations, are the strongest claims to national and individual happiness."
-George Washington

"There is a certain enthusiasm in liberty that makes human nature rise above itself, in acts of bravery and heroism."
-Alexander Hamilton

Journal

"The destiny of the world is determined less by the battles that are lost and won than by the stories it loves and believes in.

-Harold Goddard

America: Share the Story

*"Tell me a fact and I will learn. Tell me a truth and I will believe.
But tell me a story and it will live in my heart forever."*
-Indian Proverb

PREPARATION

In the late 1800s and early 1900s, there emerged a golden age of literature. Authors of school books and general children's literature went to great lengths to write to inspire patriotism, encourage faith, and develop strong moral character. This time also sparked a revival in the art of storytelling among mothers and teachers of young children. The "Greatest Generation" is what followed. Stories are very powerful because, while information goes to the brain, stories travel directly to the heart, and it's our hearts that inspire our thoughts and direct our actions.

When we share the stories of America with our children—the real story—they will gain a love and appreciation not only for their country but for who they are as Americans. Stories show our children what good looks like, what courage looks like, what faith looks like, what patriotism and virtue look like. And they will grow to emulate those virtues that penetrate their hearts through the stories we share.

To prepare yourself to lead the presentation, please review and consider the following material. NOTE: Video links and additional resources are available on the Hostess Resource Center at MomsforAmerica.us

- Read "The Story that Unites Us" found in the Supplemental Materials of this presentation. Read through the sampling of stories and choose the ones you want to share. A suggested idea is to assign a story to individual members of your group to read and share at the meeting

- View the video *The Power of a Story* provided in the Hostess Resource Center on the Moms for America® website www.MomsforAmerica.us

- Read the Forward, Challenge, and Introduction from the *5000 Year Leap;* mark any sections you would like to share in your meeting

- Optional: If available, read vignettes 2.5, 3.4, 4.2, 4.3, 4.5, and 4.6 of *Promises of the Constitution*

- Bible References—Deut. 4:9, 6:7, 11:19, Matt. 13:34, Mark 4:2-3

- Review the quotes provided in the Supplemental Materials section of this presentation

Home Assignment

Story A Day! Each day until the next meeting read aloud with your family, a story from "Stories of American History" by Mara Pratt or one of the stories from the Freedom Series (available on the Moms for America webstore)

Personal Study

Read "Are You Just Reading to Them" Supplemental Material of this Presentation

Family Enrichment

Build your family Liberty Library! Having good books on our shelves is an excellent way to preserve the stories of America and pass on the light of liberty by sharing them with our children for generations to come. Visit the Moms for America web store or check out the list of recommendations on the Cottage Meeting Resource Center.

The purpose of this presentation is to introduce the powerful influence of stories in promoting liberty and raising patriots. Stories are a powerful medium to teach the three pillars of liberty, and storytelling is the most effective method for planting seeds in the heart.

KEY POINTS

- Jesus Christ, the master teacher, used stories and parables to teach his message

- Remembering the stories of faith, virtue, and patriotism from our past is the bridge that allows us to secure liberty for our future

- A presentation of facts will educate the mind, but a story will educate the heart, and the heart is the core of human motivation and behavior

MEETING OUTLINE

Welcome & Gathering

We recommend starting your meeting with a prayer and the Pledge of Allegiance.

 **Show Video:** *Great American Story: Land of Hope* by Hillsdale College (link provided in the Hostess Resource Center)

> *"Freedom is never more than one generation away from extinction. We didn't pass it to our children in the bloodstream. It must be fought for, protected, and handed on for them to do the same, or one day we will spend our sunset years telling our children and our children's children what it was once like in the United States where men were free." -Ronald Reagan*

> *What must we do to preserve liberty in America? How can sharing the American Story promote a love of liberty?*

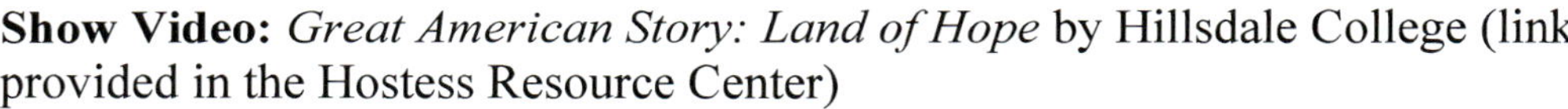 **Show Video:** *The Power of a Story* (available in Hostess Resource Center)

 **Group Discussion**

> *How do stories shape our nation?*

> *What is the story that unites us as a people?*

- Reference the *5000 Year Leap* and share the highlighted sections from Forward, Challenge, and Introduction in leading the discussion

- See Bible Reference—Deuteronomy 4:9; 6:7

Sharing the Story

Read "The Story that Unites Us" provided in the Supplemental Materials of this Presentation. Share the stories you pre-selected to read as a group. If you have a copy of *Promises of the Constitution*, you can also reference the stories found in the following vignettes:

- 2.5 Life Among the Puritans

- 3.4 The War for Independence

- 4.2 Miracle of the Cannon

- 4.3 The Battle for Boston

- 4.4 The Miracle on Long Island

- 4.5 The Miracles at Trenton & Princeton

- 4.6 Valley Forge

  How has our story changed? How can we preserve our story? How can sharing the story of America heal our nation and sustain a free society?

Summary

Summarize your thoughts on the material covered in this presentation

- Give the Home Assignment for the next meeting

- Announce date, time and location for next meeting

Take Home Assignment: Encourage attendees to share the stories from our meeting or Mara Pratt's *American History Stories*

ADDITIONAL PRESENTATION IDEAS

Why Not Just Give them A Book?

Reading aloud with your children is a powerful way to connect, communicate and foster strong bonds with your children. While encouraging children to read is good thing, it is reading to them that develops that life-long love of reading and thirst for good books. You won't need to convince children to read. They will naturally be drawn to it. The quality of things you read makes a big difference as well as the time you spend talking about what you read.

- Read "Reading Aloud to Your Children" provided in the Supplemental Materials section of this presentation

- What are the benefits of reading aloud to your children? What additional benefits come from telling a story from the heart? What makes a good story? How can you enrich the experience of reading with your children?

- Read "Are You Just Reading to Them?" provided in the Supplemental Materials section of this presentation

- Read Matthew 13:34 and Mark 4:2

MINI COTTAGE IDEAS

Mini Cottages are designed especially for moms of preschoolers and moms who work full-time jobs. Moms simply read and/or watch the same materials at home, on their own, then meet together once a week in a playdate or over lunch during the workday to discuss what they read. The articles and videos are short and can usually be read and/or viewed in less than hour. Below are some suggestions to host mini cottage discussions under the "America: Share the Story" theme.

- Read "The Story that Unites Us" (Discuss: How has our story changed, How can sharing the story of America heal our nation and sustain a free society?)

- Read & Discuss "Are You Just Reading to Them?"

- Share the Story: have the ladies in your group choose their favorite stories from those provided in the Supplemental Materials or those they are familiar with. You can also read the stories from *Promises of the Constitution* in the following Vignettes 2.5, 3.4, 4.2, 4.3, 4.5, 4.6

- View the Videos *The Great American Story: Land of Hope* and *The Power of a Story* provided in the Hostess Resource Center; meet and Discuss

COTTAGE MEETING BOOK CLUB

For those who like the book club format, we've compiled a list of great books to help you gain an appreciation and foundational understanding of the concepts presented in "America: Share the Story."

The 5000 Year Leap: A Miracle That Changed the World

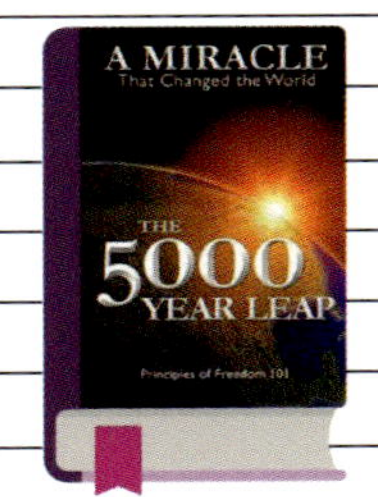

- Read the Forward, Challenge, and Introduction

Promises of the Constitution

Review the following vignettes:

- 2.5 Life Among the Puritans

- 3.4 The War for Independence

- 4.2 Miracle of the Cannon

- 4.3 The Battle for Boston

- 4.4 The Miracle on Long Island

- 4.5 The Miracles at Trenton & Princeton

- 4.6 Valley Forge

Stories of American History by Mara L. Pratt

If you are looking for that perfect little treasure of American history stories—this is it! *The American History* series by Mara Pratt has been loved and cherished by homeschoolers for years. Now, through Libraries of Hope, you can get all four volumes of this inspirational series in one book. History is brought to life in these beautiful stories, creating a wonderful introduction to American history for children of all ages. It is great for story time, but the short, easy-read chapters are also perfect for sharing at the dinner table, in the car, or at bedtime. (Included in the Hostess Kit and available through the MFA online store)

The Freedom Series by Libraries of Hope

We cannot recommend this beautiful collection of history classics strongly enough! The Freedom Series is a 12 volume, beautifully bound collection of books full of stories written in the golden age of literature (late 19th and early 20th centuries) when authors wrote to inspire patriotism, encourage faith, and develop strong character. Every American family should own a set of these books. The stories are disappearing way too quickly, and including these history classics in your home library is the perfect way to preserve these stories for ourselves and our posterity. An excellent foundation to your own Home Liberty Library. Available through Libraries of Hope www.LibrariesOfHope.com

Restoring the Art of Storytelling in the Home by Marlene Peterson

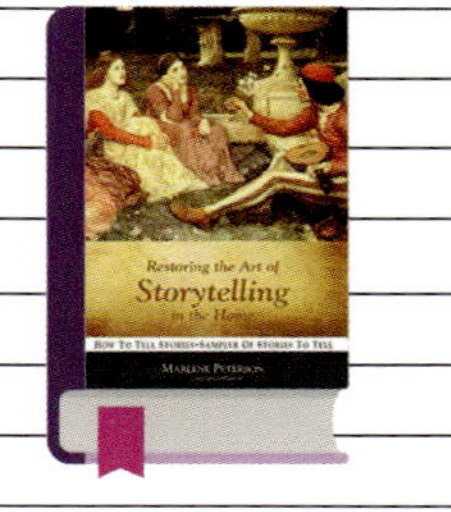

A revival in the art of storytelling among mothers swept America in the early 1900's. Story groups were formed to practice and perfect the art. While storytelling has seen a new revival in the last thirty years, it has yet to reach where it can do the most good—the home. Much of the training available is aimed at the professional storyteller or for using stories in business, education, or healthcare. Yet, in times past, the art of storytelling yielded its greatest masterpieces by the fireside while the listener was held close to a mother's heart. Two things have been lacking in sparking a new revival: a beginner's guide to using the art at home and simple access to stories that work well for telling. *Restoring the Art of Storytelling in the Home* has been created to fill those needs. Part One introduces you to the power of a story as well as basic guidelines for storytelling and age-appropriate stories. Part Two contains over one hundred stories reworked for telling by the gifted storytellers of a hundred years ago. They provide a perfect tutorial for anyone interested in re-learning the art.

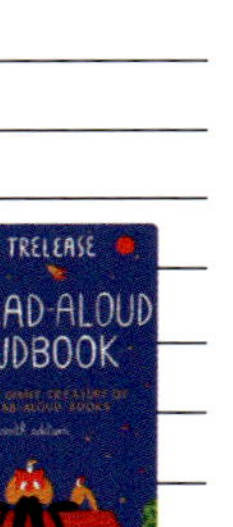

***The Read-Aloud Handbook* by Jim Trelease** is a classic handbook on reading aloud to children. In this beloved, enduring guide, Trelease shares his inspiring message, backed by delightful anecdotes as well as the latest research, and

- Explains how reading aloud awakens children's imaginations and improves their language skills

- Shows how to begin reading aloud and which books to choose

- Suggests ways to create reader-friendly home, classroom, and library environments

- Gives tips on luring children away from the television

- Shows how to integrate silent reading with read-aloud sessions

- Offers an up-to-date treasury to 1,000 books that are great for reading aloud—from picture books to novels—and highlights some of Trelease's favorites by theme: friendship, sports, dogs, fairy-tale parodies, and more.

The Patriot's Reading List

"The Patriot's Reading List" is a great resource for families and individuals seeking good books to read and share with their families. It is a compilation of books, films, and resources that we have used in our own homes. The list has a variety of reading materials from children's picture books to novels and non-fiction. The list is categorized by age and content subject for convenience. Available for download in the Hostess Resource Center

COTTAGE MEETING FOR KIDS

Cottage Meeting for Kids is a liberty promoting program for the entire family and focused on children from preschool to teens. It is full of great stories and fun activities to help children gain a love of liberty. Families can join together each month for an Activity Day to share the concepts they've learned and enhance them through group activities. Here are some ideas to promote the concepts presented in "America: Share the Story." You can find additional ideas, outlines and activities on the Moms for America® website under "Cottage Meetings for Kids."

- Read *American History Stories* by Mara Pratt with your children

- Watch *Schoolhouse Rock: America Rock* video shorts with your children and talk about them together

- Make a space in your home to start your own Liberty Library. Make your children a part of the decision and adding books to the shelf. They may have favorites they want to add. Visit the Hostess Resource Center to get our Big List of recommended classics for all ages

- Talk to your children about what makes a classic book. A classic book isn't necessarily an old book, although the old writers did write in higher quality. Classics are chosen by their quality for things like: it holds a truth, teaches a lesson, inspires us to greatness, helps us learn from the story, a book or story you can read again and again

- Encourage the children to share their favorite stories; have them write or tell their own story

- A fun project is to create a Family Story Book with each child having their own section about when and where they were born, their favorite color, favorite food, something they treasure, etc. You can add pictures to create a memory book, create it as a scrapbook, or make a digital scrapbook using online programs such as Shutterfly or Mixbook

Book & Movie List

Suggested books and readings for children all ages to nurture a love of liberty in the home.

Rush Revere Series
by Rush Limbaugh

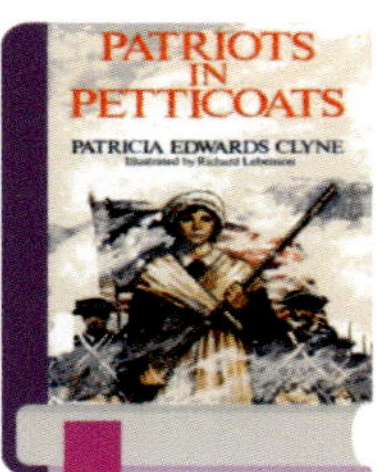

Patriots in Petticoats
by Patricia Edwards Clyne

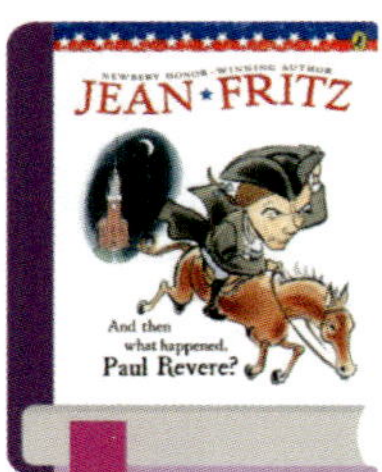

And Then What Happened, Paul Revere
by Jean Fritz

Can't You Make Them Behave, King George
by Jean Fritz

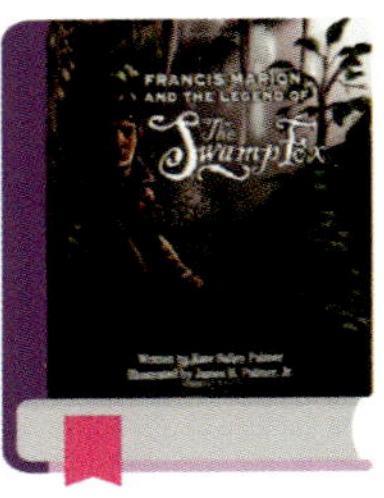

**Francis Marion and the
Legend of the Swamp Fox**
by Kate Salley Palmer

**The Bulletproof
George Washington**
by David Barton

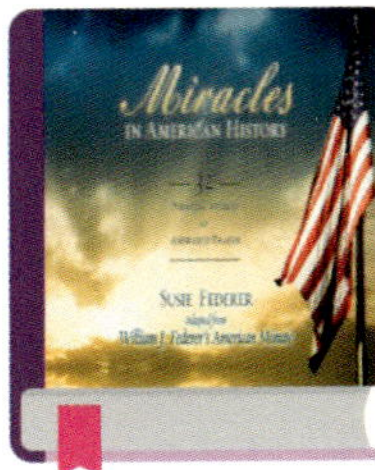

**Miracles in
American History**
by Susie Federer

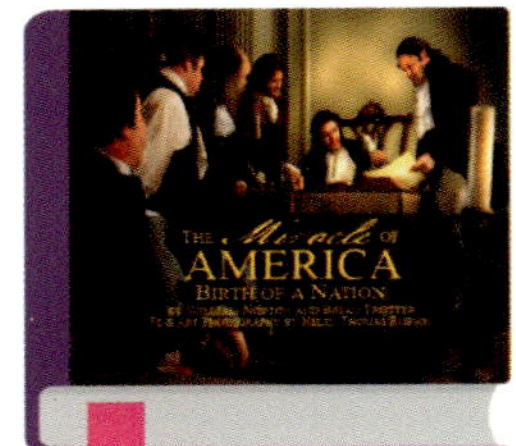

The Miracle of America
by William Norton &
Brian Trotter

Schoolhouse Rock: America Rock

In the 1970's ABC aired a series of animated shorts called Schoolhouse Rock. The series included sciences, vocabulary, and American history. The Great American Melting Pot is one of the segments under America Rock. The American Melting Pot was something all children knew and understood. It was taught in school, promoted in media and culture. In the 1990's, the story changed. The Melting Pot became the tossed salad-all mixed together, never united. It was a small way teacher's unions could begin rewriting the story of America in the hearts of America's children. Imagine if the true story of the Melting Pot were promoted today, how it could unite us once again as a people. This video is a great place to start.

SUPPLEMENTAL MATERIALS

The Story that Unites Us

BY KIMBERLY FLETCHER

Harold Goddard said, "The destiny of the world is determined less by the battles that are lost and won than by the stories it loves and believes in."

The story of America is an epic tale of freedom, courage, heroes, and patriots—men, women, and children who united together for a common cause, bound by the united agreement that all men are equal under God. The American story is unique in all the world; it is the story that unites us as people. Unfortunately, it is a story that is largely no longer told—especially to our children. How can we believe in a story when we don't even know the story?

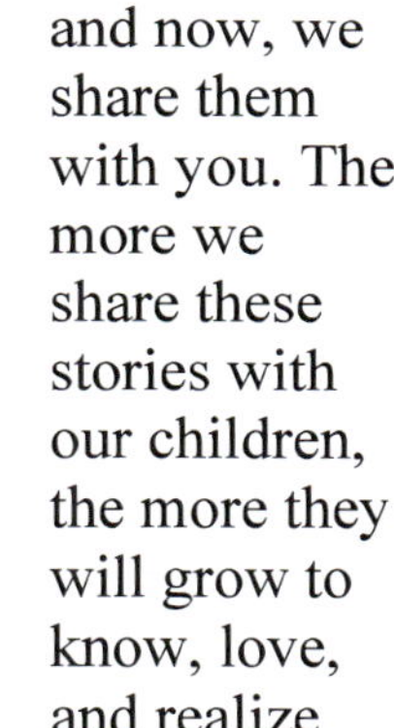

Since the beginning of Time and across the globe, stories have been the most effective means of passing values and traditions from generation to generation. As the old Indian Proverb states: "Tell me a fact, and I will learn. Tell me a truth, and I will believe. But tell me a story, and it will live in my heart forever." And it is our hearts, after all, that guide our actions.

Author Vaughn J. Featherstone lamented, "Our concern isn't about the flames of freedom which burn in our generation. The concern is that in the upcoming generation, the fire has never been kindled." As mothers, we are in a unique and powerfully influential position to promote a love of liberty in the hearts of our children simply by the stories we share. It's time to kindle those flames. This section is full of great stories, articles, and resources to do just that.

We have provided a sampling of our favorite stories. We hope you enjoy them as much as we do. They have touched our hearts and the hearts of our children, and now, we share them with you. The more we share these stories with our children, the more they will grow to know, love, and realize the beauty of our united story.

Elbridge S. Brooks, author of *True Stories of Christopher Columbus* (published 1892), ends his book with a powerful charge, "Happier than any fairytale, more marvelous than any wonder book, the story of the United States of America begins 'Once upon a time' and has come to the point where it depends upon the boys and girls who read it to say whether or not they shall 'live happily ever after.'"

I'm rooting for that "happily ever after." How about you?

A Miracle at Boston

In October 1746, French Duke of d'Anville sailed for New England, commanding the most powerful fleet of the time. He had 70 ships with 13,000 troops. In fact, it was "the largest fleet ever to be sighted from American soil." They started for Boston. The Duke intended that they avenge themselves for the loss they had suffered in Louisburg. They planned to recapture Louisburg, Nova Scotia, and destroy [all the English Colonies] from Boston to Georgia.

The situation was bleak for the Colonists. They had no chance of matching the power of the huge fleet on their own. Massachusetts Governor William Shirley gathered all the men, ammunitions, and supplies he could find; he then turned the situation over to the Lord by declaring the 16th of October, 1746, a Universal Day of Fasting. He would have everyone pray and fast for deliverance.

Everywhere, men observed it, thronging to the churches. In Boston, the Reverend Thomas Prince from the high pulpit of the Old South Meetinghouse prayed before hundreds. The morning was clear and calm; people had walked to church through sunshine. 'Deliver us from our enemy!' the minister implored. 'Send thy tempest, Lord, upon the waters to the eastward! Raise thy right hand. Scatter the ships of our tormentors and drive them hence. Sink their proud frigates beneath the power of thy winds!'

He had scarcely pronounced the words when the sun was gone, and the morning darkened. All the church was in a shadow. A wind shrieked around the walls—sudden, violent—hammering at the windows with a giant hand. No man was in the steeple—afterward the sexton swore it—yet the great bell struck twice, a wild, uneven sound. Thomas Prince paused in his prayer, both arms raised. 'We hear thy voice, O Lord!' he thundered triumphantly. 'We hear it! Thy breath is upon the waters to the eastward, even upon the deep. Thy bell tolls for the death of our enemies!' He bowed his head; when he looked up, tears streamed down his face. 'Thine be the glory, Lord. Amen and amen!'

… All the Province heard of this prayer and this answering tempest.

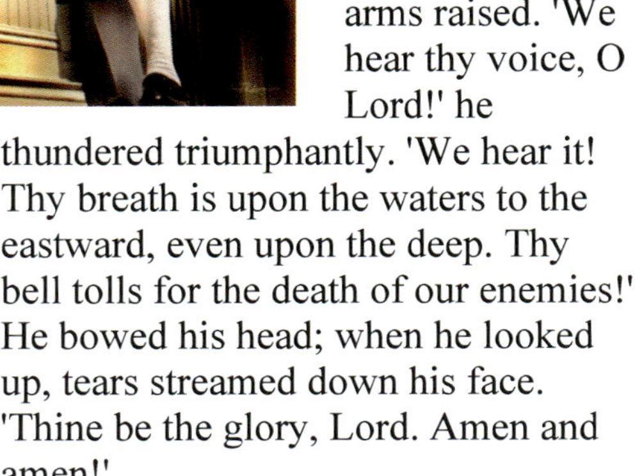

Governor Shirley sent a sloop, the *Rising Son*, northward for news … she brought news so good it was miraculous—if one could believe it … the whole fleet was nearly lost and the men very sick with scurvy or some pestilential fever. Their great admiral, the Duc d'Anville, was dead.

A week later, the news was confirmed by other vessels entering Boston from the northeastward. D'Anville was indeed dead; it was said he had poisoned himself in grief and despair when he saw his men dying round him. Two thousand were already buried, four thousand were sick, and not above a thousand of the land forces remained of their fleet. Vice-Admiral d'Estournelle had run himself through the heart with his sword. The few remaining ships, half-manned, were limping off to the southwestward—headed, it was thought, for the West Indies.

Pestilence, storm, and sudden death—how directly and with what extraordinary vigor the Lord had answered New England prayers! The country fell on its knees…. A paper with d'Anville's orders had been found, instructing him to take Cape Breton Island, then proceed to Boston to 'lay that town in ashes and destroy all he could upon the Coast of North America; then proceed to the West Indies and distress the Islands.'

Ten-year-old John Adams was in the church during this famous prayer and later declared, "That day, I became a patriot."

*Story from Catherine Drinker Bowen, John Adams, Grosset & Dunlap, N.Y., 1950, pp. 5, 10-11

The Faith of Columbus

On August 3, 1492, a small fleet set sail from Spain. The entire fleet consisted of three small ships, the *Nina*, *Pinta*, and *Santa Maria*. The ships were small in size (less than seventy-five feet long and twenty-five across) and were typical of ships that sailed the Mediterranean Sea at the time. The three vessels were manned by a combined crew of eighty-eight men.

Instead of turning west, they travelled 700 miles south to the Canary Islands off the Northwestern coast of Africa. In that way, they were able to catch the northeast trade winds, which would propel them all the way to the Americas. On September 6th, after restocking provisions and making repairs, they left the safety of the civilized world and headed west.

In order to convince Queen Isabella of Spain to invest in the expedition, Christopher Columbus had promised the trip from the Canaries to the Indies would be a "few days." He believed that Asia was only 2,400 miles away. But after the few days had past and they traveled further (as they believed) than man had ever sailed, the crew became increasing uncomfortable. To lessen their fears, Columbus purposely reported the length of each day's voyage as shorter than they had actually traveled. Numerous false sightings of land also caused morale

to suffer. By the last week of September, the men could see their supplies diminish, and clear signs of mutiny were appearing among the crew. The spirit of adventure and the promise of shared wealth soon turned to whispered threats and grumbling.

On October 8th, the captains of the *Nina* and *Pinta* demanded a meeting. They insisted that the search for land be abandoned. Columbus agreed they would turn homeward if land was not found within 3 days. He also avoided complete mutiny of his own crew by agreeing to turn back after 2 or 3 days.

Columbus was resolute! Later, in a letter to the Spanish hierarchy, he wrote, "Our Lord unlocked my mind, sent me upon the sea, and gave me fire for the deed. Those who heard of my emprise called it foolish, mocked me, and laughed. But who can doubt but that the Holy Ghost inspired me?" His quest for the voyage was also explained in his writings, "The fact that the gospel must be preached in so many lands in such a short time—this is what convinces me." Unwavering, yet running out of time, Columbus went to his cabin and, in his words, "prayed mightily to the Lord."

Finally, on October 11th, a little after midnight, crew members found a sprig of green with a tiny white flower floating in the water. Later, a piece of floating board was discovered, then a little stick which appeared to have been carved into the shape of a man. Finally, at 2:00 AM on October 12th, under a moon slightly past full, a sailor called out, "Land! Land on the horizon!" The expedition, led by Christopher Columbus, had discovered America.

Years later, when alone and frustrated, Columbus told of hearing a "Compassionate voice" that addressed him saying, "O fool, and slow to believe and to serve thy God . . what did He do more for Moses, or for David his servant, than He has done for thee?"

Columbus had opened the doors to the most phenomenal spread of Christianity since the time of the early apostles and set the stage for the greatest nation in the history of the world. To us and generations to come, the words of Columbus continue to encourage us: "No one should fear to undertake any task in the name of our Savior, if it is just and the intention is purely for His holy service."

To read Christopher Columbus's story and other stories like this, see *The Light and the Glory* by Peter Marshal and the *Freedom Series* from Libraries of Hope.

A Gunpowder Story

BY JOHN ESTEN COOKE

The following short story is an adapted version by author Frances Jenkins Olcott in her book *Good Stories for Great Holidays* (1914). It is a story about a young girl whose courage saves several patriot families and protects an important fort in the Revolutionary War.

In the autumn of 1777, the English decided to attack Fort Henry at Wheeling in northwestern Virginia. This was an important border fort named in honor of Patrick Henry, and around which had grown up a small village of about twenty-five log houses.

A band of Indians, under the leadership of one Simon Girty, was supplied by the English with muskets and ammunition and sent against the fort. This Girty was a white man who, as a boy, had been captured by Indians and brought up by them. He had joined their tribes and was a ferocious and bloodthirsty leader of savage bands.

When the settlers at Wheeling heard that Simon Girty and his Indians were advancing on the town, they left their homes and hastened into the fort. Scarcely had they done so when the savages made their appearance.

The defenders of the fort knew that a desperate fight must now take place, and there seemed little probability that they would be able to hold out against their assailants. They had only forty-two fighting men, including old men and boys, while the Indian force numbered about five hundred.

What was worse, they had but a small amount of gunpowder. A keg containing the main supply had been left by accident in one of the village houses. This misfortune, as you will soon see, brought about the brave action of a young girl.

After several encounters with the savages, which took place in the village, the defenders withdrew to the fort. Then a number of Indians advanced with loud yells, firing as they came. The fire was returned by the defenders, each of whom had picked out his man and taken deadly aim. Most of the attacking party were killed, and the whole body of Indians fell back into the near-by woods and there awaited a more favorable opportunity to renew hostilities.

The men in the fort now discovered, to their great dismay, that their gunpowder was nearly gone. What was to be done? Unless they could get another supply, they would not be able to hold the fort, and they and their women and children would either be massacred or carried into captivity.

Colonel Shepherd, who was in command, explained to the settlers exactly how matters stood. He also told them of the forgotten keg of powder that was in a house standing about sixty yards from the gate of the fort.

It was plain to all that if any man should attempt to procure the keg, he would almost surely be shot by the lurking Indians. In spite of this, three or four young men volunteered to go on the dangerous mission.

Colonel Shepherd replied that he could not spare three or four strong men, as there were already too few for the defense. Only one man should make the attempt, and they might decide who was to go. This caused a dispute.

Just then, a young girl stepped forward and said that she was ready to go. Her name was Elizabeth Zane, and she had just returned from a boarding-school in Philadelphia. This made her brave offer all the more remarkable since she had not been bred up to the fearless life of the border.

At first, the men would not hear of her running such a risk. She was told that it meant certain death. But she urged that they could not spare a man from the defense, and that the loss of one girl would not be an important matter. So after some discussion, the settlers agreed that she should go for the powder.

The house, as has already been stated, stood about sixty yards from the fort, and Elizabeth hoped to run thither and bring back the powder in a few minutes. The gate was opened, and she passed through, running like a deer.

A few straggling Indians were dodging about the log houses of the town; they saw the fleeing girl, but for some reason, they did not fire upon her. They may have supposed that she was returning to her home to rescue her clothes. Possibly they thought it a waste of good ammunition to fire at a woman, when they were so sure of taking the fort before long. So they

looked on quietly while, with flying skirts, Elizabeth ran across the open, and entered the house.

She found the keg of powder, which was not large. She lifted it with both arms, and, holding the precious burden close to her chest, she darted out of the house and ran in the direction of the fort.

When the Indians saw what she was carrying, they uttered fierce yells and fired. The bullets fell like hail about her, but not one so much as touched her garments. With the keg hugged to her bosom, she ran on and reached the fort in safety. The gate closed upon her just as the bullets of the Indians buried themselves in its thick panels.

The rescued gunpowder enabled the little garrison to hold out until help arrived from the other settlements near Wheeling. And Girty, seeing that there were no further hopes of taking Fort Henry, withdrew his band.

Thus, a weak but brave girl was the means of saving strong men with their wives and children. It was a heroic act, and Americans should never forget to honor the name of Elizabeth Zane.

Oh Say, Can You See

In 1814, Great Britain was again at war with America. Although the United States had won their independence 29 years earlier, Great Britain was enraged at America's demands for an independent Canada, and America's continued friendship and free trade with France galled them. In April, 1814, the London Times reported, "There is no public feeling in this country stronger than that of indignation against the Americans." Conflict between the two nations had erupted into full-scale war. The defeat of Napoleon's "Grand Army" had freed an additional 14,000 veteran British soldiers to join in the battle against America. By April, Great Britain was well entrenched in America and was winning the war.

The newly arriving soldiers pillaged the East coast of the United States, burning ships at anchor, razing manufacturing plants, torching private homes, and taking what property they could carry away. On August 24th, after a short battle, British forces set fire to Washington D.C., plundered the city, and burned the White House, most of the public buildings, and many private homes. The British next set their sights on Baltimore, some 30 miles northeast of the nation's capital.

Baltimore is situated on a beautiful natural harbor on the Patapsco River, which flows into Chesapeake Bay. Because of its location, Baltimore was a major port city that carried on extensive trade with France—which is why the British particularly disliked the people of Baltimore. The rag-tag American militia, shopkeepers, and farmers built trenches and defended the city from a land invasion. Fort McHenry guarded the city from a waterborne attack. Flying above the fort was a huge American Flag. The flag was 30 feet tall, 42 feet long, and made of 400 yards of cloth. The 2 foot tall stars were "spangled" (off-set at different angles so they would appear to twinkle when the flag was blown). It had been specially made so large that the British would have no difficulty in seeing it from a distance.

On Sunday, September 11th, the first ship in the British fleet arrived at the mouth of the Patapsco River as the people of Baltimore were attending church. On hearing that the British had arrived, church services adjourned all over the city. The Reverend John Gruber concluded his services with the prayer, "May the Lord bless King George, convert him and take him to heaven, as we want no more of him."

At 5:46 AM on September 13th, most of the fleet of 50 British ships opened fire on Fort McHenry. Their long-range cannons could fire 400 pound cannon balls a distance of 2½ miles with accuracy. But because the cannons from the fort drove the fleet back to a 4-mile circumference, their cannons were less than accurate. British gunners hoped to make each shrapnel-filled bomb explode shortly before impact by correctly trimming the length of each fuse. British cannons shot over 3,000 cannon balls towards Fort McHenry throughout the day, and continued until early the next morning. Many bombs exploded in midair, far from the fort, others continued burning after impact and were doused with water to keep them from exploding. Miraculously, four

inches of heavy rain also extinguished many of the bombs. At 1:00 AM, all grew silent.

From the deck of the *Minden*, Francis Scott Key watched the bombardment of Fort McHenry. As a young attorney, he was aboard to negotiate the release of prisoners. From his vantage point, the silence was worse than the bombardment. An amphibious nighttime assault was ordered, and the troops rowed for shore.

The city of Baltimore, as well as the British fleet, waited through the long night to see whose flag would be flying. At day break, a single cannon shot was heard from the fort, signifying that the fort was occupied, but by whom? Finally, as the early morning mist and smoke began to clear, Key saw through the distance the stars and stripes still flying over the fort, and the British rowboats in retreat. Now confident of a complete American victory, Key took an old letter from his pocket and began to write on the back of the words of *The Star-Spangled Banner*. Only four

Americans had been killed in the long assault, yet the battle was the turning point of the war.

"Oh, say can you see by the dawn's early light; What so proudly we hailed at the twilight's last gleaming? Whose broad stripes and bright stars thru the perilous fight; O'er the ramparts we watched were so gallantly streaming?

And the rocket's red glare, the bombs bursting in air; Gave proof through the night that our flag was still there. Oh, say does that star-spangled banner yet wave; O'er the land of the free and the home of the brave?"

In 1931, President Herbert Hoover signed a bill declaring this as our national anthem. Long let it wave!

A Story of George Washington

STORY FROM *AMERICAN HISTORY STORIES* VOLUME 1 BY MARA L. PRATT
(AVAILABLE THROUGH LIBRARIES OF HOPE)

During the Revolution, George Washington was one day riding by a group of soldiers who did not know him. They were busily engaged in raising a beam to the top of some military works. It was a difficult task, and often the corporal's voice could be heard shouting, "Now you have it!" and "All ready! Pull!"

Washington quietly asked the corporal why he didn't help them. "Sir," the corporal angrily replied, "do you not realize that I am a corporal?"

Washington politely raised his hat saying, "I did not realize it. Beg your pardon, Mr. Corporal."

Then dismounting his horse, General Washington himself fell to work and helped the men until the beam was raised. Before leaving, he turned to the corporal and, wiping the perspiration from his face, said, "If ever you need assistance like this again, call upon Washington, your commander-in-chief, and I will come."

The confused corporal turned red, and then white, as he realized that this was Washington himself to whom he had been so pompous; and we hope he learned a lesson of true greatness.

Capture of Fort Ticonderoga

"In Vermont, called… the Green Mountain state, the men had formed themselves into a company under their colonel, Ethan Allen, and called themselves the Green Mountain Boys.

On the morning of the very day of the meeting of Congress that made George Washington Commander in Chief, Ethan Allen, with a detachment of these volunteers, set out to surprise Fort Ticonderoga.

Entering the Fort in the night, Ethan Allen went straight the commander's quarters, and in a voice like thunder, so his followers say, demanded the instant surrender of the fort.

The commander, frightened and only half dressed, threw open his door, saying, 'By whose authority do you'—But Allen broke in upon him with, 'In the name of the Great Jehovah and the Continental Congress do I command you to surrender.' No resistance was attempted; and so, a large quantity of cannon and ammunition which the English had stored there, and which just then was so much needed by the troops at Boston, fell into the hands of the Americans without the loss of a single man."

Reading Aloud to Your Children

BY PAMELA ROMNEY OPENSHAW

Reading aloud to your children, from both fiction and nonfiction books, is a powerful tool to bind people together and enhance their intellectual development. These benefits can strengthen classroom learning experiences and enrich families.

Intellectual development comes from reading aloud together. The combined sensations of speaking, hearing, and seeing deepen the learning process and embolden the concepts presented. Important ideas are solidified, applications to those concepts can be discussed, and creativity can be fostered through the common reading experience.

Reading aloud brings other benefits to families when parents gather their children together and share a good book. Whether one-on-one or as a group, parents can strengthen moral behavior through this family experience. Discussions before or after provide opportunities to teach moral concepts. The emotions aroused, particularly by good fiction, give a child experiences in times, events, and circumstances beyond his own world. He develops maturity and experience outside his own sphere.

Two experiences from my life illustrate these points. The first took place in a third grade classroom decades ago. As a student teacher, I had chosen to read

Charlotte's Web, by E.B. White, aloud to my class during the last ten minutes of each school day.

We were on the last chapter of the book, when Charlotte was dying as Wilbur met her ongoing posterity. Our classroom clock ticked mercilessly toward the daily bus departures as I raced to finish the book, fearful of stopping a page or two shy of the end. The twenty-eight children in the classroom sat immobile, mesmerized by the emotional ending. They hardly seemed to breathe. Triumphantly, I finished the last sentence and looked into the eyes of the children, made tender by Charlotte's death and Wilbur's pain and consolation. The PA system blared its message that the buses were almost ready to depart, but not one child moved, held by the emotions within.

As I looked into the eyes of each child, I felt a love for each of those children that endures to this day. Reading good literature together has that effect.

The second instance came as a mother. I read faithfully to our children every school morning for decades. Our home was organized on a firm schedule, and we all had morning tasks, the most joyful of which was our twenty minutes spent reading together. We read the scriptures for ten minutes, then read a good book for another ten, ending with kneeling family prayer before we scattered to the four winds until nightfall.

That day we were concluding the book *Johnny Tremain* by Esther Forbes. Our five-year-old son David sat to my immediate right. As we finished the final words of the book, an aura of reverence—for Johnny Tremain, for our country and its revolutionary history, for our common familial bond—held us silently spellbound.

A full minute passed as each of us turned inward to capture tender personal feelings. David broke the prolonged silence with a deep, reverential sigh that poured from his little body. He turned his face upward as I looked down to gaze into his eyes. With awe, he exclaimed: "Oh, mommy! That was the bestest book in the whole world!"

Twenty-three years later, that memory was still fresh in my mind as I gave David a new copy of Johnny Tremain on his wedding day, and we reminisced over the power of that moment.

Such is the might of reading together. I encourage you to make these experiences a part of your life.

Are You "Just" Reading to Them? GIGO

BY RACHEL DEMILLE
THOMAS JEFFERSON EDUCATION, TJED.ORG

So much has been said about the importance of reading to our kids, and those of us who do can attest that it's a formative experience—on so many levels:

- Bonding

- Laughing

- Making memories

- A shared language

- Gratitude

- Reliving the past

- Pity and compassion

- Empathy for others

- Tenderness

- Shared stories/quotes/inside jokes

- Moments of transparency and unguarded confiding

- Feelings of righteous outrage and commitment to make a difference

- Self discovery and desire to improve

- Exploring new ideas/places/words/peoples/images

- Connecting with our ancestors/predecessors

- Deepened affection for family

- and so much more…

It occurred to me one day last week, when I was teaching a little lesson for a group of friends and their kids (we take weekly turns for an hour of class before the kids play together), that I do something a little more than just reading. It's one of those things that comes so naturally that sometimes you forget to even comment on it or suggest it to others.

As I taught our little group about the the power of stories to help us "Remember," I retold the traditional folktale of the *Three Little Pigs*—not the Disney version, but the one where the piggies actually get gobbled up because their houses were not made to last. And then I did what I always do: I started to ask questions about the story.

We had a discussion about it. In technical mentoring terms, we had a "debriefing." It took longer to discuss the story and listen to the responses from the kids and their moms than it did to tell the thing, and it could have gone on for three times as long. There is so much to talk about when you have a good quality story!

I found a version on the web that's really close to the one I read to the kids. (see Hostess Resource Center for the link)

Some of the things we discussed:

- Why did the piggies leave their first home?

- Where did the little pigs get the materials to build their houses?

- Does it seem strange that the man gave away the straw/wood/bricks just because the pigs needed them and asked for them—without paying?

- Do you think the man would have given away the materials if they hadn't asked?

- Who in our lives gives us what we need, just because we ask?

- Why is asking an important part of that process?

- How did the pigs get the houses? [They built them]

- How much did they cost? [Only the cost of their labor]

- So basically, they all cost the pigs the same amount; which house was the most valuable, and why?

- Why would a pig ask for free materials of lesser value, and put his effort into building a house that doesn't actually do what a house should do—protect and shelter?

- Do we ever ask for things that aren't of lasting value?

- Do we ever put our effort into things that don't serve our interests? How/What?

- Did the unfortunate piggies try to avoid the wolf? Why were they unable to do so? [Because they had not prepared adequately]

- Did the wise piggy try to avoid the wolf? How? [He put in extra effort to use the resources he had been freely given by the man so that the wolf wouldn't be able to enter his home. He also made plans and sacrifices in an effort to never be in the same place with the wolf when he had to leave his home.]

- What happened to the foolish piggies? Does misfortune ever come to those who mean well but do less than they could?

- How does this apply to us?

There are many more questions that could come from such a story. But, obviously, just any old version of the story doesn't provide such fertile thought. Some common versions are stripped of the details that make this one such a great discussion. This is why we recur to the classics (See Hostess Resource Center for list of recommended Classics). They stay around generation after generation, retelling after retelling, because they have more than a bossy moral at the end; they have myriad open questions embedded in the details.

Not all stories are created equal; not all reading times are created equal. It sort of brings to mind the computer science term, "Garbage in, garbage out." The common acronym is: GIGO. It means, the quality of output is determined by the quality of input. How many times have we pulled out our hair in frustration because our computer (or vacuum, or car, or…) isn't reliably doing what we need it to do? Somewhere in the programming, design, construction, or planned obsolescence of the tool we were confronted with its limitations. And yet, a sleek, well designed program can really make your life a dream and simplify your work; and there's

nothing quite so glorious as a vacuum or car that you absolutely love!

When it comes to family reading time (or personal reading, or leisure pursuits), are we choosing materials freely available to us that don't serve our interests? Are we putting in the time and effort but getting inferior results?

GIGO. The lesson of the 3 Pigs tells us this:

- Choose the highest quality materials

- Put in the extra effort to put them to work (Don't just read; interact. Don't just lecture; listen.)

- Shun, dismiss, and expel the influences that distract, compete, or deceive

I think sometimes moms and dads feel overwhelmed, frustrated, or disillusioned with their family's education and have no idea that the fix could be as simple as having a family reading time with a great classic. Consider: if I had chosen a different version of the 3 Little Pigs, what kind of discussion might have ensued? How might I have spent that 30 minutes? What additional effort or floundering might I have gone to and never had such an enriching and bonding experience with my kids and friends?

To my way of thinking, it would have been a lot harder, and a lot less fulfilling. When we're engaged with a great classic, I don't have to have 7 different lessons going on for 7 different kids at home. They each take from that experience something that applies to them specifically. In fact, my 18-year-old daughter happened to pass by the parlor while I was leading the 3 Pigs discussion, and she stayed to take it in. It was every bit as interesting and relevant for her as it was for my neighbor's 4-year-old. She commented to me afterward that she hadn't realized how much there was to think about in that story! My response: that's the power of classics and mentors. GIGO. Quality in, quality out.

And in this case, quality also translates to all the wonderful feelings and experiences I listed at the beginning of this article. After such a discussion, the natural result is a spirit of harmony and productivity that never fails to lead to other wonderful projects and happy times throughout the rest of the day. Isn't that more productive and less stressful than the alternative?

What do you think will happen to your family's education when you input the classics and debrief with interactive listening? What will the output be? Sounds like a good time to employ the scientific method….

RELATED QUOTES

"If history were taught in the form of stories, it would never be forgotten."   **-Rudyard Kipling, The Collected Works**

"Let me tell the stories and I care not who writes the textbooks."   **-G. Stanley Hall**

"When the world is in chaos, and not able to locate its identity, its the storytellers that bring it back to center. Because storytellers are the keepers of the culture."   **-Michael Meade**

"The decline of literature indicates the decline of a nation."   **-Johann Wolfgang von Goethe**

"The destiny of the world is determined less by the battles that are lost and won than by the stories it loves and believes in."   **-Harold Goddard**

"Storytelling is the most powerful way to put ideas into the world today."   **-Robert McAfee Brown**

"The stories we tell literally make the world. If you want to change the world, you need to change your story. This truth applies both to individuals and institutions." **-Michael Margolis**

"People think that stories are shaped by people. In fact, it's the other way around."   **-Terry Pratchett**

"People are hungry for stories. It's part of our very being. Storytelling is a form of history, of immortality too. It goes from one generation to another."   **-Studs Terkel**

"There's always room for a story that can transport people to another place."   **-J.K. Rowling**

"After nourishment, shelter and companionship, stories are the thing we need most in the world."   **-Philip Pullman**

"The purpose of a storyteller is not to tell you how to think, but to give you questions to think upon." **-Brandon Sanderson, The Way of Kings**

"Stories have to be told or they die, and when they die, we can't remember who we are or why we're here."   **-Sue Monk Kidd, The Secret Life of Bees**

"Storytelling is the essential human activity. The harder the situation, the more essential it is."   **-Tim O Brien**

"Happier than any fairy tale, more marvelous than any wonder book, the story of the United States of America begins 'Once upon a time' and has come to the point where it depends upon the boys and girls who read it to say whether or not they shall 'live happily ever after.'"
-Elbridge S. Brooks
The True Story of Christopher Columbus

FROM THE FOUNDERS

"Honesty is the first chapter in the book of wisdom."
-Thomas Jefferson

"If we are to guard against ignorance and remain free, it is the responsibility of every American to be informed."
-Thomas Jefferson

"Every child in America should be acquainted with his own country. He should read books that furnish him with ideas that will be useful to him in life and practice. As soon as he opens his lips, he should rehearse the history of his own country." **-Noah Webster**

"The philosophy in the classroom of this generation is the philosophy of government in the next." **-James Madison**

Journal

"Enjoy the little things, for one
day you may look back and
realize they were the big things."

-Robert Brault

Capture the Sunshine

"Never lose an opportunity of seeing anything beautiful, for beauty is God's handwriting."

-Ralph Waldo Emerson

PREPARATION

- To prepare yourself to lead this presentation please review and consider the following material

- Read "Mans Search for Meaning," "The Friendship Train," and "Be the Change" provided in the Supplemental Materials of this presentation; mark any sections you want to highlight in your meeting discussion

- Read "Birdman from Alcatraz" and "The Nobleman and the Seed"

- View the video *Capture the Sunshine* provided in the Hostess Resource Center on the Moms for America® website www.MomsforAmerica.us

- Bible References—James 1:17, Psalms 100, Acts 16:23-25, James 5:13-15, Luke 17:11-19

- Optional: Review *Promises of the Constitution* Vignettes 2.5 and 3.12

- Review the Preface to the *5,000 Year Leap*; highlight areas you want to include in your discussion

PURPOSE

The purpose of this presentation is to introduce the essential need of "sunshine" in our lives; just as a plant needs sunshine to grow healthy and strong. We will look at how beauty in art and music will nurture the growth of liberty within the hearts of people. We will discuss why expressions of gratitude and recordings of inspirational thoughts are essential to capturing the sunshine in our lives.

KEY POINTS

- Just as a plant needs sunshine to grow, people also need "light" in their lives for liberty to grow in their hearts

- Beauty, inspiration, and gratitude can be likened to the "light" required for the nurturing of liberty

- "Capture" is an action verb that suggests we must reach outside ourselves to find "light" in our environment

Home Assignment

As a family, visit a music, dance or theatrical performance. While live drama is a definite unique experience, if you can't attend a live performance there are some great films of musicals that are well worth viewing. Top of our list would be *"Seven Brides for Seven Brothers"*, *"The Sound of Music"*, *"Marry Poppins"*, *"The Wizard of OZ"*, *Fiddler on the Roof"*, *The Greatest Showman*, and *"Singing in the Rain"*

Personal Study

Read *The Present* by Spencer Johnson and/or *Freedom Factor* by Gerald N. Lund

Family Enrichment

View the videos in the Cottage Meeting Resources on the MFA website to choose the ones you would like to share with your family. Choose a patriotic song you can share with your children. As a family, discuss the blessings of being an American and ways we can show gratitude for our blessings, individually and as a family.

MEETING OUTLINE

Welcome & Gathering

We recommend starting your meeting with a prayer and the Pledge of Allegiance.

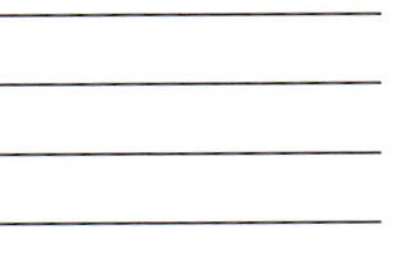

Show Video: *Capture the Sunshine* (available in Hostess Resource Center)

Hostess Presentation and **Group Discussion**

Read or Summarize: "Man's Search for Meaning"

> *"Man is originally characterized by his 'search for meaning' rather than his 'search for himself.' The more he forgets himself—giving himself to a cause or another person—the more human he is. And the more he is immersed and absorbed in something or someone other than himself the more he really becomes himself."*
>   *-Viktor Frankl*

How can finding a cause outside ourselves be likened to "capturing the sunshine?"

How does service to others promote a free society?

Read as a Group: "The Birdman of Alkatraz", "The Nobleman and the Seed" and, "Man's Search for Meaning" provided in the Supplemental Materials section of this presentation.

How can beauty nourish the heart towards a love of liberty?

How can we be the light in the darkness?

Ghandi said, "We must be the change we wish to see in the world." How can we be the change we want to see?

Read: "Be the Change" provided in the Supplemental Materials section of this presentation.

Share: Highlights from *Raising Patriots* chapter "Making Good Use of the Harvest"

How can beauty nourish the heart towards a love of liberty?

How can we invite and promote beauty in the lives of family members?

The Founders of our country chose to seek the "light" in the dark environment of tyranny and oppression. How might we follow their example and do the same?

Read or Summarize "The Friendship Train" provided in the Supplemental Materials section of this presentation. If desired, you can share the film reels of the Friendship Train provided in the Hostess Resource Center on the MFA website.

Summary

Summarize your thoughts on the material covered in this presentation.

- Give the Home Assignment for the next meeting

- Announce date, time, and location for next meeting

ADDITIONAL PRESENTATION IDEAS

The Good, True, and Beautiful

Beauty isn't usually associated with freedom. However, when we read stories of those who triumphed over trials, it was often the beauty they found in their everyday lives that gave them hope. When communism and Marxism took root in the world, hope was a dangerous threat to their objective.

On January 10, 1963, Representative Albert Sydney Herlong Jr., a Democratic Congressman (1949-1969) introduced "Current Communist Goals" into the Congressional Record. The list was an excerpt from the book *The Naked Communist* written by Cleon Skousen. Goal #23 reads, "Control art critics and directors of art museums. Our plan is to promote ugliness, repulsive, meaningless art."

- **View and Discuss** the following videos provided in the Hostess Resource Center

  - *Mysteries at the Museum*—Pavel Jordanowitch

  - "Why is Modern Art so bad?"

- What is the difference between classic and modern art?

- How can beauty enrich our lives? How can it help us see and share the light in the darkness of the world or our own pain and trials? View the following Videos:

  - *Tree Change Dolls* provided in the Hostess Resource Center

  - *Lindsay Sterling "Hallelujah"*

Spirit of Gratitude & Forgiveness

A spirit of gratitude has been known to lift people from discouragement and depression. Why is acknowledging God's hand in our lives important? How can music help lift our spirits during times of challenge? How can serving others help us develop a spirit of gratitude?

- Review the following Bible References: James 1:17, James 5:13-15, Acts 16:23-25, Psalms 100, Parable of the Lepers"—Luke 17:11-19

- Read "We're Not Poor" provided in the Supplemental Materials section of this presentation

- Read and Discuss "Beauty Sweetens Life"

- Read "Forgiveness" by Corrie Ten Boom provided in the Supplemental Materials section of this presentation. How can forgiveness help us reach a higher level of freedom? See Bible References Acts 26:19, Colossians 3:13, Luke 6:37, Ephesians 4:31-32, Luke 17:3-4

- Discuss the following Quotes

  > *"I think the first step is to understand that forgiveness does not exonerate the perpetrator. Forgiveness liberates the victim. It's a gift you give yourself." -T. D. Jakes*

  > *"Forgiveness has nothing to do with absolving a criminal of his crime. It has everything to do with relieving oneself of the burden of being a victim—letting go of the pain and transforming oneself from victim to survivor." -C.R. Strahan*

MINI COTTAGE IDEAS

Mini Cottages are designed especially for moms of preschoolers and moms who work full-time jobs. Moms simply read and/or watch the same materials at home, on their own, then meet together once a week in a playdate or over lunch during the workday to discuss what they read. The articles and videos are short and can usually be read and/or viewed in less than hour. Below are some suggestions to host mini cottage discussions under the "Capture the Sunshine" theme.

- Read & Discuss "Corrie Ten Boom on Forgiveness" provided in the Supplemental Materials of this presentation. How does forgiveness play a role in healing?

- Read "Being the Change" provided in the Supplemental Materials of this presentation; watch the Video *Playing in the Subway* (link provided in the Hostess Resource Center. How do our busy lives distract us from the beauty around us? What can you do be the change beginning in your own home and family? How can you bring beauty into your home?

- One of the Communist Goals referenced in the *Naked Communist* by Cleon Skousen (introduced into the Congressional Record) was to control art critics and directors of art museums, stating, "Our plan is to promote ugliness, repulsive, meaningless art" (The full list of Communist Goals is provided in the supplemental materials section of Presentation 2 "Liberty Begins at Home"). View the Videos *Mysteries at the Museum*: Pavel Jordanowitch and *Why is Modern Art So Bad?* (Video links provided in the Hostess Resource Center)

- View the videos *Tree Change Dolls* and *Lindsay Sterling "Hallelujah"* (Video links provided in the Hostess Resource Center). How can beauty enrich our lives? How can it help us see and share the light in the darkness of the world or our own pain and trials?

COTTAGE MEETING BOOK CLUB

For those who like the book club format, we've compiled a list of great books to help you gain an appreciation and foundational understanding of the concepts presented in "Capture the Sunshine."

The 5000 Year Leap: A Miracle That Changed the World

- Review Principles Preface and Principle 9

Promises of the Constitution

- Review the following vignettes: 2.5 and 3.12

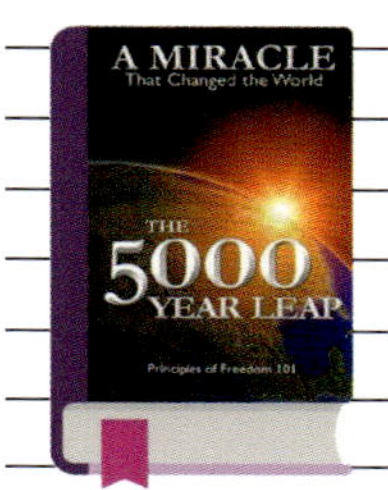

Poems of American History by Brander Matthews

What a masterpiece this book is! Brander Matthews has taken the best-loved poems and stories of America and combined them with the beautiful artwork of N.C. Wyeth. This turn of the century classic has been reproduced especially for children by Libraries of Hope and is sure to become a well-loved treasure with your little ones. Imagine a picture book with classic art by a famous artist to tell and retell the stories of America. This is a must for every budding patriots home library-a true gem!

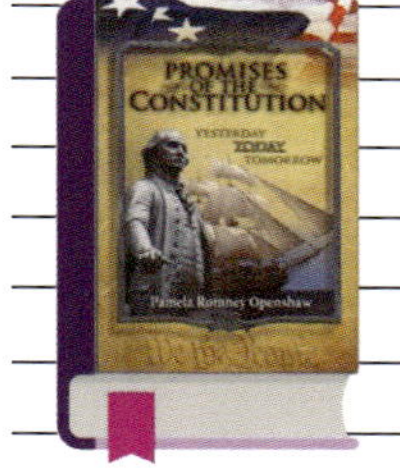

The Freedom Factor by Gerald N. Lund

The Freedom Factor, a gripping novel of courage and love that will leave you deeply grateful for the Founding Fathers and the Constitution of the United States. Nathaniel Gorham, an original Founding Father, visits young Bryce Sherwood, a rising aide to a Washington senator and a key player in an attempt

to pass an amendment that would eliminate the checks and balances built into the Constitution. When Bryce refuses to change his position, Gorham transports him into a world where the Constitution was never ratified. In this strange world of oppression and fear, Bryce begins to learn the true meaning of the Constitution and the price of freedom. Through this riveting story the author creates an understanding of the important nature of beauty and gratitude in our lives and why the Constitution of the United States is so vitally important to us personally—and our families.

Heart Throbs

In 1905, a popular magazine ran a contest asking Americans to submit their favorite clipping, story, or anecdote—something that had touched their hearts. *Heart Throbs* is the publication of the winners. As you read through what inspired Americans then and what they valued, you can't help but wonder what the current version would look like. How different are we? *Heart Throbs* is a beautiful compilation of inspiring works that it gives us a tangible idea of what Americans used to value. If people today were to submit the poem or story that touched their heart, what would it look like? It's an interesting question to pose as you read through the book

Man's Search for Meaning by Viktor Frankl

Psychiatrist Viktor Frankl's memoir has riveted generations of readers with its descriptions of life in Nazi death camps and its lessons for spiritual survival. Between 1942 and 1945 Frankl labored in four different camps, including Auschwitz, while his parents, brother, and pregnant wife perished. Based on his own experience and the experiences of those he treated in his practice, Frankl argues that we cannot avoid suffering, but we can choose how to cope with it, find meaning in it, and move forward with renewed purpose. Frankl's theory—known as logotherapy, from the Greek word logos ("meaning")—holds that our primary drive in life is not pleasure, as Freud maintained, but the discovery and pursuit of what we personally find meaningful.

The Ultimate Gift by Jim Stovall

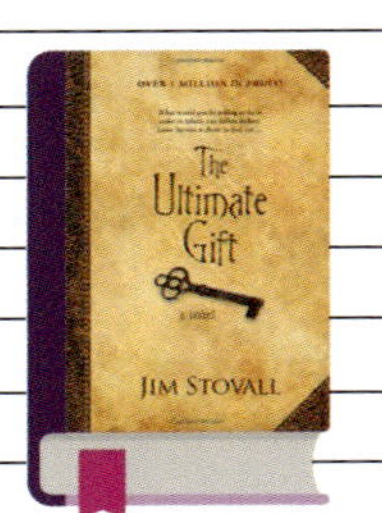

What would you do to inherit a million dollars? Would you be willing to change your life? Jason Stevens is about to find out in Jim Stovall's *The Ultimate Gift*. Red Stevens has died, and the older members of his family receive their millions with greedy anticipation. But a different fate awaits young Jason, whom Stevens, his great-uncle, believes may be the last vestige of hope in the family. *The Ultimate Gift* is a fictional story, but it teaches a lesson that is very real. Your heart will change as you journey with Jason to find the Ultimate Gift.

The Present Spencer Johnson

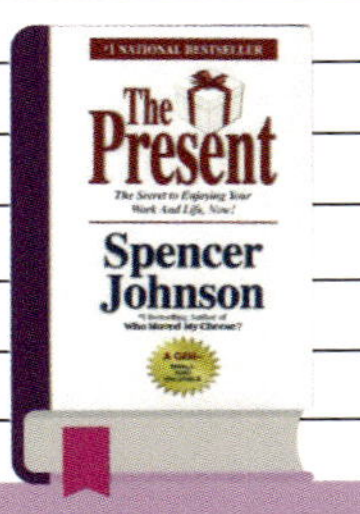

The Present is an engaging story of a young man's journey to adulthood, and his tireless search for The Present, a mysterious and elusive gift he first hears about from a wise old man. This Present, according to the old man, is the most valuable gift a person can receive. Why? Because it is the one thing that doesn't change in changing times. As the young boy becomes a man, he grows disillusioned with his work and his life. So he returns to ask the old man to help him find The Present. The old man responds, "Only you have the power to find The Present for yourself." Heeding the old man's advice, the young man embarks on a worldwide search for this magical gift that remains unchanging in a changing world and holds the secret to personal happiness and lifelong success. Like the young man, you may find that it is the best gift you can ever give to yourself—and to those you care about.

The Hiding Place by Corrie Ten Boom

When the Nazis invaded Holland, Corrie Ten Boom's quiet life turned into a nightmare. Because she made her home a "hiding place" for Jews, she and her family were sent to a concentration camp. Refusing to despair, Corrie discovered how Jesus can turn loss to glory! This unforgettable story will move you to tears and to joy. This is a book that will literally change your life.

Read-a-loud Book *The Giver* by Lois Lowry

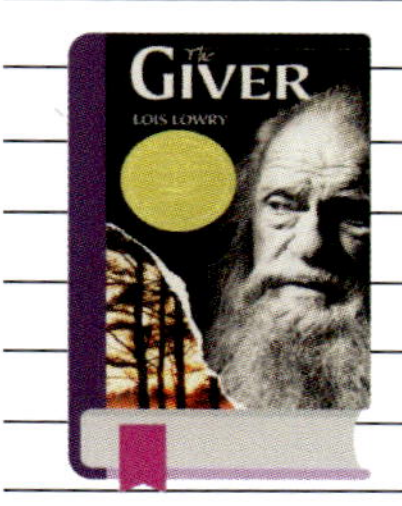

The Giver, the 1994 Newbery Medal winner, is one of the most influential novels of our time. The haunting story centers on twelve-year-old Jonas, who lives in a seemingly ideal, if colorless, world of conformity and contentment. Not until he is given his life assignment as the Receiver of Memory does he begin to understand the dark, complex secrets behind his fragile community. There are three companion novels to *The Giver,* including *Gathering Blue, Messenger,* and *Son.* The book was adapted into a film, creating a great comparison discussion to read the book and then watch the movie.

COTTAGE MEETING FOR KIDS

Cottage Meeting for Kids is a liberty promoting program for the entire family and focused on children from preschool to teens. It is full of great stories and fun activities to help children gain a love of liberty. Families can join together each month for an Activity Day to share the concepts they've learned and enhance them through group activities. Here are some ideas to promote the concepts presented in "Capture the Sunshine." You can find additional ideas, outlines and activities on the Moms for America® website under "Cottage Meetings for Kids."

- Read *The Giver* and/or *The Hiding Place* as a family

- Mahatma Gandhi, "You must be the change you wish to see in the world." Learn about individuals who, through their lives, became the change for good they wanted to see. Some ideas are Irene Sendler, Harriett Tubman, Martin Luther, Penelope Barker, James Madison, and Joan of Arc.

- Choose films and books from the recommended lists to share as a family

- Make colorful butterflies and other art projects. See Hostess Resource Center and Cottage Meetings for Kids for additional project ideas

Book & Movie List

Suggested books and readings for children all ages to nurture a love of liberty in the home.

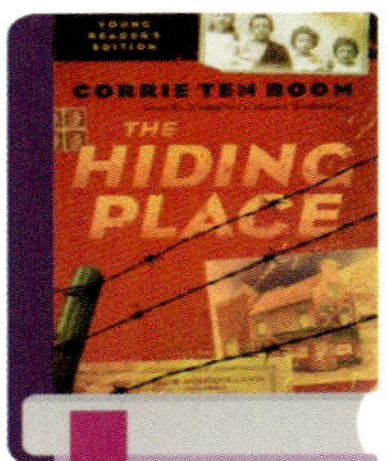

The Hiding Place
by Corrie Ten Boom

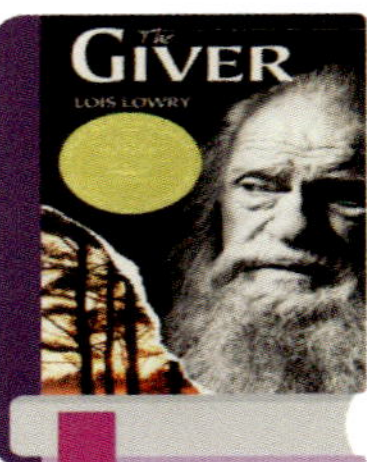

The Giver
by Lois Lowry

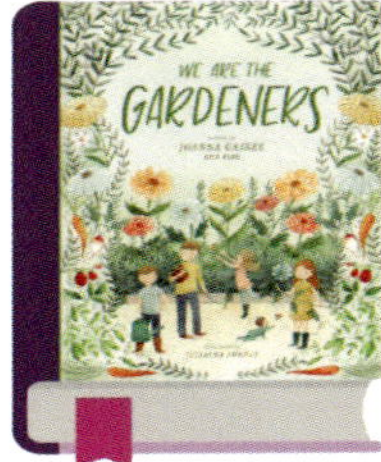

We Are the Gardeners
by Joanna Gaines

The Jolly Pocket Postman
by Janet and Allan Ahlberg

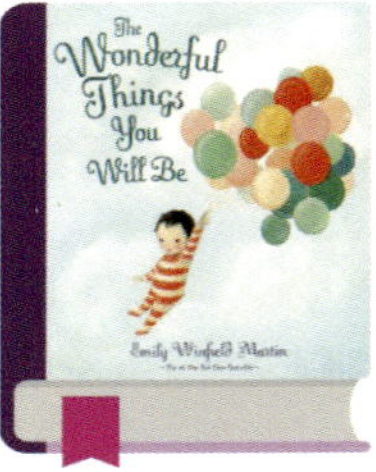

The Wonderful Things You Will Be
by Emily Winfield Martin

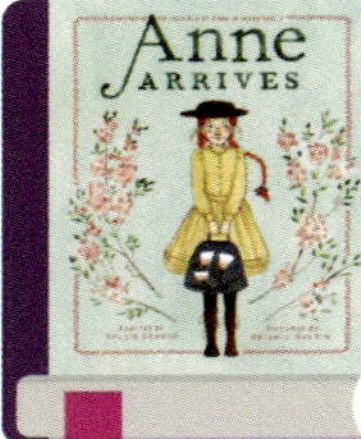

Anne Arrives
by Kallie George

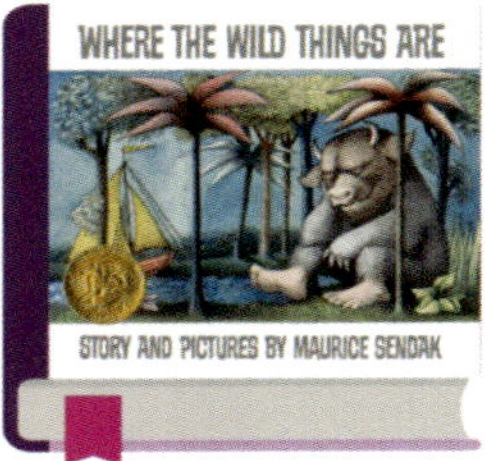

Where the Wild Things Are
by Maurice Sendak

Lola Dutch
by Kenneth and Sarah Jane Wright

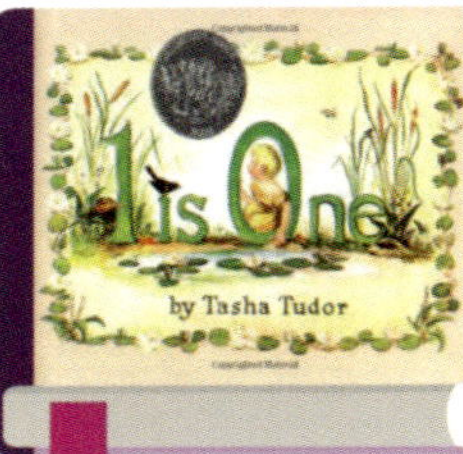

1 is One
by Tasha Tudor

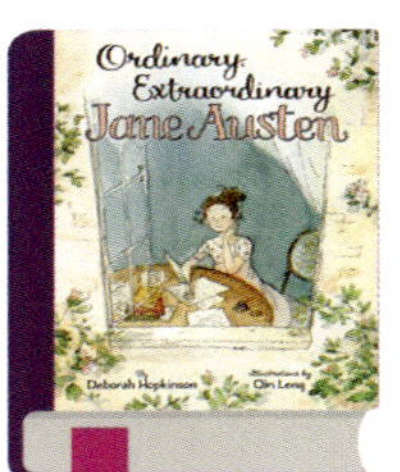

Ordinary, Extraordinary Jane Austen
by Deborah Hopkinson

Sleeping Beauty

Beauty and the Beast

Miracle at Midnight
1998

The Giver
2014

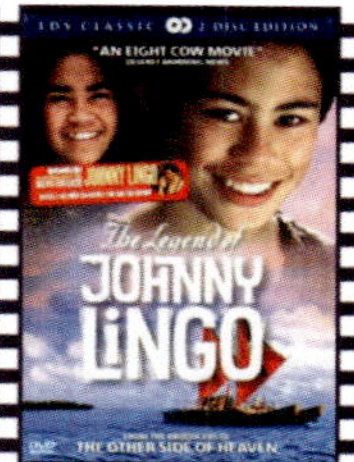

Johnny Lingo
2003

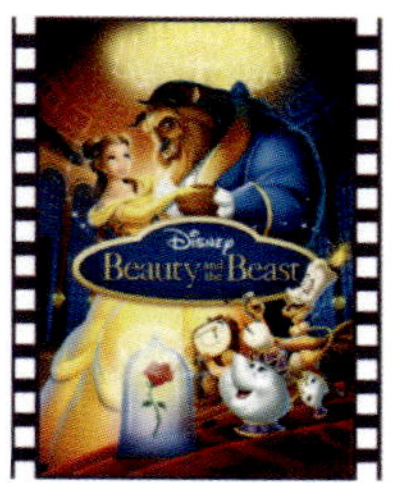

Beauty and the Beast
1991 animated

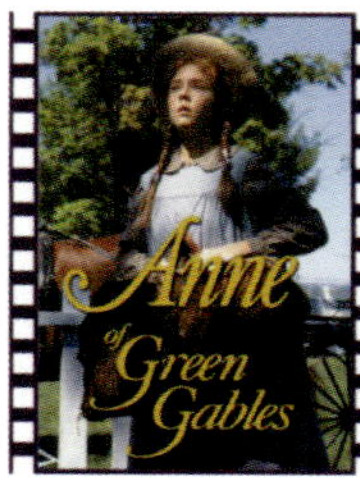

Anne of Green Gables
1985 Miniseries

Pete's Dragon
2016

**Seven Brides for
Seven Brothers**
1954

The Sound of Music
1965

Mary Poppins
1964

The Wizard of OZ
1939

Fiddler on the Roof
1971

Singing in the Rain
1952

Pollyanna
1960

Nannie McPhee
2005

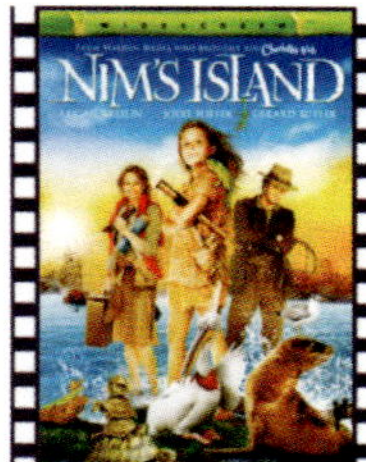

Nim's Island
2008

The Beauty of Freedom

"When you think of freedom, beauty isn't something that usually comes to mind. And yet, beauty is a powerfully freeing element.

While reading a book on the Russian Revolution, I came across an interesting tidbit about Lenin, who was known for his cold, cruel abusive nature. He once admitted after listening to a Sonata by Beethoven, "I can't listen to music too often. It affects your nerves; makes you want to say stupid nice things and stroke the heads of people who could create such beauty while living in this vile hell."

Contrast that with Viktor Frankl, a Jewish neurologist who spent three years in Nazi concentration camps. In his book, "Man's Search for Meaning," Dr. Frankl found those that weathered the storm of the camps could find beauty in the simplest things-memories of family, a blade of grass, a sunset. For some this was survival, for others it generated feelings of profound gratitude. Dr. Frankl witnessed the way those who held on to these things-those who had purpose in their life-seemed not only to bear their horrific burdens better than most, but also, at great personal sacrifice, helped and comforted others.

"We who lived in concentration camps," he recalled, "can remember the men who walked through the huts comforting others, giving away their last piece of bread. They may have been few in number, but they offer sufficient proof that everything can be taken from man but one thing: the last of the human freedoms-to choose one's attitude in any given set of circumstances; to choose one's own way."

Even an evil man like Lenin recognized the heart-warming influence of beautiful music. It's sad and horribly tragic that there are those who prefer coldness to warmth. But it also shows that these inspiring influences can reach even the hardest of hearts.

Martin Luther King asserted, "Music is a discipline, and a mistress of order and good manners, she makes the people milder and gentler, more moral and more reasonable.

The Friendship Train:
A Bright Light in America's History

"You've probably never heard of it. Most people haven't."

That's how Dorothy Scheele, curator of the Friendship Train website, introduces one of the most amazing, yet mostly forgotten, stories from American history. It was Dorothy and another American, Earl Bennet Sr. (now passed on), who dedicated their lives to preserving this beautiful story.

I found out about it through Turner Classic Movies' old newsreels. I was so moved by the story that I immediately went to my computer and began googling everything I could find on the Friendship Train. What I found were the websites of two incredible Americans who spent years collecting stories, photos, and news footage so the Friendship Train would not be forgotten.

The year was 1947. The people of the world were still recovering from the ravages of World War II. Europe was hit especially hard. Drew Pearson, a popular American journalist, while touring post-war Europe, noticed the Communists were being lauded for delivering a few carloads of grain, and it deeply

troubled him. He knew America could do better.

On Oct. 11, 1947, Drew Pearson opened his famous radio show with his vision of the "Friendship Train," a cross-country collection of food from the people of America to the people of Europe. This project would be much different than the proposed Marshall Plan, which was government imposed and government regulated. While the Marshall Plan was government-to-government, the Friendship Train would be people-to-people.

Pearson sent out the call asking Americans to donate food from their homes, kitchens, gardens, and fields, and the American people responded beyond all expectations. Immediately, communities formed plans to collect food, coordinating efforts to meet up with the Friendship Train along the

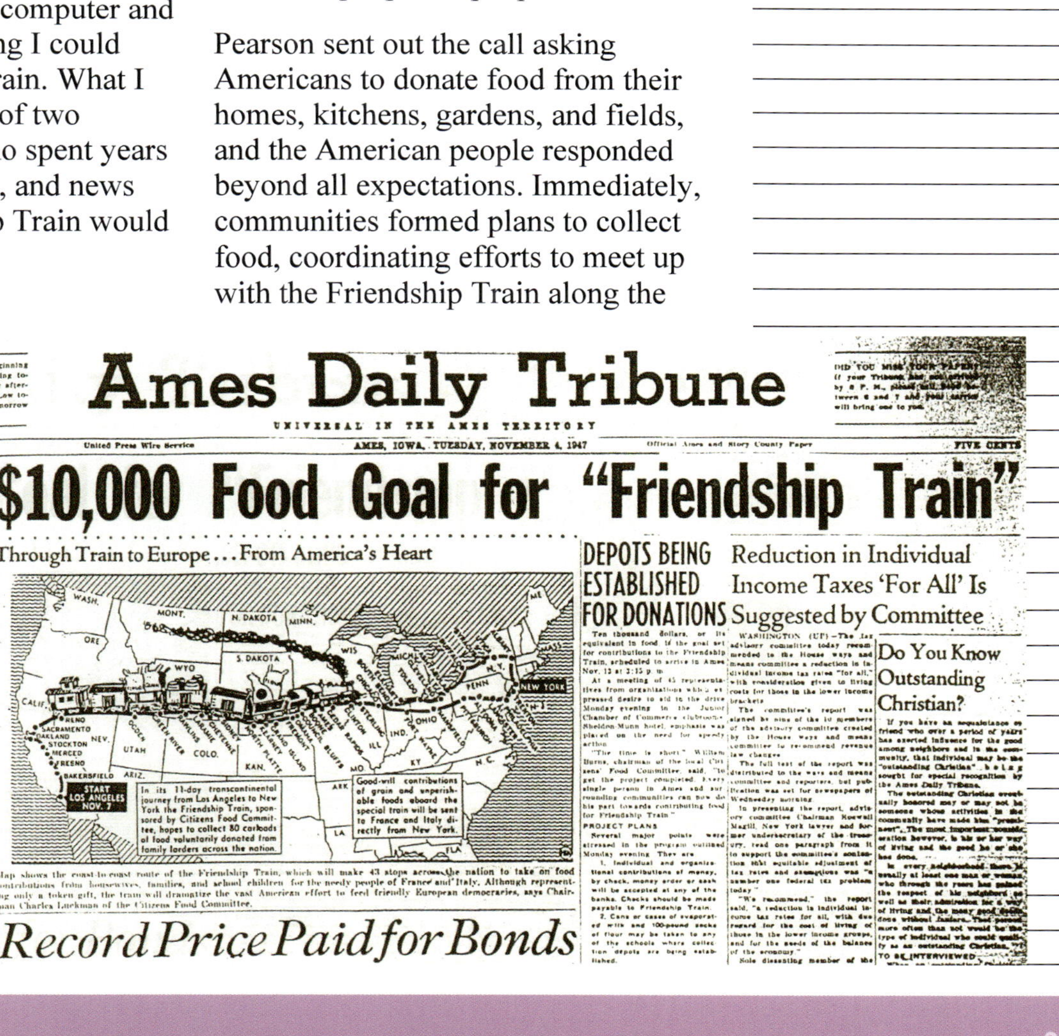

published route. On Nov. 7, 1947, five weeks after Pearson's announcement, the Friendship Train began its incredible journey across America, beginning in Los Angeles with a spectacular Hollywood send-off. All along the route, ordinary Americans brought bags of flour from their homes, vegetables from their gardens, and canned goods from their storehouses. It was an amazing site.

Eleven days after leaving Los Angeles, the Friendship Train arrived in New York City to great fanfare. Drew Pearson, who was there to greet the train, never could have imagined what he saw. The goodwill and compassion of ordinary American citizens far exceeded his expectations. The 80 boxcars he had hoped to fill grew to 270 boxcars filled with merchandise worth $40 million.

Every package on the train was labeled with the same message:

"All races and creeds make up the vast melting pot of America, and in a democratic and Christian spirit of good will toward men, we, the American people, have worked together to bring this food to your doorsteps, hoping that it will tide you over until your own fields are again rich and abundant with crops."

No money was ever spent for the project: the food, trains, ships—everything was donated for the cause; even the unions participated. When this demonstration of brotherly kindness arrived in Europe on December 18, the people were overcome with gratitude.

The French people were so moved they organized a gratitude project— the Merci Train. Forty-nine boxcars were filled—one for each of the 48 states, the 49th shared between Washington, D.C. and the territory of Hawaii. The people of France had very little after the war, so they gave what they had—precious pieces of their lives. Despite their dire circumstances, over 6 million families contributed some 52,000 gifts, which

included things like children's drawings, hand crocheted doilies, and 50 rare paintings. Also included were a jeweled Legion d'Honneur once presented to Napoleon, a Louis XV carriage, and the bugle which signaled the Armistice signing.

By 1948, the boxcars were filled to capacity and loaded onto the ship *Magellan*. When the ship sailed from France, 9,000 gifts had to be left on the docks because there wasn't enough room for them. When the ship arrived in New York, it was greeted by waves of Air Force planes and a parade of boats with the *Magellan* boldly displaying the message, "Merci, America!"

In the next several weeks, each state held parades and ceremonies as they welcomed their designated boxcar. Many of the states who received these beautiful gifts of gratitude still have their box car, and the items it carried, lovingly preserved and on display. North Dakota has an impressive interactive display of the 500 gifts they received. I wanted to drive to North Dakota to see their train when I remembered that every state had received one. I looked up the Nebraska Train, where I live, to find out where I could see it. What I found, however, was not at all what I expected.

According to the Merci Train website, Nebraska's boxcar was shunted from place to place…first to the state historical society, then to the Nebraska Forty and Eight Society, and finally to a playground in Lincoln. In 1951, an attempt was made to return it to the historical society, but they didn't want it. So, it was sold to an Omaha junkyard for $45. Its wheels and metal parts were pounded into scrap and its body converted into a storage shed. Its humiliation finally ended in 1961 when the junkyard was relocated, and the box car was demolished.

My heart sank as I read the story of the fate of this priceless gift given to the people of Nebraska. I thought of all those families who showed up by the thousands at train stops across our state to give what little they could to their brothers and sisters across the sea. What would they think of how we treated this precious gift?

It reminds me of what is happening in America today. Generations ago, families sacrificed everything to give us the precious gift of freedom. They signed their lives away when they put their names to the Declaration of Independence, and they dedicated their lives to the creation of a more perfect union with the United States Constitution. And just like the Nebraska Train, some carelessly

dismiss it as old, out of date, and discard it as scrap.

I am deeply grateful for two people who decided keeping the story of the Friendship and Merci Trains alive was worth their time. I am so grateful to be a recipient of the blessings of liberty America offers. And, in spite of everything our country now faces, it is truer now more than ever—the United States is still the freest place on earth, and our freedom, our legacy of liberty, is something worth holding on to.

An Unexpected Pleasure

In the summer of 2019, our family took a vacation to Oregon. We spent seven days enjoying the breathtaking vistas, landscapes, and coastal towns that make up western Oregon. Then, while driving through the small town of North Bend, a quick image passed my view. "Stop the van!" I yelled out, pleading with my husband to turn around and go back.

"What's the matter?" he asked.

"It's the train! It's their train," I shouted, pointing behind me.

I had heard the story, was inspired by it, shared it with my children, wrote about in media, and here, in North Bend, Oregon, I had the amazing opportunity to see one of the remaining Merci Trains!

Our children jumped from the van to see what it was that causing all my excitement, and then they saw it too. My husband went into the visitor center and found that the woman who ran the center knew nothing about the story behind the train. After my husband repeated the story he heard me tell so many times the woman was speechless. "I had no idea," she said. "I thought it was just a train car." She was so inspired by the story that she said she was going to have it printed on a flyer to hand out to visitors and present it at the next meeting of the City Counsel. And I left with an awesome picture to add to my memory book.

Being the Change

It's hard to see all the darkness flooding our world today and not become overwhelmed by it. In just five short months our entire world has turned upside down with Covid-19, riots across the country, and anything related to God being attacked, defamed, defaced. How did we get here? As I've pondered that question over the last few months, something Victor Hugo once said kept filling my mind, "Even the darkest night will end, and the sun will rise."

As I've pondered his words, I've come to understand how this simple sentiment has the power to literally turn the world around—and it begins with us!

The time of the Judges was one of the darkest periods in Biblical history. It has been referred to as "the Dark Ages of Israel." People lived by their own interpretation of right and wrong. The younger generation forsook their faith and history. Anarchy ensued, absolutes truths of right and wrong were done away and everyone justified their own behavior. Every evil flooded the nation, and it truly was the darkest of times. But then, we turn the page to the Book of Ruth, who we learn lived in the time of the Judges. What an amazing story of light during a dark time.

As I thought more about being the light, it reminded me of an experience I had a few years ago. My husband, Derek, has always wanted to see the Grand Canyon, but I was never interested. After all, it's just a big crack in a desert. You look at it, leave, and check it off your bucket list. I just didn't see the big deal.

We passed by the Canyon many times on the way back and forth from the west to east coast to visit family. We even stayed in Arizona a couple of times with my husband's sister. For 25 years, we passed by that crack in the desert, and though my husband always said he wanted to see it, we never stopped because I wasn't interested. Then, a few years ago, my son moved to Phoenix, and we decided to visit him. As we were planning our trip, my husband brought up the Grand Canyon yet again. It obviously meant a lot to him, and after 25 years, I was tired of hearing about it. "Okay," I said, "Let's go see the crack in the desert."

We arrived at the Grand Canyon just before sunset, and my husband insisted we drive straight to the Canyon before checking into the

hotel. I was bit irritated with the delay after the long drive, but the kids were excited about it, and Derek really wanted to go, so I put on my happy face and decided to make the best of it. Derek sprinted past me as we got out of the car, and the kids followed right behind him. "Honestly," I thought rolling my eyes at their excitement, "it's just a crack in the desert."

We walked along a treed path until we came to an opening with an overlook

and there, as the path widened, I had my first look at the wonder of the Grand Canyon. A lump formed in my throat as I realized just how foolish and shortsighted I'd been. It was absolutely beautiful beyond description. I was simply awestruck. As we walked back through, the path I noticed a sign that said, "Sunrise 6:10." I reached for my husband's hand and motioned toward the sign. "I want to come back," I said. He just smiled.

The next morning, I was the one sprinting past everyone, not wanting to miss a thing. I was insistent we arrive at 6:00am so I could capture every moment. It was a bit harder navigating the path in the dark, but it was worth it. My husband and I sat arm in arm in anticipation of the first ray of sun over the horizon. My heart leaped as the dark sky flowed to pink, and there before my eyes, I saw the sun, in all its splendor, rise above the majestic grandeur of the Grand Canyon. Tears filled my eyes. I was absolutely speechless. How do you describe such a breathtaking scene in words?

An immense feeling of joy and profound gratitude welled up inside me. There before me, in that moment in time, I was witness to the majesty of God's hand! I will never forget that moment; it changed me.

As I stood watching that beautiful scene, no problem seemed too big, no burden too heavy. I found myself counting every blessing, and I wanted to be more and do more to show gratitude for each one. Then a quote by Thomas Tapper came to my mind: "*There will now and again come to us a scene, a remembrance, so full of beauty and pleasure that we shall feel rich in the possession of it.*"

And in that moment, that is exactly how I felt.

Our world has changed dramatically in a short time, but for a moment, let's look back and remember what our world was like before Covid-19. There's an excellent video on YouTube titled the *The Great Realization*. It depicts, in powerful imagery, the change that swept across the world in 2020. The change was the realization that we had become too busy, too disconnected, too self-absorbed, then poses the question: when the doors open, do we want to go back to the same?

We are surrounded by beauty. The majesty of God's hand is all around us. For 25 years, I ignored it, dismissed it as unimportant. For 25 years, I missed being in the presence of ultimate beauty, denied by my own short sightedness the feeling of a peace I can't explain. That day at the Grand Canyon changed me. It made me realize the importance of beauty and light in our lives. It helped me understand that, no matter how dark things become, I can be the light where I am. I can be the change I want to see in the world. It begins with me.

We're bombarded daily by the impact of media and culture on our lives. Advanced technology has rendered us incapable of escaping it. We can seek retreat in our churches, homes, or private schools, but the world is always there, influencing our children and intruding upon our lives. Escaping the world is not the answer. We can't escape from the world, nor does God want us to, but we can learn how to successfully navigate through it and lift others along the way.

So, what do we do? How can we be the light in the darkness? How can we create the change?

First, we need to start with us. We can decide to give into the darkness posting nasty comments or derogatory statements on social media just like everyone else OR we can use it as a medium to promote the good, true, and beautiful. We can choose to be angry and resentful OR we can choose to be kind. We can become argumentative when people attack us OR we can choose to be silent and pray for them. We can be the frown, OR we can be the smile; the choke hold OR a warm hug. It may not happen right away, but over time and with consistent love, even the angriest people will be drawn to the light.

Second, we need to create havens of love and light in our homes—places where our children, friends, and neighbors will feel peace and want to gather.

The environment we create in our homes is the very thing that has the power to change the world—in one generation. The books we read, music we play, the pictures on our walls, are the very things that create that environment. When our children see beauty, they will gravitate to it. When they see pictures of Jesus with children, they will come to know Him and know that He loves them. When they hear patriotic music, they will become patriots. When they see artwork depicting courage, grace, love, and beauty, they will want to emulate it. We are creating the future of America right now, in our homes, today. If we don't like what we see in the world, it is we who have the power to change it!

In these dark times—knowing they *would* be dark times—God has raised up a mighty generation of mothers to be the light where we are and create the change HE wants to see in the world. He is counting on us.

In the time of the Judges there was Ruth. Today, there is you!

Man's Search for Meaning

BY KIMBERLY FLETCHER

I was sitting in Church one day when our pastor suggested that during that week when we pray individually and as a family that we devote our prayers solely to thanking God for all our blessings. This was a message I have become familiar with around Thanksgiving, but this was August—nowhere near Turkey time. And the Pastor's message had nothing to do with gratitude; it was all about the "pure in heart." But as I listened to my heart as he expounded on his message, it suddenly became clear to me that a pure heart is directly connected with how grateful we are.

I recently read the book *Man's Search for Meaning* by Viktor Frankl and found an even deeper understanding of the truthfulness of the tie between gratitude and a pure heart and how it directly impacts our actions.

Viktor Frankl was a Jewish neurologist and psychiatrist who spent three years laboring in four different concentration camps, including Auschwitz and Dachau. Dr. Frankl spends the first half of his book describing his experiences in the various camps where he was confined. The unique thing about this book, however, is that—unlike other books that depict personal experiences in the concentration camps—this one is presented in third person. Dr. Frankl shares his experiences as if an observer looking in—not only at the other members of the camp, but at himself as well.

He observed the behaviors of those in the camp and witnessed how differently inmates reacted and responded to their brutal surroundings. What he learned and came to understand through his experiences led to his revolutionary theory known as logo-therapy, from the Greek word logos or "meaning." Unlike Sigmund Freud, who maintained that our primary drive in life is pleasure, Dr. Frankl, through his own experience and personal discovery, found that it wasn't pleasure but purpose that gave meaning to life. Men who lived and suffered in the very same conditions would either give up, succumb to their worst selves, or in rare occasions, rise above their surroundings. Dr. Frankl realized it was something in the heart, something more powerful than the brutality and dire nature of their surroundings—a sense of peace within the storm.

Those that weathered the storm could find beauty in the simplest things—memories of family, a blade of grass, a sunset. For some, this was survival, for others, it generated feelings of profound gratitude. Dr. Frankl witnessed the way those who held on to these things, those who had purpose in their life, seemed not

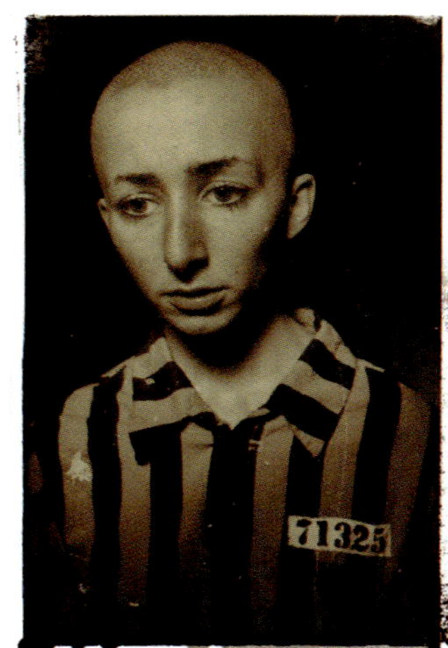

only to bear their horrific burdens better than most, but also, at great personal sacrifice, helped and comforted others. He shares this in his book. "We who lived in concentration camps," he recalled, "can remember the men who walked through the huts comforting others, giving away their last piece of bread. They may have been few in number, but they offer sufficient proof that everything can be taken from man but one thing: the last of the human freedoms—to choose one's attitude in any given set of circumstances, to choose one's own way."

This, then, is the ultimate depth and definition of freedom. It is not the circumstances without but the determination within that ultimately defines who we are and the kind of person we will be. It is our freedom to choose not necessarily our specific conditions and environment, but how we will meet them. No one can take that away.

Viktor Frankl shares thoughts about his experiences in his book *Man's Search for Meaning*.

"...there were always choices to make. Every day, every hour offered the opportunity to make a decision, a decision which determined whether you would or would not submit to those powers which threatens to rob you of your very self, your inner freedom; which determined whether or not you would become the plaything of circumstance, renouncing freedom and dignity to become molded into the form of the typical inmate...

"...Even though conditions such as lack of sleep, insufficient food, and various mental stresses may suggest that the inmates were bound to react in certain ways, in the final analysis it becomes clear that the sort of person the prisoner became was the result of an inner decision and not the result of camp influence alone.

"Dostoevski said once, "There is only one thing that I dread: not to be worthy of my sufferings." These words frequently came to my mind after I became acquainted with those martyrs whose behavior in camp, whose suffering in death, bore witness to the fact that the last inner freedom cannot be lost. It can be said that they were worthy of sufferings; the way they bore the suffering was a genuine inner achievement. It is this spiritual freedom that cannot be taken away, that makes life purposeful.

"The way in which a man accepts his fate and all the suffering it entails, the way in which he takes up his cross gives him ample opportunity even under the most

As I read Viktor Frankl's words, I suddenly realized just how beauty, gratitude, and freedom all tied together. No matter what trial, challenge, or suffering we may face, there is always something we can point to to be grateful for. Even when things are going well for us, we often forget the beautiful gift that gratitude is. When we focus on our blessings, when we take time to feel and show gratitude for those blessings, then we transcend beyond ourselves. Not only do we appreciate all we have so much more, we also develop a deep desire to share what we have with others. This allows our natural selfish nature to evolve into selflessness. Suddenly, we then find more beauty in life. We see it more often and more clearly in all that is around us and beauty becomes not just what we see outside, but what is actually in our hearts—it becomes our inner compass, who we are. Beauty in music, art, and nature penetrates our very soul when we have a spirit of gratitude. We see things differently. We face things differently.

The more grateful we are, the more we see and feel beauty around us—not just in the things we see, but in our interactions with others, in the trials we face. We look beyond ourselves, beyond our own suffering, and instead of thinking of nothing but how miserable our conditions are, we think of the ways we can lift and help others who are suffering. We have a desire to serve more, to give more, to love more.

It has been said that gratitude is the cure for pride. I believe this with all confidence. But I also believe it is so much more. It is the cure for selfishness, for self-pity, doubt, and despair. It allows us to see beyond our suffering. We actually become grateful for the opportunity to be challenged, wonder what we can learn from it, how we can remain true to ourselves in spite of it, and become a better person because of it. That is what Viktor Frankl learned; that is what he shares in his book.

It was the beauty within the hearts of the prisoners in the concentration camps that led them to think beyond themselves, to rise above and see beyond their dire conditions, to bear their burdens and see the need in others more than themselves—even though they were suffering equally, and sometimes even more. They found their purpose, their meaning, and beauty filled their souls—it became who they were inside, and no concentration camp could take that away. When we can reach that place, we can find beauty in everything, no matter how hard the world tries to hide it, and we will be filled with profound gratitude. When we reach that place, we will have reached the pinnacle of self-governance, and we will at last comprehend the true depth and nature of freedom.

The Nobleman and the Seed

Once there was a nobleman with power and riches. He loved everything. Of learning and art and all such things had he had partaken. But the times were troubled in his country, and for some reason, he lost all he had and was imprisoned. Then, there was scarcely anything in his life. All he had was the cell, the prison yard, and, now and again, a word or two from his keeper. The cell was small and gloomy, the keeper silent, the yard confined and so closely paved with cobblestones that one could barely see the earth between them.

One day, as he walked in his yard, the man noticed that, between two of the stones, there seemed to be something. He looked closer. With the greatest attention, he studied it, then he knelt on the rough stones and looked and looked again. His heartbeat and his hands trembled, but with a touch as gentle as one could give, he moved a grain or two of soil, and there beneath was something that the poor captive cried out for joy to see—a tiny plant. As if in a new world, and certainly as if another man, he cared daily for the tender little companion that had come to share his loneliness; he thought of it first in the morning and last at night. He gave it of his supply of water, and as a father, he watched over it.

The plant grew until, one day, the man saw that the little plant must either die or have more room. But it could not have more room unless a cobblestone was removed. Now this could only be done with the consent of the emperor. It took many long weeks of correspondence, but he did get his request to the Emperor, and the Emperor gave his permission. So, the plant was given more room, but even more, the prisoner himself was given more room—he was liberated.

Just because the seed of a beautiful thing came to life in his tiny world, he found love for it. And that love gave him a new life because he cared for something—something outside himself. And it filled his life with beauty and hope. That love which is given outside of oneself reveals the beauty of the world.

The Bird Man of Alcatraz

FROM THE BOOK *WILLPOWER IS NOT ENOUGH*
BY A. DEAN BYRD AND MARK D. CHAMBERLAIN

After numerous violent crimes, a man was doomed to a life in prison. For months, he lived a mean, narrow, pitiful existence. His hate festered and anger continued to dominate his life.

Then, one day, a sign of hope and life came into the desolate environment of his cinder-block cell: a tiny, injured bird fluttered in. The helpless creature somehow touched a seed of compassion within the inmate, and he began to care for it, nursing it back to health. A capacity to nurture and love began to sprout and take root within him. Another bird came to rest at his window. He fed it, and it returned. Soon, he was talking about his birds with other inmates. He learned to control his temper and relate more agreeably with the guards—at first to gain favors for his birds but more genuinely as time went on.

More birds came, and he gradually built up a small aviary in his cell. When some of his birds began to die, he learned everything he could about bird diseases. He experimented with treatments and found those that worked. He learned to write more effectively so he could communicate his passion for his birds. He published articles about his methods of caring for them, corresponded with a woman who was a fellow bird-lover, and even developed a relationship with her that resulted in her visiting the prison.

As his story unfolds, it becomes clear that the more time he spent with his birds, the more human he became. While this is a tragic story, in a sense, it is also a story of great hope. The changes in the Birdman began when a visit from a small bird ignited a small spark of gratitude. This feeling opened the door for a sense of purpose to swell within his heart and displace the elements of darkness.

"Discovery of purpose is like a dose of sunshine that propels men and women forward to new heights of achievement. When we are deeply involved in a positive purpose, our souls and even our bodies, it seems, resonate with the power and energy of God."

-A. Dean Byrd and Mark D. Chamberlain

Victor Marie Hugo
"God is behind everything."

Victor Hugo was born February 26, 1802. He has been hailed as the greatest of the Romanticist poets. He is best known for writing *Cromwell* (1827), The *Hunchback of Notre Dame* (1831) and the highly famed classic *Les Miserables* (1862), an epic story of redemption set in Paris after the French Revolution.

Hugo's father was a general in Napoleon's army, and Hugo himself supported Bonaparte. However when Napoleon Bonaparte turned out to be a tyrant, Hugo fiercely opposed him, and because of his opposition, was forced into exile for 19 years.

In his Preface to *Cromwell*, Victor Hugo wrote: "Lastly, this threefold poetry flows from three great sources—The Bible, Homer, Shakespeare...The Bible before the Iliad, the Iliad before Shakespeare."

Victor Hugo stated, "England has two books, the Bible and Shakespeare.

England made Shakespeare, but the Bible made England."

Over 3 million people attended Hugo's funeral in Paris.

Some famous quotes from Hugo and his writings are:

"Music expresses that which cannot be put into words and that which cannot remain silent."

"Even the darkest night will end and the sun will rise."

"People do not lack strength, they lack will."

"Certain thoughts are prayers. There are moments when, whatever be the attitude of the body, the soul is on its knees."

"Laughter is sunshine, it chases winter from the human face."

We Were Not Poor

BY MARLENE PETERSON

Many families are going to feel the crunch of our current economic downturn this Christmas. Not being able to provide the gifts we may want to give to our children adds to the stress of the holiday season.

But as it is with most challenges, this one can be turned to great good. We often hear talk that Christmas has become too commercial and materialistic. Maybe this is the year to stop a cycle of spending that has gotten out of control.

One year, our family met the challenge by coming up with an alternate plan. It was the children who suggested that each family member draw one name and shop for that person. Each person was to shop for three gifts. . . . from a thrift store. The traditional Christmas sweater was substituted with the 'Ugly Christmas Sweater'. After finding the ugliest sweater possible, several 'accessorized' their sweater with additional features that suited the personality of the recipient. The second gift was a book bought from the same store, with a price limit of $2.00. And finally, each person carefully selected a gift of their choosing-maximum spending limit: $2.00.

Presents were wrapped and placed under the tree. Christmas Eve was spent taking turns reading aloud from a heart-warming story*—free on the internet—about gifts and true giving. Christmas morning was filled with a lot of laughter and fun. The joy of the day was spending time with family.

Being poor is a state of mind. As one mother expressed it, "We're not poor....we just don't have any money." By focusing on treasures of a different kind, we can feel rich even if our bank accounts say otherwise. A line from Gershwin's Porgy and Bess says it best: "The things that I prize, like the stars in the skies, are all free."

Maybe this is the year to start filling the hearts of our children with treasure that has nothing to do with money; treasure that stands independent from stock market trends and global dollar values.

Of course, finding joy in the simple things of life, like a walk in the rain or a beautiful sunset, comes to mind. Or, as was said of George Bailey in *It's a Wonderful Life*, he was the richest

man in town because of the love of friends.

But also consider the great worth of a mind and heart stocked full of images of great art, the melodies of inspirational music and the beautiful words of great literature. These were pleasures only the very elite could afford in years past. The humblest home of today has access to masterpieces that even the kings and queens of yesterday would have been jealous of. Today, our children can be inspired by works of great art that, in previous days, hung on walls of palaces of the world and could only be viewed by royalty. They can listen to a steady stream of symphonies that, in former days, were reserved for aristocracy. We can hit a playback button and listen to favorites over and over again. All their wealth couldn't buy that privilege. The noblest and greatest thoughts of the greatest minds and hearts that ever lived upon this world are available to us today—for free. Today's children can literally rub shoulders with the giants of civilization. Even with no money in the bank account.

And the world's greatest treasure is already found in 98% of American homes. The most deeply moving music that has ever been composed, the most inspiring art that has ever been painted, and the most exquisite words that have ever been written have found their inspiration in the Bible. As Lincoln exclaimed, "the Bible is the best gift God has ever given to man." People of yesterday paid a dear price to read it. Readers of the Wycliffe Bible were burned with copies round their necks. Husbands were made to witness against their wives and children forced to light the death-fires of their parents. Possessors of the banned book were hunted down as if they were wild beasts. Considerable sums of money were paid for the privilege of reading even a few sheets of manuscript. A farmer might give up a load of hay for permission to read it for a certain period one hour a day. Today, this great gift sits unopened in too many American homes.

A well-stocked mind and heart is equipped to find hope in the direst of circumstances. Marie Antoinette expressed, "What a resource amid the casualties of life is a well-cultivated mind! One can then be one's own companion and find society in one's own thoughts." Victor Frankl observed a small group of prisoners in those horrible death camps of Nazi Germany who secretly gathered together to recite poetry, sing songs, and act in improvised plays even though such activities were forbidden and punishable by death. Instinctively, they understood that the soul's weapon in the fight for self-preservation is art and beauty.

As it has been said, maybe the richest man is not he who has the most, but the one who needs the least.

No matter what the condition of our bank accounts, may this coming season and the year to follow find us pouring lasting riches into the hearts of our children, for then it will be said of us that we truly are the richest nation in the world.

The Life and Adventures of Santa Claus by Amelia C. Houghto

Beauty Sweetens Life

ADAPTED FROM AN EXCERPT OF THE BOOK
MUSIC TALKS WITH CHILDREN BY THOMAS TAPPER, WRITTEN IN 1897

Sometimes when I am in a great gallery, the thought is very strong in me that many (ever and ever so many) people, in all countries and in all times, have so loved the beautiful as to devote their lives to it. Painters, who have made pictures to delight men for generations, looked and looked and prayed to find the beautiful. And we must believe that one looks out of the heart to find the beautiful or finds only the common. And the sculptor who have loved marble for the delight they have in beautiful forms, they, too, with eyes seeking beauty, and hands so gentle upon the marble, that it almost breathes for them, they, too, have loved the beautiful.

But commoner ones have the tenderest love for what is sweet and fair in life—people who are neither painters nor sculptors. In their little way—but in a very true way—they have sunlight in their hearts, and with it, love for something. Perhaps it is a flower, or a sunrise, or a mountain scene. The beautiful may be covered up with everything that is able to keep it down, but it is always there.

Beauty sweetens life; it makes even a common life bright. And when we have it in us, it is like golden sunlight in the darkness of pain, affliction, loneliness, or suffering. The great advantage of beauty in all good things in our lives is the good it may bring to others. It is not just the joy and comfort it brings to ourselves that makes beauty so powerful an influence for good, but the joy and comfort it brings to those we share it with.

The beautiful music we may sing or play is not to show who we are or what we can do—it will, of course, do these things—but it is to be a blessing to those who listen. And how are blessings bestowed? Out of the heart.

Guideposts Classics: Corrie ten Boom on Forgiveness

ORIGINALLY PUBLISHED IN GUIDEPOSTS MAGAZINE

In this Guideposts Classics, Corrie ten Boom learns a lesson about forgiveness.

It was in a church in Munich that I saw him, a balding heavyset man in a gray overcoat, a brown felt hat clutched between his hands. People were filing out of the basement room where I had just spoken, moving along the rows of wooden chairs to the door at the rear.

It was 1947, and I had come from Holland to defeated Germany with the message that God forgives.

It was the truth they needed most to hear in that bitter, bombed-out land, and I gave them my favorite mental picture. Maybe because the sea is never far from a Hollander's mind, I liked to think that that's where forgiven sins were thrown.

"When we confess our sins," I said, "God casts them into the deepest ocean, gone forever."

The solemn faces stared back at me, not quite daring to believe. There were never questions after a talk in Germany in 1947. People stood up in silence, in silence collected their wraps, in silence left the room.

And that's when I saw him, working his way forward against the others. One moment I saw the overcoat and the brown hat; the next, a blue uniform and a visored cap with its skull and crossbones.

It came back with a rush: the huge room with its harsh overhead lights, the pathetic pile of dresses and shoes in the center of the floor, the shame of walking naked past this man. I could see my sister's frail form ahead of me, ribs sharp beneath the parchment skin. Betsie, how thin you were!

Betsie and I had been arrested for concealing Jews in our home during the Nazi occupation of Holland; this man had been a guard at Ravensbrück concentration camp where we were sent.

Now he was in front of me, hand thrust out: "A fine message, fräulein! How good it is to know that, as you say, all our sins are at the bottom of the sea!"

And I, who had spoken so glibly of forgiveness, fumbled in my pocketbook rather than take that hand. He would not remember me, of course—how could he remember one prisoner among those thousands of women?

But I remembered him and the leather crop swinging from his belt. It was the first time since my release that I had been face to face with one of my captors, and my blood seemed to freeze.

"You mentioned Ravensbrück in your talk," he was saying. "I was a guard in there." No, he did not remember me.

"But since that time," he went on, "I have become a Christian. I know that God has forgiven me for the cruel things I did there, but I would like to hear it from your lips as well. Fräulein"—again the hand came out— "will you forgive me?"

And I stood there—I whose sins had every day to be forgiven—and could not. Betsie had died in that place— could he erase her slow terrible death simply for the asking?

It could not have been many seconds that he stood there, hand held out, but to me it seemed hours as I wrestled with the most difficult thing I had ever had to do.

For I had to do it—I knew that. The message that God forgives has a prior condition: that we forgive those who have injured us. "If you do not forgive men their trespasses," Jesus says, "neither will your Father in heaven forgive your trespasses."

I knew it not only as a commandment of God, but as a daily experience.

Since the end of the war, I had had a home in Holland for victims of Nazi brutality.

Those who were able to forgive their former enemies were able also to return to the outside world and rebuild their lives, no matter what the physical scars. Those who nursed their bitterness remained invalids. It was as simple and as horrible as that.

And still, I stood there with the coldness clutching my heart. But forgiveness is not an emotion—I knew that too. Forgiveness is an act of the will, and the will can function regardless of the temperature of the heart.

"Jesus, help me!" I prayed silently. "I can lift my hand. I can do that much. You supply the feeling."

And so—woodenly, mechanically—I thrust my hand into the one stretched out to me. And as I did, an incredible thing took place. The current started in my shoulder, raced down my arm, sprang into our joined hands. And then this healing warmth seemed to flood my whole being, bringing tears to my eyes.

"I forgive you, brother!" I cried. "With all my heart!"

For a long moment, we grasped each other's hands, the former guard and the former prisoner. I had never known God's love so intensely as I did then.

And having thus learned to forgive in this hardest of situations, I never again had difficulty in forgiving: I wish I could say it! I wish I could say that merciful and charitable thoughts just

naturally flowed from me from then on. But they didn't.

If there's one thing I've learned at 80 years of age, it's that I can't store up good feelings and behavior—but only draw them fresh from God each day.

Maybe I'm glad it's that way. For every time I go to Him, He teaches me something else. I recall the time, some 15 years ago, when some Christian friends whom I loved and trusted did something which hurt me.

You would have thought that, having forgiven the Nazi guard, this would have been child's play. It wasn't. For weeks, I seethed inside. But at last, I asked God again to work His miracle in me. And again it happened: first the cold-blooded decision, then the flood of joy and peace.

I had forgiven my friends; I was restored to my Father.

Then, why was I suddenly awake in the middle of the night, hashing over the whole affair again? My friends! I thought. People I loved! If it had been strangers, I wouldn't have minded so.

I sat up and switched on the light. "Father, I though it was all forgiven! Please, help me do it!"

But the next night I woke up again. They'd talked so sweetly too! Never a hint of what they were planning. "Father!" I cried in alarm. "Help me!"

His help came in the form of a kindly Lutheran pastor to whom I confessed my failure after two sleepless weeks.

"Up in that church tower," he said, nodding out the window, "is a bell which is rung by pulling on a rope. But you know what? After the sexton lets go of the rope, the bell keeps on swinging. First ding then dong. Slower and slower until there's a final dong and it stops.

"I believe the same thing is true of forgiveness. When we forgive someone, we take our hand off the rope. But if we've been tugging at our grievances for a long time, we mustn't be surprised if the old angry thoughts keep coming for a while. They're just the ding-dongs of the old bell slowing down."

And so it proved to be. There were a few more midnight reverberations, a couple of dings when the subject came up in my conversation. But the force—which was my willingness in the matter—had gone out of them. They came less and less often and at last stopped altogether.

And so I discovered another secret of forgiveness: that we can trust God not only above our emotions, but also above our thoughts.

And still, He had more to teach me, even in this single episode. Because many years later, in 1970, an American with whom I had shared the ding-dong principle came to visit me in Holland and met the people involved. "Aren't those the friends who let you down?" he asked as they left my apartment.

"Yes," I said a little smugly. "You can see it's all forgiven."

"By you, yes," he said. "But what about them? Have they accepted your forgiveness?"

"They say there's nothing to forgive! They deny it ever happened. But I can prove it!" I went eagerly to my desk. "I have it in black and white! I saved all their letters and I can show you where—"

"Corrie!" My friend slipped his arm through mine and gently closed the drawer. "Aren't you the one whose sins are at the bottom of the sea? And are the sins of your friends etched in black and white?"

For an anguishing moment I could not find my voice. "Lord Jesus," I whispered at last, "who takes all my sins away, forgive me for preserving all these years the evidence against others! Give me grace to burn all the blacks and whites as a sweet-smelling sacrifice to Your glory."

I did not go to sleep that night until I had gone through my desk and pulled out those letters-curling now with age-and fed them all into my little coal-burning grate. As the flames leaped and glowed, so did my heart.

"Forgive us our trespasses," Jesus taught us to pray, "as we forgive those who trespass against us." In the ashes of those letters, I was seeing yet another facet of His mercy. What more He would teach me about forgiveness in the days ahead, I didn't know, but tonight's was good news enough.

When we bring our sins to Jesus, He not only forgives them, He makes them as if they had never been.

RELATED QUOTES

"America is a tune. It must be sung together."
-Gerald Stanley Lee, Crowds

"May you have the strength of faith, be surrounded by the love of family and know the beauty of freedom." **-Kevin Hall**

"Enjoy the little things, for one day you may look back and realize they were the big things." **-Robert Brault**

"The average man does not want to be free. He simply wants to be safe." **-H.L. Mencken**

"Man is originally characterized by his 'search for meaning' rather than his 'search for himself.' The more he forgets himself-giving himself to a cause or another person-the more human he is. And the more he is immersed and absorbed in something or someone other than himself the more he really becomes himself." **-Viktor Frankl, Man's Search for Meaning**

"These monuments are not merely pretty things, not merely valued signs of man's creative power. They are expressions of faith, and they stand for man's struggle to relate himself to his past and to his God." **-Robert M. Edsel, The Monuments Men**

"There will now and again come to us a scene, a remembrance, so full of beauty and pleasure that we shall feel rich in the possession of it." **-Thomas Tapper**

"Discovery of purpose is like a dose of sunshine that propels men and women forward to new heights of achievement. When we are deeply involved in a positive purpose, our souls and even our bodies it seems, resonate with the power and energy of God." **-A. Dean Byrd and Mark D. Chamberlain.**

"Courage for the great sorrows of life, and patience for the small ones, and when you have laboriously accomplished your daily task, go to sleep in peace. God is awake." **-Victor Hugo**

"God is behind everything." **-Victor Hugo, Les Miserables**

"Where words fail...Music Speaks." **-Hans Christian Anderson**

"The main object of every school should be, not to provide the children with the means of learning a livelihood, but to show them how to live a happy and worthy life, inspired by ideals which exalt and dignify both labor and pleasure. To see beauty and to love it is to possess large securities for such a life.

It is undeniable that the American democracy . . . has thus far failed to take proper account of the sense of beauty as means of happiness and to provide for the training of that sense."
-Charles Eliot

"The pursuit of truth and beauty is a sphere of activity in which we are permitted to remain children all our lives."
-Albert Einstein

"You must be the change you want to see in the world."
-Mahatma Gandhi

"We could never learn to be brave and patient if there were only joy in the world."
-Helen Keller

"The ultimate measure of a man is not where he stands in moments of comfort and convenience, but where he stands at times of challenge and controversy."
-Martin Luther King Jr.

"Everything can be taken from a man but one thing: the last of the human freedoms—to choose one's attitude in any given set of circumstances, to choose one's own way."
-Viktor E. Frankl, Man's Search for Meaning

"The happiest people are those who do the most for others. The most miserable are those who do the least."
-Booker T. Washington

"I shall allow no man to belittle my soul by making me hate him."
-Booker T. Washington

"I think music in itself is healing. It's an explosive expression of humanity. It's something we are all touched by. No matter what culture we're from, everyone loves music."
-Billy Joel

"A song will outlive all sermons in the memory."
-Henry Giles

"It is time for parents to teach young people early on that in diversity there is beauty and there is strength."
-Maya Angelou

"When I admire the wonders of a sunset or the beauty of the moon, my soul expands in the worship of the creator."
-Mahatma Gandhi

The boys [and girls] of the rising generation are to be the men [and women] of the next, and the sole guardians of the principles we deliver over to them.

-Thomas Jefferson

A Time to Sow

"All great change in America begins at the dinner table."

~Ronald Reagan

PREPARATION

Providing quality family time and an organized environment is essential when nurturing a love of liberty in the home. Family dinner hour is a simple, yet profoundly effective, way to connect as family and provide teaching moments. It is also an excellent opportunity to promote good manners. There is a plethora of subjects that can be addressed under this topic. The Hostess Resource Center has several additional resources and presentation ideas on topics such as home management and organization, time management, chore charts, family devotionals, and daily schedules. We encourage you to visit the "Time to Sow" section and explore all the great resources available to support your home and family.

To prepare yourself to lead this presentation please review and consider the following material.

- Read "Family: It's About Time" and "4 Tricks to Getting Family to the Table" found in the Supplemental Materials of this presentation

- View the video *What Are We Sowing?* and the video shorts *The Importance of Family Meals* and *Family Dinner Dilemma* provided in the Hostess Resource Center on the Moms for America® website www.MomsforAmerica.us

- Review the *Table Talk Sampler* (provided in the Hostess Kit and also available as a pdf download on the Hostess Resource Center)

- Read Principle 21 of the *5,000 Year Leap*

- Review Bible References—Gen 18:19, Prov. 24:3, Josh 24:15, Prov. 22:6

- Review the quotes provided in the Supplemental Materials of this presentation

- Optional: Review *Promises of the Constitution* Vignettes 13.3, 13.4, 13.5, 13.7, 14.5

Home Assignment

Read *"Table Talk Sampler"* (can be downloaded from HFA website)
Make an effort to eat dinner together as a family each day until the next meeting. Use the Table Talk Sampler during family dinner time to spark conversation. Share your experiences at the next meeting.

Personal Study

Review Nicholeen Peck's audio seminar *"Teaching Self Government"*

Family Enrichment

Watch the "Family Dinner" and "Manners" videos listed in Cottage Meeting Resources under "A Time to Sow" on the MFA website. Discuss the ideas presented in the videos, why manners are important and what the phrase "Your manners are showing" means.

Prepare a family activity to learn proper table setting techniques, napkin folding, etc. Set the table nice for a special dinner with fancy dishes sparkling cider, etc. The kids will love it-and wonder what's up.

The purpose of this presentation is to introduce the power of family dinner hour and quality family time to strengthen your family and promote a foundation of freedom in the home. The concept of self-government will also be introduced.

KEY POINTS

- Quality family time is found in the small and simple things that are repeated consistently over time

- The family dinner hour is one of the best environments to teach and discuss principles that are important to the family

- The things taught and nurtured in the home today become the foundation of society in the future

MEETING OUTLINE

Welcome & Gathering

We recommend starting your meeting with a prayer and the Pledge of Allegiance.

Show Video: *What Are We Sowing?* (Available in Hostess Resource Center)

Group Discussion

Read (or have someone read): "Family: It's About Time" provided in the Supplemental Materials of this presentation.

Most parents agree that leading and directing a family can be a daunting and overwhelming task.

> *How can the principles of self-government help parents lead their family towards stability and freedom? (Refer to Proverbs 22:6)*

Share: sections you highlighted in Principle 21 of the *5000 Year Leap*

> *How can problem solving at a family level contribute to strong local self-government? Why is this important to the preservation of liberty?*

With so many distractions and negative influences in our children's lives and the constant blatant attack on the institution of family, a return to the family dinner hour is not only well overdue, but also vital to the success of a civilized society—and the preservation of liberty itself.

Introduce *Table Talk: 30 Days of Stories, Quotes, and Questions to Spark Conversation at the Dinner Table*

Table Talk Sampler is a great resource to encourage family mealtime and recognize the power of family dinner hour. The first part of the book introduces the concept of family dinner hour through history and explains why eating together as a family will help save America. The second part of the book is filled with questions, stories, and quotes to stimulate dinner conversation for 31 days of family dinners. The resource section in the back of the booklet lists additional resources you can use to continue your experience.

Read or Review: "4 Tricks to Getting Family to the Table"

Share Videos: *The Importance of Family Meals* and *Family Dinner Dilemma* provided in the Hostess Resource Center on the Moms for America® website

Optional: Reference *Promises of the Constitution* Vignettes 13.3, 13.4, 13.5, 13.7, 14.5

NOTE: *Table Talk* is a great resource to get you started on sparking conversation at the dinner table. Three other great resources are *Catechism on the Constitution, Promises of the Constitution,* and *American History Stories* by Mara Pratt. All these great resources are available in the Moms for America® online store. You can just read one vignette, one story, or pose one question to start the conversation, hen keep it going with mix-or-match or by going through each book.

Summary

Summarize your thoughts on the material covered in this presentation

- Give the Home Assignment for the next meeting

- Announce date, time, and location for next meeting

ADDITIONAL PRESENTATIONS

Manners Matter

In preparation for your Cottage Meeting, view the 30 minute video *Manners & Civility* by David Barton (provided in the Hostess Resource Center of the Moms for America® website).

Hostess Presentation & Group Discussion: Manners & Civility

Show Video: *Manners & Civility* by David Barton

Reference the following quotes and scriptures as you lead the discussion:

- Romans 12:10; 1 Corinthians 15:33; Proverbs 13:20; Proverbs 29:11; Philippians 4:8

- "I like to see a man proud of the place in which he lives. I like to see a man live so that his place will be proud of him." -Abraham Lincoln

- "If your boys wrangle and contend at home, if they cannot discuss with dignity the little questions that arise in their daily intercourse with one another, be sure they will not honor the nation when they take their places in senate halls to discuss the great problems that confront civilization."
  -C.E. Sargent, Our Home

- "Adore God. Reverence and cherish your parents. Love your neighbor as yourself, and your country more than yourself."
  -Thomas Jefferson

How do manners influence society and culture? How does teaching your children good manners lead them to be good citizens? How can teaching and promoting good manners in the home create a peaceful environment and strengthen family relationships? What are examples of good manners and etiquette we can teach our children to help them understand, grow, and flourish in the four areas Thomas Jefferson mentions?

A House United

When we find outstanding resources, we share them. Teaching Self-government is one of those gems.

Nicholeen Peck is the founder of Teaching Self-Government and the author of *A House United*. The book and accompanying audio series are absolutely phenomenal. Nicholeen has been teaching self-government skills to people all over the world for 15 years, and now, you can get the secrets to her success in her book *A House United* and her audio seminar *Teaching Self-Government*.

Nicholeen Peck and her husband Spencer were foster parents to several children—including troubled teens—along with parenting four of their own children. The Pecks have taught children with ADHD, OCD, kleptomania, compulsive lying, anger control issues, etc. Nicholeen said, "I taught behaviors, not medication. They would come to us on many medications and usually leave not on any medications. Many children are misdiagnosed. They just need to learn cause and effect better."

We highly encourage parents to get the book, take the course, and visit the Teaching Self-Government website to take advantage of the excellent resources you will find there. This could be an entire series of Cottage Meetings.

Self-Government Works is another excellent resource for parents and teachers to help youth understand the concepts of self-government in a free society. The program, created by Bill Norton in cooperation with Bellevue University and the Center for Self-Governance, takes middle and high school aged youth on a journey from freedom to tyranny and back to freedom. Youth will discover the key concepts to a free society as liberties are slowly taken from them. They will experience tyranny and oppression and, through the principles taught, navigate their way to freedom.

Youth who participate in the program not only grasp the concept of self-governance, they also leave with a deep love of liberty and commitment to preserving it. Due to generous benefactors, the program is available to schools, teachers, churches, and families at no charge. Several families can unite together to host the program, as you need a minimum of 9 youth to participate in the simulations.

MINI COTTAGE IDEAS

Mini Cottages are designed especially for moms of preschoolers and moms who work full-time jobs. Moms simply read and/or watch the same materials at home, on their own, then meet together once a week in a playdate or over lunch during the workday to discuss what they read. The articles and videos are short and can usually be read and/or viewed in less than hour. Below are some suggestions to host mini cottage discussions under the "A Time to Sow" theme.

- Watch the video *What Are We Sowing* and read "Family: Its About Time"

- Watch the video *Manners & Civility* by David Barton

- Visit Nicholeen Pecks website *Teaching Self-Government*

- View the Videos and Resources in the Hostess Resource Center under this topic

- Read the Introduction to *Table Talk* (pdf download provided in the Hostess Resource Center)

- Read "Good Manners Makes Good Citizens" provided in the Supplemental Materials of this presentation

- Read & Discuss "Fortifying Our Homes" by Lisa Cummins provided in the Supplemental Materials of this presentation

- Read & Discuss "Mind Your Manners" by Cherie Cawley provided in the Supplemental Materials of this presentation

COTTAGE MEETING BOOK CLUB

For those who like the book club format, we've compiled a list of great books to help you gain an appreciation and foundational understanding of the concepts presented in "A Time to Sow."

The 5000 Year Leap: A Miracle That Changed the World

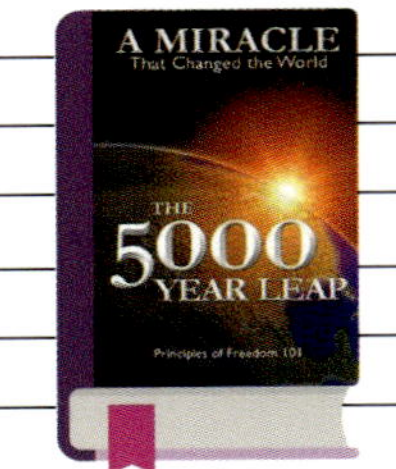

- Review Principle 21

Promises of the Constitution

- Review the following vignettes: 13.3, 13.4, 13.5, 13.7, 14.5

Table Talk: 30 Days of Stories, Quotes, and Questions to Spark Conversation at the Dinner Table

Table Talk is a great resource to encourage family mealtime and recognize the power of family dinner hour. The first part of the book introduces the concept of family dinner hour through history and explains why eating together as a family will help save America. The second part of the book is filled with questions, stories and quotes to stimulate dinner conversation for 31 days of family dinners. The resource section in the back of the booklet lists additional resources you can use to continue your experience (Available in the Moms for America® Store in hard copy and as pdf download in the Hostess Resource Center).

The Food Nanny Rescues Dinner by Liz Edmunds

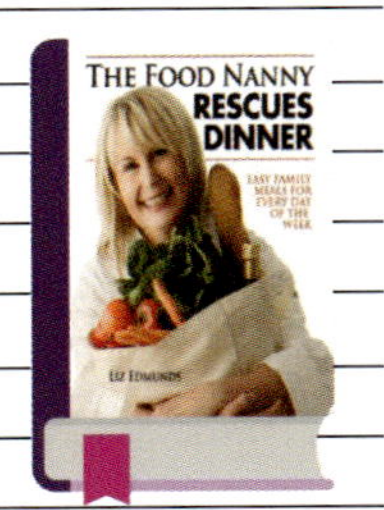

With the idea that shared family meals are the cornerstone of good parenting and relationships, self-styled "food nanny" Liz Edmunds offers up a collection of 200 classic family favorites in this terrific home resource. Deciding what to make is always the most wearisome part of preparing a meal. But unlike other books that offer only good-looking recipes, this cookbook offers a revolutionary template for scheduling fun food themes for each night of the week. With readily available ingredients in mind, this handy collection also provides fun and delicious recipes appropriate for every theme—hungry kids will look forward to a family dinner at home, especially when they know what to expect! Complete with tips to help every parent get organized, equip the kitchen, supply the pantry, involve other family members in the preparations, and forge family bonds around the dinner table, this book arrives family-tested and kid-approved. Excellent book! Highly recommended.

***A House United* by Nicholeen Peck**

Parenting: A House United is based on Nicholeen's popular seminar series Teaching Self-Government. This book shows parents the communication skills they need to teach their children to govern themselves. With the proper family environment and understanding of childhood behaviors, homes can become happier. Even if families simply implement some of Nicholeen's tested parenting principles, their family life will improve. Nicholeen's candid storytelling style and experience with tough teens makes the book usable and a joy to read for all. Even if you have heard Nicholeen speak before, you can't pass this book up. It promises new stories, examples, valuable question and answers, and further insights never before shared.

COTTAGE MEETING FOR KIDS

Cottage Meeting for Kids is a liberty promoting program for the entire family and focused on children from preschool to teens. It is full of great stories and fun activities to help children gain a love of liberty. Families can join together each month for an Activity Day to share the concepts they've learned and enhance them through group activities. Here are some ideas to promote the concepts presented in "A Time To Sow." You can find additional ideas, outlines and activities on the Moms for America® website under "Cottage Meetings for Kids."

- Meet as a family to create a Family Mission Statement. What is your mission? What is important to you? To your children? Get everyone involved in the discussion. You can also create a Family Slogan.

- Mealtime is a fantastic opportunity to teach good manners, foster respectful communication, and strengthen family relationships. Good manners and etiquette taught in the home will lead to good citizens, respectful adults, and a more civil society. A fun idea is to plan and hold a formal family dinner. You can choose a theme, like a tea party or tuxedo night, or a time period like the Elizabethan era or colonial America; kids love to dress up. As you prepare, you can teach the children proper table setting, dinner décor, and discuss proper etiquette. Check out the Hostess Resource Center for fun ideas and resources.

- Read & Discuss the *Magic Mask* provided in the Supplemental Materials of this presentation

Book List

Suggested books and readings for children all ages to nurture a love of liberty in the home.

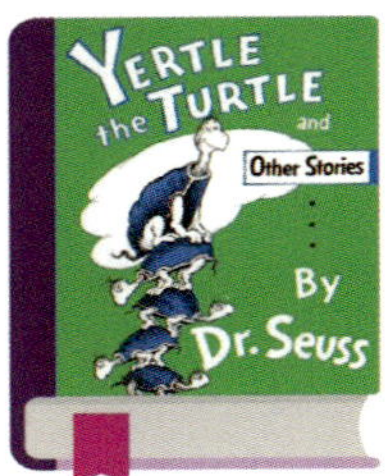

Yertle the Turtle
by Dr. Suess

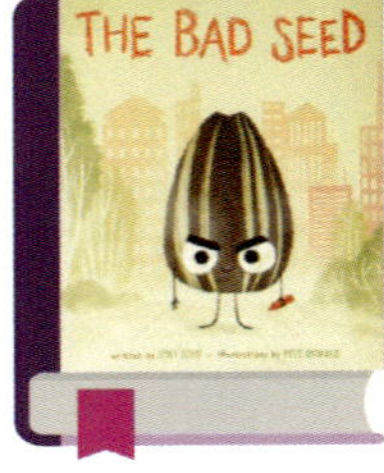

The Bad Seed
by Jory John

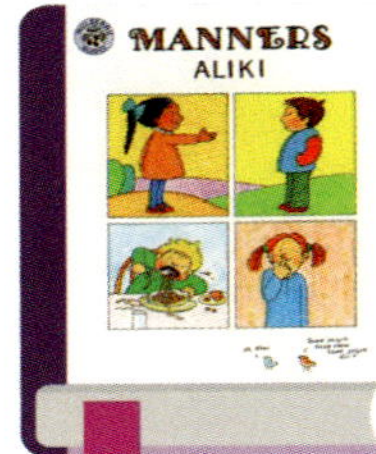

Manners
by Aliki

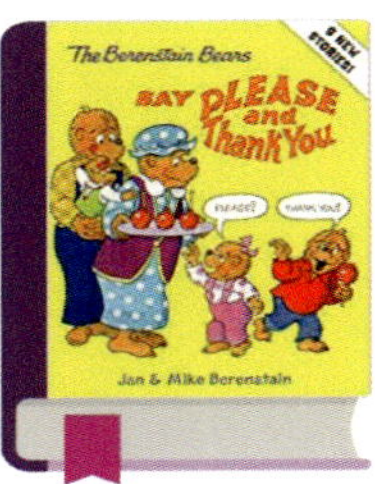

**The Berenstain Bears
Say Please and Thank You**
by Stan Berenstain

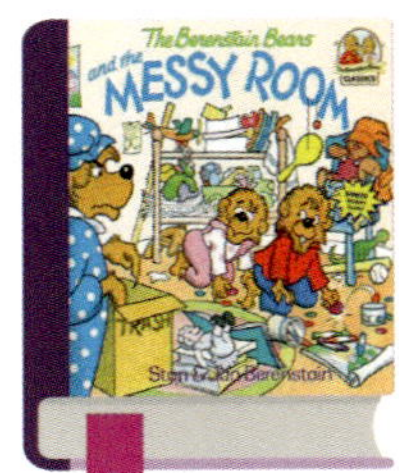

**The Berenstain Bears
and the Messy Room**
by Stan Berenstain

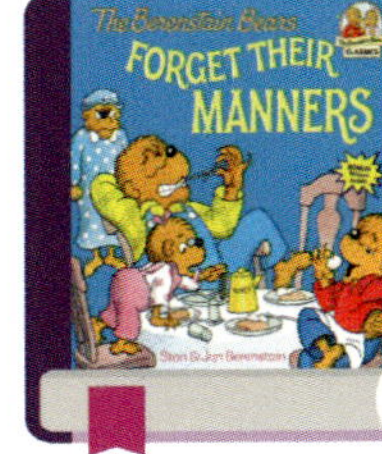

**The Berenstain Bears
Forget their Manners**
by Stan Berenstain

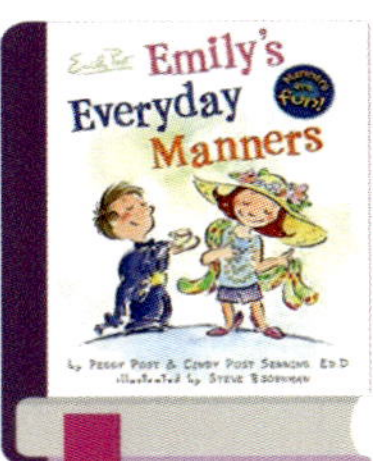

Emily's Everyday Manners
by Peggy Post and
Cindy Post Senning

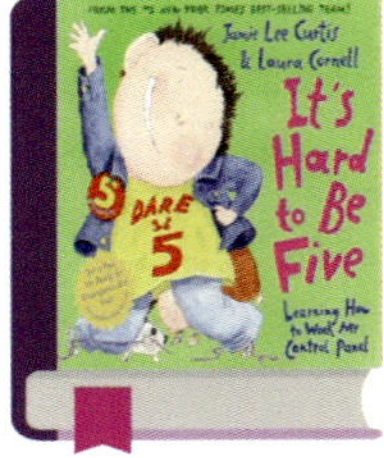

It's Hard to Be Five
by Jamie Lee Curtis and
Laura Cornell

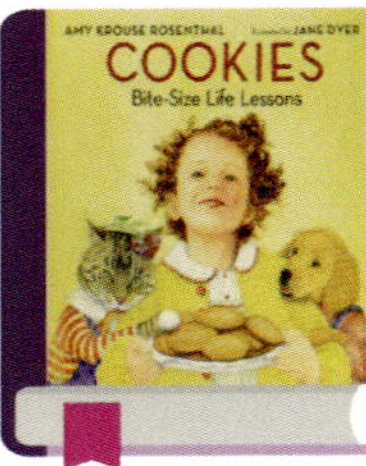

Cookies: Bite-Size Lessons
by Amy Krouse Rosenthal

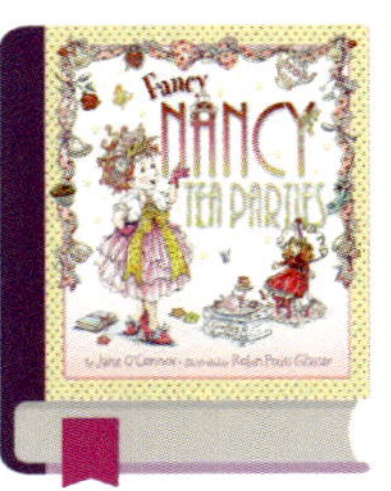

**Fancy Nancy:
Tea Parties**
by Jane O'Connorg

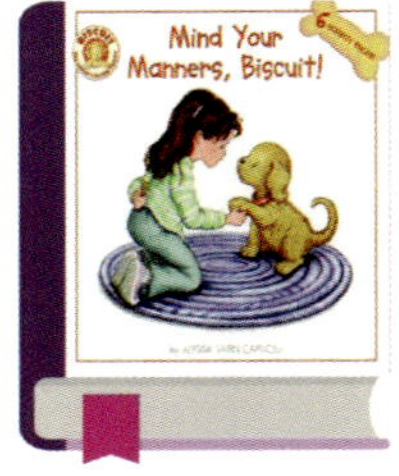

**Mind Your Manners,
Biscuit!**
by Alyssa Satin Capucilli

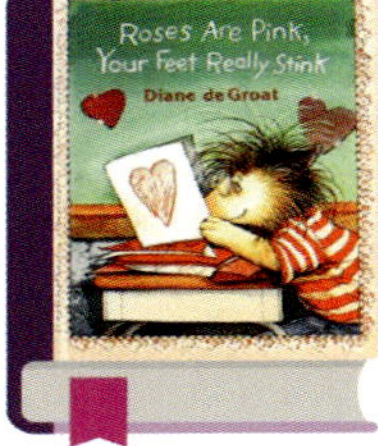

**Roses Are Pink,
Your Feet Really Stink**
by Diana deGroat

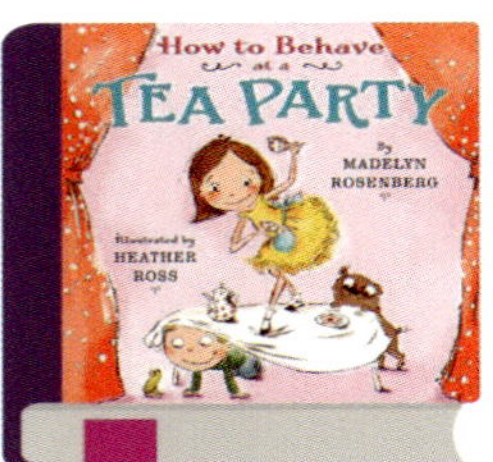

**How to Behave
at a Tea Party**
by Madelyn Rosenberg

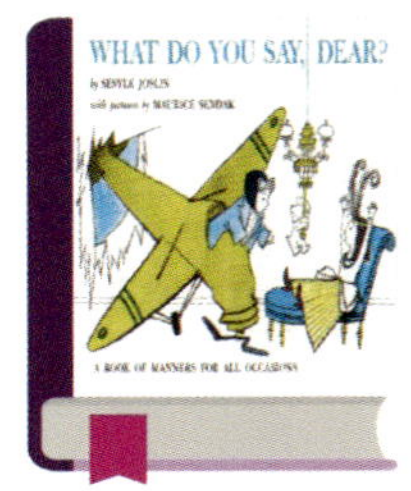

**What Do You Say,
Dear?**
by Sesyle Joslin

SUPPLEMENTAL MATERIAL

Family: It's About Time!

It is no surprise that we live in a fast-paced world filled with extremely busy schedules. Just keeping up with the kids' activities alone can leave us feeling like little more than a human taxi. With so many things pulling for our time and filling our days, finding time for family can be a difficult challenge. But we don't need to take a vacation, make big plans, go long distances, or spend a lot of money to have quality time as a family. We just need to schedule the time and take advantage of all those precious little moments of quality time that pass us by because we didn't even realize they were there. In order to spend more time together as a family, we may need evaluate how we spend our time—and re-evaluate our expectations of the time we spend together.

Quality time doesn't need to be complicated, it can be as simple as a conversation while setting the table or an evening walk in the neighborhood. It isn't as important how we spend the time as it is how often we spend it. Without quantity of time, there cannot be quality time. And the more time we spend as a family, the more well-adjusted our children will be, and the better citizens they will become; there have been many studies to prove this.

Quality family time does not need to have a specific agenda or planned activity. This time can be spontaneous and varied in length from a few minutes to several hours, depending on the situation.

- Here are just some ideas of how you can create or take advantage of time with your family

- Plan a monthly "family night" where you play board games, or an outside game such as kick ball, basketball, etc.

- Pizza Movie Night—a great activity for the whole family. You can all choose the movie together it can be a new movie just out or a favorite you already have. You can even make it a special treat and let the kids eat in the Living Room while they watch the movie. Adding their favorite soda to the meal is an extra special treat (sippy cups or cups with straws are good idea for the little ones)

- Have your children help with a home project, such as repairing something or painting a room

- Make dinner together as a family, each person can take a part of the meal to make or everyone can share the preparations together

- Attend a concert or sporting event; there a lot of great inexpensive activities put on by local schools and community centers you can attend and even participate in

- Have a special breakfast together and go all out with their favorites eggs, bacon, waffles, strawberries—whatever they like

- Pitch a tent in the backyard and go "camping"

- Go for a nature walk or a hike; pack a lunch and enjoy the adventure

- Do a movie marathon of your favorite movie series, such as *Star Wars,* and stay up late

- Volunteer as a family at a food bank, retirement home, park clean-up, or other community service opportunity

- Read together. Reading to children about something they have seen or done is often interesting to children. Talk with your child about what you have just read. Reading together encourages children's interest in reading

- Go places and do things together. Visit parks, libraries, the zoo, museums and other places of interest. Allow children to have a part in the planning of these outings so that it becomes partly their activity as well

When you do go on hikes or outings together, take a camera whenever possible. Reviewing the photo albums full pictures from the places you've been and things you've seen is a great activity all on its own. Children also enjoy looking through baby books—their own and their siblings.

There are so many great ways to connect and spend quality time together as a family. So turn off the TV, put those electronics away, and make time to connect. Every moment together as a family is a gift—whether playing, chatting, or simply being together—cherish every moment you have together, and take the time to savor the moment and enjoy your family.

Good Manners Makes Good Citizens

"Your boys are soon to take the reins of this high mettled steed, America. A nation's only hope is in them, and their only hope is in you; and the instruments which God has put into your hands with which to fit them for this high office, are the influences of the home.

If your boys wrangle and contend at home, if they cannot discuss with dignity the little questions that arise in their daily intercourse with one another, be sure they will not honor the nation when they take their places in senate halls to discuss the great problems that confront the civilization of the...century.

You, today, are writing on the yielding tablets of their hearts and minds the preface to the next volume of our nation's history."

-C.E. Sargent, *Our Home,* 1888

4 Tricks to Getting Family to the Table

BY ALICE OSBORNE

I recognize life is hectic for most of us, and habits can be hard to break—the non-dinner hour habit more specifically. A Harvard study found that something as basic as eating together consistently fostered many wonderful things for families, not the least of which is the important conversations that ensue while enjoying a good meal.

Many a child's character and esteem have been strengthened through meal-time discussions. So I thought it would be helpful to share some tricks my friends and I have used over the years that might help you in making the family dinner hour possible.

1: Get in the habit of making a morning announcement to everyone leaving for the day what the evening menu is (this means you need to have planned ahead—you actually need to KNOW what's for dinner). "We're having Chicken & Rice Casserole, and cherry pie with ice cream tonight! See you for dinner!" Another common approach to this routine is to assign days of the week to specific meals: "Don't forget this is chili-and-homemade-cornbread-smothered-in butter-and-honey night! See you for dinner!"

This reminds me of a heart-warming experience I had the other day while driving through our neighborhood after work. I came up on a couple of 10-year-old neighbor boys pedaling like crazy towards home. I slowed up, rolled down my window, and called to them, "Hey guys, where you headed so fast?" Josh answered, "Hi Mrs. Osborne. It's Sloppy Joe night. We gotta get home for dinner!" "And I've been invited!" Josh's pal, Kevin shouted out. Now THAT'S what I'm talkin' about!

Some moms use a chalk, bulletin, or white board to post the day's meal—

kind of like a restaurant: TODAY'S FAMILY SPECIAL: Crock-pot Spare Ribs, Baked Potatoes, Angel Food Cake with Strawberries and Cream. Everyone leaves for their appointed destinations feeling all is right in the world—mom's on the job!

2: Set the table. It sends a quiet message that dinner hour is important and those coming to the table are special and deserve this extra effort. And it can be a lot of fun as well—it lends itself nicely to holiday themes, birthdays, and other special days. Let your creativity run with this part of the family dinner hour.

We never had much money as the kids were growing up, so meals were generally very basic—nothing fancy, gourmet-ish, or worth accolades—but the table was always set, even if it was with paper plates. There were usually candles lit, paper napkins neatly folded underneath the forks, and glass-glasses (as opposed to plastic) at each setting. And place settings were always sitting on inexpensive plastic or vinyl placemats (ala K-Mart or Walmart). When I worked outside the home, I would set the dinner table before I left for work in the morning. As the kids got older, they shared the table-setting responsibility.

Also, a set table signals to the family as they pass by the kitchen or dining area that you're serious about the family dinner goal (and they should be as well) and is a visual reminder of where they need to be at the appointed hour.

3: As you begin your meal preparations, start with frying some onions (even if you're not using them in the meal—they can always be frozen for another time). Food aromas say "Hang in there…dinner's coming!" and this calms anyone in the family that doesn't deal well with hunger pangs. My son Philip, for instance, always the sweetest and most pleasant child, did a Dr. Jekyll and Mr. Hyde turn when he was hungry. I found if he could smell something cooking, and

see visual evidence that dinner was pending, his crankiness calmed right down. And of course, food aromas create an anticipation of what's to come—always a good thing when you want folks to "buy in" to what you're attempting.

4: Introduce fun traditions and the element of surprise on a regular basis. One mom I know hides an almond in her tapioca or cream pudding desserts, or a quarter in the cake, for the Monday dinner every week. The person finding the almond or quarter is the week's "lucky kid" and they can choose one chore to remove from their weekly chore list. You can bet they show up to dinner! Another mom likes to write little notes to her kids and tuck them under their dinner plate. And another friend likes to give goofy names to the elements of her dinners (Head-hunter Stew, Chocka-Rocka-Docka Chocolate Cake, Razza-Ma-Tazz Ravioli, etc.). Kids love this stuff and the ambiance it creates.

Family dinner hour is a lost tradition that you can help bring back, one meal at a time. So try these tricks and see how they make YOUR family dinner hour possible.

The Magic Mask

There was once a great and powerful prince. He had hundreds of soldiers in his army, and with their help, he had conquered vast strips of country, over which he ruled. He was wise as well as brave, but, though all men feared his iron will and respected his strong purpose, no one loved him. As he grew older, he became lonely and unhappy, and this made him sterner and colder, and more severe than ever. The lines about his mouth were hard and grim, there was a deep frown on his forehead, and his lips rarely smiled.

Now it happened that, in one of the cities over which he had come to rule, there was a beautiful princess whom he wished to have for his wife. He had watched her for many months as she went about among the people, and he knew that she was as good and kind as she was beautiful. But, because he always wore his armor and his heavy helmet when he rode through his dominions, she had never seen his face.

The day came when he made up his mind that he would ask the lovely princess to come and live in his palace. He put on his royal robes and his golden coronet; but when he looked at his reflection in the glass, he could see nothing but what would cause fear and dislike. His face looked hard and cruel and stern. He tried to smile, but it seemed an unnatural effort and he quickly gave it up. Then a happy notion came to him. Sending for the court magician, he said to him: "Make for me a mask of the thinnest wax so that it will follow every line of my features, but paint it with your magic paints so that it will look kind and pleasant instead of fierce and stern. Fasten it upon my face so that I shall never have to take it off. Make it as handsome and attractive as your skill can suggest, and I will pay for it any price you choose to ask."

"This I can do," said the court magician, "on one condition only. You must keep your own face in the same lines that I shall paint, or the mask will be ruined. One angry frown, one cruel smile will crack the mask and ruin it forever; nor can I replace it. Will you agree to this?"

The prince had a strong will, and never in his life had he wanted anything so much as he now wanted the princess for his wife. "Yes," he said, "I agree. Tell me how I may keep the mask from cracking."

"You must train yourself to think kindly thoughts," said the magician, "and, to do this, you must do kindly deeds. You must try to make your kingdom happy rather than great. Whenever you are angry, keep absolutely still until the feeling has gone away. Try to think of ways to make your subjects happier and better. Build schools instead of forts, and hospitals instead of battleships. Be gracious and courteous to all men."

So the wonderful mask was made, and when the prince put it on, no one would have guessed that it was not his true face. The lovely princess, indeed, could find no fault with it, and she came willingly to be his bride in his splendid palace. The months went on, and though, at first, the magic mask was often in danger of being destroyed, the prince had been as good as his word, and no one had ever discovered that it was false. His subjects, it is true, wondered at his new gentleness and thoughtfulness, but they said: "It is the princess who has made him like herself."

The prince, however, was not quite happy. When the princess smiled her approval of his forbearance and goodness, he used to wish that he had never deceived her with the magic mask. At last he could bear it no longer, and summoning the magician, he bade him remove the false face.

"If I do, your Royal Highness," protested the magician, "I can never make another. You must wear your own face as long as you live."

"Better so," cried the prince, "than to deceive one whose love and trust I value so greatly. Better even that she should always despise me than that I should go on doing what is unworthy for her sake."

Then the magician took off the mask, and the prince in fear and anguish of heart sought his reflection in the glass. As he looked, his eyes brightened and his lips curved into a radiant smile, for the ugly lines were gone, the frown had disappeared, and his face was molded in the exact likeness of the mask he had worn so long. And, when he came into the presence of his wife, she saw only the familiar features of the prince she loved.

Discussion Questions:

How did the prince's countenance change? Why did it change? What made the prince look old and mean? How did the love of the Princess influence the prince?

All boys are princes and all girls are princesses because we are all children of a king! What can we do behave more like princes and princesses? How does true royalty conduct themselves and treat others?

Mind Your Manners

BY CHERIE CAWLEY

Imagine being seated at the dinner table with someone who decided to donate millions of dollars to your organization or support your start-up company you've been laboring over for years and now you've finally had your big break. Would you say please and thank you every time something was passed to you? Would you be as polite as possible? Of course you would! Not because you are pretentious but because you are grateful for the opportunity to be in the situation, and you want to put your best foot forward.

Now head to your own dinner table. Amidst the craziness happening with littles—or, for that matter, teenagers—do you speak kindly to one another? Are manners only relevant in big situations or are they important in the small ones? Are manners even relevant in today's society? Absolutely. Here are 3 great reasons for sowing the seeds of gratitude in your home.

Number one, manners show appreciation. Plain and simple. Manners, like holding the door open for someone older than you, not speaking with your mouth full, and saying please and thank you consider other people around you and show them value. I've read that people may perceive it as old fashioned to do these things, but is it really old fashioned to be respectful of those around us? I don't think it's ever old fashioned to treat others as we want to be treated.

Number two, manners show that you have self-control. Our society has become very "feeling driven." Doing only what we feel like shows very little self-restraint. Obviously, there are deeper issues we could dive into here, but self-control means you are able to bypass that "I don't feel like it" feeling and do the right thing such as writing a thank you note to someone for a gift. It is easy for children to think money and gifts grow on trees, especially very young ones. Teaching them to bypass what they feel by choosing gratitude gives them a lifelong tool.

Lastly, manners actually show self-respect. I know it sounds backward, but if you have come to a place in life where you know sacrifice and hard work pay off, you know

that presenting your best, hardworking self helped make a path for you. Along that path, if you had enough drive and respect for yourself, you most likely used manners. Otherwise, many of those doors and opportunities might have been shut. If you respect yourself, you show constraint and appreciation for other people. "What goes around comes around" is often very true.

Even if you are convinced manners are worth your training and investment for your children, it can be daunting to start! If you haven't been intentional about manners in the past—don't stress. We all begin somewhere. If you have young children, it is easy to teach them to say please and thank you. The best way to implement this is to model in your own language toward them. For example, "Would you please pick up that toy, Hannah?" and "Thank you, Ethan, for bringing Mom your shoes."

Manners will pay off when they head to school, interact at church, and can even be helpful on the playground! If your children are older and you have

taught manners in the past but see that middle schooler or high school aged child begins to slack, give them a vision for their future. Ask your middle school child why manners matter in their everyday life of being grateful, and if your high schooler has a job, give them a vision of manners along with their diligence at work. Give them examples of how these two aspects of holding a job go a long way with employers and bring them favor for raises and better positions. If they are working a customer service job, this can bring more tips and respect from customers. Remember, even when we use manners, there will be instances when others do not appreciate this intentionality. BUT…we don't live by other's standards. We live by our own standards, so we respect others and ourselves enough to use manners even when they are not returned.

The easiest rule to follow with manners is the golden one: treat others as you want to be treated. Attitudes of gratitude will always be in style for every generation. If you are looking for resources to help implement manners in your home, check these out:

Toddlers/Young Children:

Kindness Rules by Eunice Moyle and Sabrina Moyle

Llama Llama by Anna Dewdney

howdoesshe.com/18-fun-activities-that-teach-good-manners/

Middle School Aged Children:

Dude, that's rude! (Get Some Manners) by Elizabeth Verdick

365 Manners Kids Should Know by Sheryl Eberly

www.nea.org/tools/lessons/learning-and-practicing-good-manners-grades-6-8.html

High School Aged Children:

How Rude: The Teen Guide to Good Manners, Proper Behavior and Not Grossing People Out by Alex J. Packer

Tiffany's Table Manners for Teenagers by Walter Hoving (Former Chairman of Tiffany's of New York)

Fortifying Our Homes to Withstand the Social and Political Contention Outside It!

BY LISA CUMMINS

On a very popular conservative talk radio show, a young mom called in to the host very worried about what was going on in the media and if there was a future for her toddling daughter. This young mom was scared and did not have much hope. The host, and audience, could tell she needed faith and encouragement. He quickly changed the tone of voice; it became softer, slower, almost grandpa like. He said, "Susanne, I want you to have hope. I want you to have faith. Will you do me a favor?"

"Yes," she says.

"Will you turn off your radio, your social media, the T.V., mainstream media, for a week and pay attention to your daughter, to your family. I promise you nothing will change drastically in that week. You will not miss anything. The news does not change." The host continued, "do what ever it is that brings you joy for a week. Will you do that for me?"

"Yes," she replied.

Now, I cannot tell you what advise was given after that, as I had turned off the radio at that point rushing to my next 'must do' on my list. But I remember this man's voice getting soft and patient and kind. I also remember the feeling that what I brought into my home must be intentional.

America is a combination of everything good, beautiful, and wise with lessons-learned mixed in. It is the same with our homes. Our families, our faith, the artwork, the color, and the culture that we display in our homes represent us!

In my home, we have bright walls to reflect the sunlight. The pictures on the walls depict Christ or his teachings. We have chosen to display the Declaration of Independence and the Constitution to remind us of the freedoms that we have a responsibility to uphold. And, of course, pictures scattered around of family.

The décor includes olive wreaths that represent eternal peace, bookshelves filled with uplifting books, and music that tie in the feelings and lifts the soul. We gather as family, tell stories, play games, laugh, and reminisce.

Sometimes, just turning off the social media and the news is not enough. Sometimes, that quick get away is not enough; especially today, when government mandates and shutdowns have limited the convenience of getaway destinations.

There is no end in sight of things ever going back to the serene peace that Americans normally experience on the outside. That is the tragedy of this.

However, we can be in complete control of what happens in our homes.

American editor, lecturer, and essayist, William George Jordan (1864-1928) wrote,

"Calmness is the rarest quality in human life. It is the poise of a great nature, in harmony with itself and its ideals. It is the moral atmosphere of a life self-centered, self-reliant, and self-controlled. Calmness is singleness of purpose, absolute confidence, and conscious power—ready to be focused in an instant to meet any crisis."

Intentionally fortifying our homes prepares us to meet the contention of the world when we are ready. We guard against what comes into our homes, and our children should be taught to do the same. They have stewardship over helping to keep that peace which you have set.

By doing this, our children and our friends will recognize the difference in the feelings they experience, and the right vs wrong they see. It is a simple truth that there is nothing going on outside our home that can't be healed, countered, or curtailed inside our home. We must guard our homes, fortify our walls, and strengthen our family within to be able to overcome the propaganda, anxiety, confusion, and contention without.

I promise it will strengthen us as a community, and as a Nation, when we do!

RELATED QUOTES

"The family is the test of freedom; because the family is the only thing that the free man makes for himself and by himself."
-Gilbert K. Chesterton

"The home is the first and most effective place to learn the lessons of life: truth, honor, virtue, self-control, the value of education, honest work, and the purpose and privilege of life. Nothing can take the place of home in rearing and teaching children and no other success can compensate for failure in the home." *-David McKay*

"I have no hesitation in saying that although the American woman never leaves her domestic sphere and is in some respects very dependent within it, nowhere does she enjoy a higher station. And if anyone asks me what I think the chief cause of the extraordinary prosperity and growing power of this nation, I should answer that it is due to the superiority of their women."
-Alexis de Tocqueville, 1835

"I like to see a man proud of the place in which he lives. I like to see a man live so that his place will be proud of him."
-Abraham Lincoln

"Respect for ourselves guides our morals, respect for others guides our manners." *- Laurence Sterne*

"Kindness and politeness are not overrated at all. They're underused." *- Tommy Lee Jones*

I am a child of Royal birth.

My Father is King of Heaven and Earth.

My spirit was born in the courts on high.

A child beloved, a prince or princess am I.

"Parents, your child is the bland paper on which is to be written the record of your own lives. Be careful then what you allow to be written there, for the world will read it."
-C.E. Sargent, Our Home

"May we think of freedom, not as the right to do as we please, but the opportunity to do what is right."
-Peter Marshall

"Good manners will open doors that the best education cannot."
-Clarence Thomas

FROM THE FOUNDERS

Journal

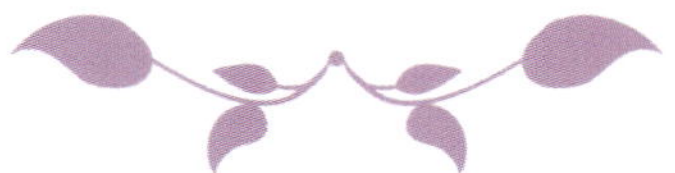

A Constitution of Government once changed from freedom, can never be restored. Liberty, once lost, is lost forever.
-John Adams

PRESENTATION TEN

The Wheat and the Chaff

"Hold on, my friends, to the Constitution and to the Republic for which it stands. Miracles do not cluster and what has happened once in 6,000 years, may not happen again."

~Daniel Webster

Separating wheat from the chaff is a common agricultural practice that is used to prepare grains for consumption. In cereals like rice, barley, oats, and wheat, the grain is surrounded by a dry husk. Before the grain can be used, the husks (or chaff) must be removed. Separating the wheat from the chaff has become a common cliché to describe the practice of distinguishing the wanted from the unwanted, the valuable from the relatively valueless.

This presentation will focus on the wheat and the chaff in our current constitution. The wheat is the original Constitution as prepared by our Founders, the chaff includes amendments and judicial interpretations that have changed the meaning and intent of the Constitution. We will explore how later amendments to the Constitution have caused us to stray from these correct principles, and how a restoration of the Constitution will guide America back to the land of liberty that it once was.

Just as the farmer needs to separate the wheat from the chaff before sending the grain to market, today's patriots must separate the original intent of the Constitution from today's interpretation if they want to be successful in preserving liberty and re-establishing America as the "one nation, under God" to which we have pledged our allegiance.

Please note: There is a lot of information provided in this presentation. You may want to divide this presentation into 2-3 meetings to provide ample discussion and exploration of the topic.

PREPARATION

In preparation to lead the Cottage Meeting Presentation, read through the presentation and highlight areas you would like to share in your meeting. To prepare yourself to lead the discussion, please review and consider the following material:

- Read "The 17th Amendment and the Destruction of Federalism" provided in the Supplemental Materials of this presentation.

- View the video *The Tale of Two Constitutions, The Most Powerful Office in the World,* and *America's Wall of Protection* provided in the Hostess

---

Home Assignment

Read Preserve, Protect & Defend by Cameron C. Taylor, view the film A More Perfect Union

Personal Study

Complete the Healing of America Cottage Series. You can join our live virtual classes or view/listen to the recorded sessions on the Moms for America website.

Family Enrichment

View the film *A More Perfect Union* with your family. (available on the MFA webstore and included in the Cottage Meeting Hostess Kit)

Use the Proclaim Liberty Discussion Guide to learn about the Constitution and the principles of Liberty our nation was founded on

Catechism on the Constitution is an excellent resource to learn about the Constitution during Family Dinner Hour

View the animated Constitution for Kids series at FreedomFactor.org

Resource Center on the Moms for America® website www.MomsforAmerica.us

- Read *5,000 Year Leap* Part 1: The Founders' Monumental Task: Structuring a government with all power in the people (Pages 7-33)

- If Available, Read through Vignettes 9.7-9.12 9.6-9.12, 10.1-10.6, 11.1-11.7, and 12.6-12.9 of *Promises of the Constitution* (NOTE: If you do not already have a copy of this book, we highly recommend obtaining one for this presentation. It is available on the Moms for America® online store.)

- Review the Quotes provided in the Supplemental Materials section of this presentation

PURPOSE

The purpose of this presentation is to introduce the Constitution of the United States as established by our Founding Fathers. The presentation uses the analogy of separating the wheat from the chaff to distinguish between the original intent of the Constitution and the alterations and misinterpretations that people equate with the Constitution today.

KEY POINTS

- By studying the Constitution from the viewpoint of the Founding Fathers, we discover the freedom formula that made the United States a free and prosperous nation

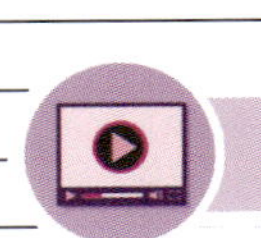

- The Founders restored the "ancient principles," or People's Law, that was practiced by the Israelites as opposed to Ruler's Law that was imposed by tyrants

- The Constitution is structured to protect the people from the human frailties of their Rulers

MEETING OUTLINE

Welcome & Gathering

We recommend starting your meeting with a prayer and the Pledge of Allegiance.

Show Video: *The Tale of Two Constitutions* by Glenn Kimber (available in Hostess Resource Center). Many people argue that the Constitution is outdated and inadequate for modern challenges. However, the Constitution we have today is quite different from what our Founders gave us.

How do the amendments and judicial interpretations of the 1900s change the original intent of the Constitution?

Group Discussion

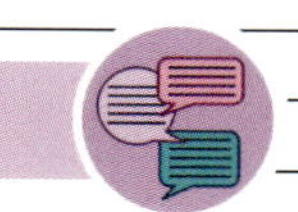

Moses was raised in Egypt and trained under "Ruler's Law" where all power resides in the ruler.

How did Jethro's counsel to his son-in-law change the system of government? How did individual responsibility and local control increase under this new system? (Reference 5000 Year Leap Part 1: The Founders' Monumental Task: Structuring a government with all power in the people)

What does the symbol of the 3 headed eagle represent? How does this explain the Legislative branch of the U.S. Government? (See 5000 Year Leap page 24-25)

Show Video: "America's Wall of Protection" (Provided in the Hostess Resource Center on the MFA website)

Summarize: "The 17th Amendment and the Destruction of Federalism" (You can send the article to the participants prior to the meeting or provide it for them to read the full article following the meeting)

What was the original intent of the Senate? How has the 17th Amendment changed the election and role of a Senator?

Show Video: *The Most Powerful Office in the World* (Provided in the Hostess Resource Center) Reference Vignettes 10.1-10.3 of *Promises of the Constitution*

What were the original duties assigned to the President? How was the president to be elected? What was the original intent of the Executive Order?

The proper role of government is to protect unalienable rights (Reference Vignettes 12.7-12.9 of *Promises of the Constitution*)

What is the danger of allowing the Supreme Court to decide our rights? What was the original intent of the Supreme Court? How have decisions of the Supreme Court altered the original intent of the Constitution?

How can Congress protect the people from Judicial Legislation? (Reference Vignettes 10.4 and 10.5 of Promises of the Constitution)

What is the Liberty Amendment? How could this amendment restore the original intent of the Constitution? (Reference Vignette 12.6 of Promises of the Constitution)

Summarize your thoughts on the material covered in this presentation.

- Give the Home Assignment for the next meeting

- Announce date, time and location for next meeting

ADDITIONAL PRESENTATION IDEAS

After learning about the Constitution in this presentation, it is very natural for you and the members of your group to want to learn more—as has been our experience in our respective groups. We highly encourage a study of the Constitution within the Cottage Meeting groups. Once you have completed the first 12 presentations, it is a great opportunity to begin a Constitution Course and/or discussion forum where you can learn and study the Constitution together as group. Moms for America® offers a 16 Week Virtual Cottage Series "The Healing of America" provided by the Thomas Jefferson Center for Constitutional Studies. The entire series is recorded and available online for you to view or listen to. You can also host the series in your home. The four books for the series are available on the Moms for America® online store.

- Host or attend a Constitution Seminar in your community. The National Center for Constitutional Studies holds both one day and half day *Making of America* seminars where they provide the presenter. It is a small fee per participant. You can provide a potluck lunch or have everyone bring their own bag lunch. The NCCS *Making of America Seminar* provides a solid foundation of the Constitution in an interactive, engaging way everyone will enjoy (Recommended for teens to adults)

- Participate in the virtual Healing of America series, list to the series online, or host the series in your home

- Use *Catechism on the Constitution* and *Promises of the Constitution* to learn and discuss the Constitution and constitutional principles in your group; both books are available in the Moms for America® online store

MINI COTTAGE IDEAS

Mini Cottages are designed especially for moms of preschoolers and moms who work full-time jobs. Moms simply read and/or watch the same materials at home, on their own, then meet together once a week in a playdate or over lunch during the workday to discuss what they read. The articles and videos are short and can usually be read and/or viewed in less than hour. Below are some suggestions to host mini cottage discussions under the "Wheat & Chaff" theme.

- Read "September 17th is Constitution Day, and It Was Started by an Ohio Mom!" provided in the Supplemental Materials section of this presentation.

What things can you do to celebrate Constitution Week with your children and/or grandchildren? Share ideas. You may consider joining with other families for an activity day.

- View the video *The Tale of Two Constitutions, The Most Powerful Office in the World,* and *America's Wall of Protection* provided in the Hostess Resource Center on the Moms for America® website www.MomsforAmerica.us

- Read *5,000 Year Leap* Part 1: The Founders' Monumental Task: Structuring a government with all power in the people (Pages 7-33)

COTTAGE MEETING BOOK CLUB

For those who like the book club format, we've compiled a list of great books to help you gain an appreciation and foundational understanding of the concepts presented in "Wheat & Chaff."

The 5000 Year Leap: A Miracle That Changed the World

- Review Part 1, Pages 7 to 33

Promises of the Constitution **by Pam Openshaw**

- Review Vignettes 9.7-9.12 9.6-9.12, 10.1-10.6, 11.1-11.7, and 12.6-12.9

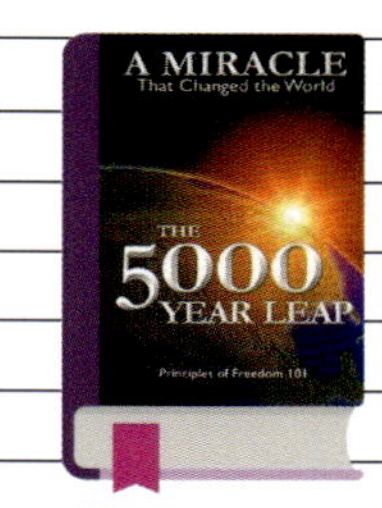

Promises of the Constitution is an outstanding resource for learning the Constitution, the history surrounding it, and the ways in which it has become twisted and ignored today. The book is written in clear, powerful 550 word vignettes in 129 topics that can be easily read in 3-5 minutes, *Promises* is enjoyable to read and makes it simple to learn the history and inspired principles of the Constitution (Available on the Moms for America® online store).

The Essential Constitution

This is a great little book put out by the Heritage Foundation. The booklet is designed to help Americans appreciate and defend the meaning and purpose of the Constitution so that they may preserve freedom for themselves and succeeding generations. You can get free copies by calling Heritage Foundation. We can also add a copy to orders from the Moms for America® online store as our supply lasts.

The Making of America

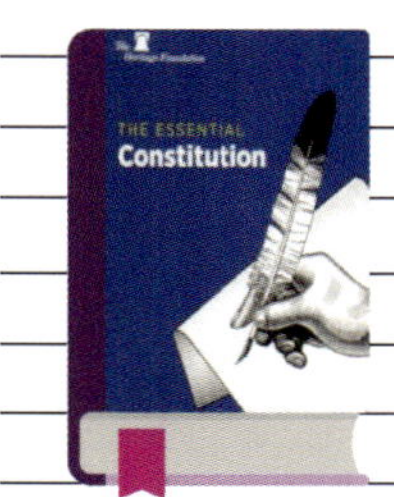

Bring the National Center for Constitutional Studies (NCCS) "Making of America: One Day Constitution Seminar" into your own home with their video presentation. Available on the Moms for America® online store and at

www.nccs.net, this kit includes the seminar guide you would receive at one of the live seminars, and a DVD recording of an all-day seminar.

This is an excellent resource for Cottage Meetings and families. If you have never attended one of these seminars, you are in for a real treat! It is an outstanding presentation and worth every minute. When using this program, you can hold it as an all-day seminar and do a pot-luck lunch, hold it in two half-day seminars, or break it up into several regular meetings. It is versatile enough to fit any format you choose.

Catechism on the Constitution

This book is designed to revive a better understanding of America's great Charter of Liberty by using one of the oldest teaching methods ever invented—asking questions. It was used so extensively by the famous Greek philosopher, Socrates, that it is often referred to as the "Socratic method of teaching"—meaning, teaching by asking questions. For over one hundred years, this book was the method used to teach America's youth to know and understand their Constitution. In 1831, when Alexis de Tocqueville came to America, he was amazed at how conversant the young people were with their charter of freedom. The Catechism was the vehicle to that learning (Available on the Moms for America® online store and through www.NCCS.net).

COTTAGE MEETING FOR KIDS

Cottage Meeting for Kids is a liberty promoting program for the entire family and focused on children from preschool to teens. It is full of great stories and fun activities to help children gain a love of liberty. Families can join together each month for an Activity Day to share the concepts they've learned and enhance them through group activities. Here are some ideas to promote the concepts presented in "Wheat & Chaff." You can find additional ideas, outlines and activities on the Moms for America® website under "Cottage Meetings for Kids."

- Watch the film *A More Perfect Union*

- The story of Olga Weber, provided in the Supplemental Materials section of this presentation, is a great introduction to Constitution Week (September 17-23) and the Ohio mom who founded it. You can celebrate Constitution Week as a family with the great books featured in our booklist.

- Another great way to celebrate the Constitution is to watch the film *A More Perfect Union* a powerful, inspiring film about the Constitutional Convention and the miracles that led to the creation and signing of that sacred document (available in the Moms for America® online store)

- Think of ways you can you do to celebrate Constitution Week with your children and/or grandchildren; you can also join with other families for a fun Constitution Celebration activity day

Book & Movie List

Suggested books and readings for children all ages to nurture a love of liberty and promote the Constitution in your home.

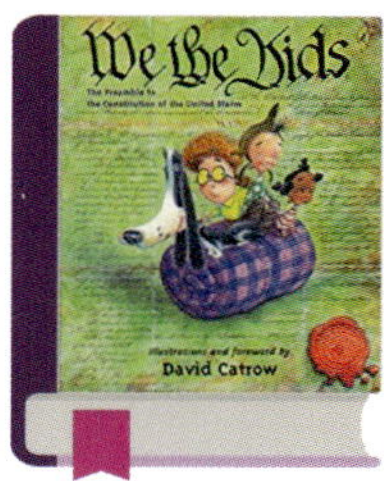

***We the Kids:
The Preamble
to the Constitution
of the United States***
by David Catrow

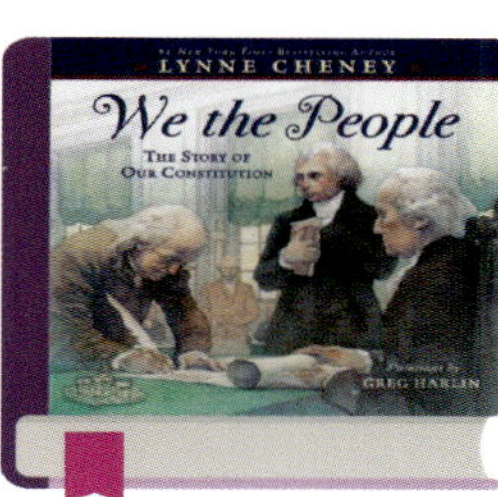

***We the People:
The Story
of Our Constitution***
by Lynne Cheney
and Greg Harlin

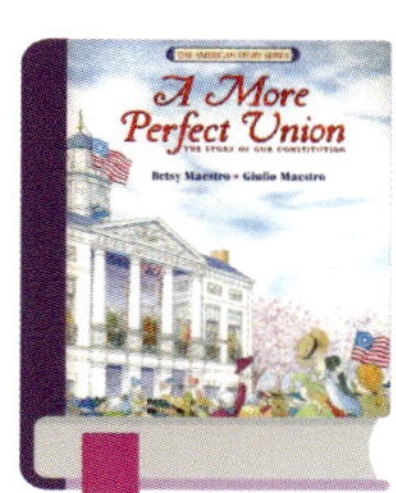

***A More Perfect Union:
The Story of
Our Constitution***
by Betsy Maestro
and Giulio Maestro

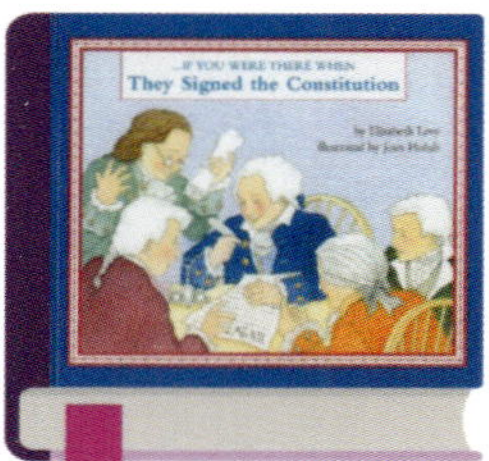

***If You Were There
When They Signed
he Constitution***
by Elizabeth Levy and Joan Holub

Our Constitution Rocks
by Juliette Turner

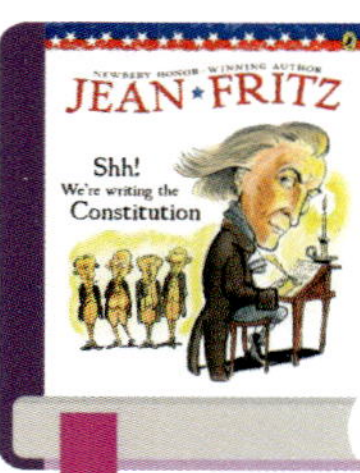

***Shh! We're
Writing the Constitution***
by Jean Fritz

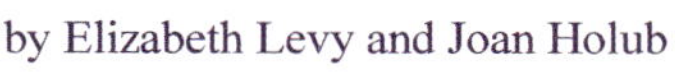

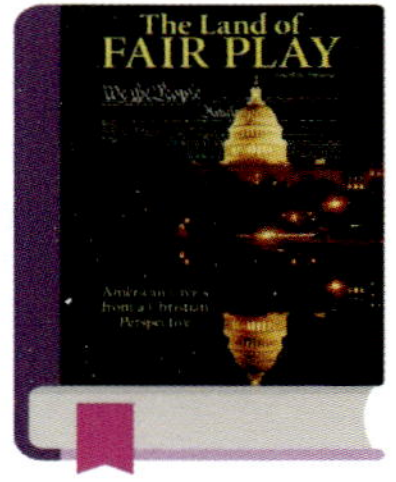

The Land of Fair Play
by Geoffrey Parsons

***A More Perfect Union:
America Becomes a Nation***
1989

Constitution for Kids
FreedomFactor.org

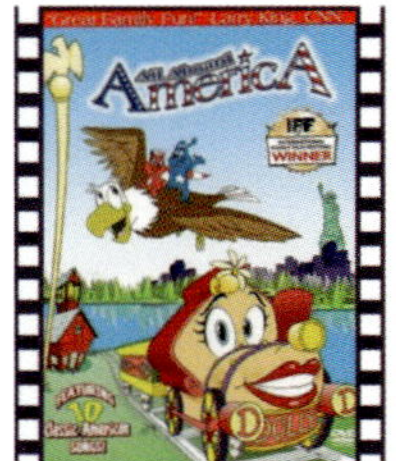

All Aboard America
2011

Liberty's Kids
2002

Seeking Golden Nuggets

Separating wheat from the chaff is a common agricultural practice that is used to prepare grains for consumption. In cereals like rice, barley, oats, and wheat, the grain is surrounded by a dry husk. Before the grain can be used, the husks (or chaff) must be removed. Separating the wheat from the chaff has become a common cliché to describe the practice of distinguishing the wanted from the unwanted, the valuable from the relatively valueless.

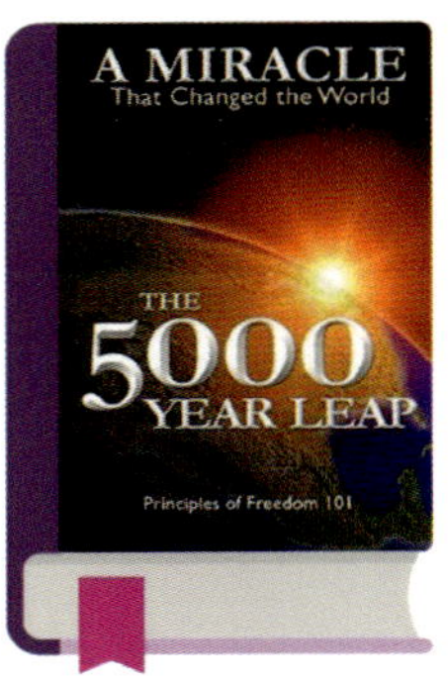

An example of a well-known author who has accomplished this great service is W. Cleon Skousen, author of *The 5000 Year Leap*. After years and years of research, he has identified the principles of freedom that were included in our U.S. Constitution; he has discovered the true character of our Founding Fathers as he read firsthand accounts of their lives and service.

Unfortunately, today's textbooks and stories about the Founding Fathers are filled with misinformation. How does the modern-day student of history know the difference between truth and falsehood? The wise student will always check the references for the material. Original source documents and firsthand accounts from those who knew the Founders will provide the most accurate information.

In speaking about his book, *The 5000 Year Leap*, Cleon Skousen said:

"After a most gratifying visit with many of the Founders through their letters, biographies, and speeches, this book has been assembled. It may appear to some to be a very modest contribution, but it has been a monumental satisfaction to the author. Never before have I fully appreciated the intellectual muscle and the quantum of solid character required to produce the first modern republic.

"I have gained a warm affection for the Founders. I have learned to see them as men imbued with all of our common weaknesses called "human nature," and yet capable of becoming victorious at a task which would have decimated weaker men. I have learned to glory in their successes and have felt an overtone of personal sorrow when they seemed to attain less than they had hoped. It has been a marvelous adventure in research to perceive the ramifications of the Founders' formula for a model commonwealth of freedom and prosperity which became the United States of America."

Moms for America encourages its members to follow the example of this great man and author. It is well worth the time and effort to find the best and most accurate sources of information. Golden nuggets of truth can be found and will enrich the lives and learning of those who search.

Something Extraordinary

The Founders of this nation accomplished something extraordinary. They created a unique political success formula that included a national government and separate state governments. They established three branches within the national system: the legislative, executive, and judicial. The United States Constitution is one of the most astounding documents ever written by man, and for two hundred years, it has withstood the test of time.

As we look back in history during the first century following the ratification of the Constitution, we can see that, by applying the principles of this new Constitutional government, a small segment of the human family, less than 6 percent, became the richest industrial nation on earth. It allowed them to originate more than half of the world's total production and enjoy the highest standard of living in the history of the world.

Today, we too can do something extraordinary: we have the power to restore the light of liberty and once again become a strong, prosperous people. Simply by learning the principles of the Constitution and sharing those divine principles with our children, we will improve humanity, increase civility, embrace individual rights, promote freedom, and secure liberty.

If freedom is to prevail, we must know and understand the Constitution, and we must preserve, defend, and protect it at all cost. If we do not, freedom will be lost, and we may not get another chance at it.

The Seventeenth Amendment and the Destruction of Federalism

NATIONAL CENTER FOR CONSTITUTIONAL STUDIES

One of the most heated topics in all of the Constitutional Convention of 1787 concerned the protection of the states from an overpowering national government. In the beginning, the large states wanted both houses of congress to be representative of the population of the different states. The small states, of course, saw this as a means by which they would be robbed of their voices and the large states would have total dominance in congress. This problem nearly split and destroyed the convention.

It wasn't until Roger Sherman of Connecticut proposed his Great Compromise that the influential leaders began to see the wisdom of this new system—the House would represent the states according to population and the Senate would represent the states equally. Each side of the issue would thus be represented. It was at this time that

Washington admitted he was wrong at first and that this new idea truly had merit in forming a more perfect union. What some may not have realized fully was the protection this new idea gave to the people against an abusive national government.

When the Founders finished their work in Philadelphia, they had created a government that was limited, divided, and balanced. Graphically, it could be represented as follows:

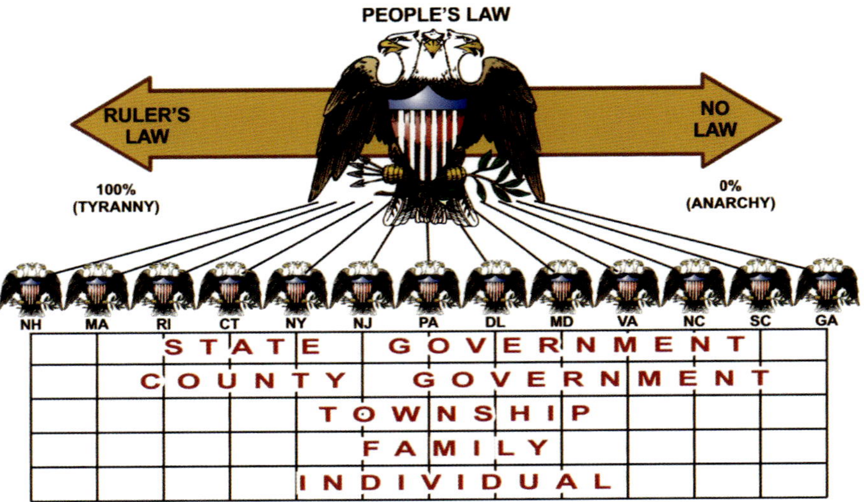

Notice how:

1.   Each level of government is separate and distinct and has its own duties which it does best.

2.   The national government is in the balanced center of the political spectrum—not too little and not too much governmental power. It is divided into three heads or branches.

3.   The lines coming from the national government stop at the states, the states deal directly with the national government, and the states provide the great bulwark of protection for the people against any overpowering move by the national government.

4.   The Senate is made up of senators who are sent by the states to see to it that the national government never intrudes into states' delegated authority and reaches down to the people; they are chosen by the state legislators who know better than the people when the national government is encroaching.

Even though Washington became a foremost proponent of the senators being chosen by the state legislatures, some of the others were slow to see the wisdom of that system. One of those was Thomas Jefferson.

Thomas Jefferson was not at the convention and was not privy to the many heated debates prior to the Great Compromise. He was a great populist and always thought representation should be by population. Even though he had tutored Madison by sending him many books prior to the convention, he still had questions about this new procedure.

When Jefferson finally returned from France, he asked Washington why the senators were not elected by the people. Washington asked him why he poured his hot drink in his saucer before drinking it. And Jefferson replied, "To cool it." "And that," Washington replied, "is what the Senate is for." The Senate is to cool down any hotheaded or imprudent legislation coming out of the House.

The Temptation of Representatives in the House

One might ask, "What is there about the House members that would engender hotheaded or imprudent legislation?" They are elected every two years, which means they have to campaign for re-election every two years. Since Representatives in the House have mostly to do with raising and spending money (all revenue bills must begin in the House) they just might be tempted to say to their constituents, "Look what I have done for you! I have brought all of this federal money down into our district, down into our schools, our towns and cities, our hospitals, our county, our health care systems, etc. Re-elect me so I can keep these monies coming to us." In other words, the House members would be the most likely ones to get the people hooked on federal money by building a "money bridge" from Washington , D.C. directly to the people. And, of course, they would fall prey to the age-old technique of taking from those who have in order to give more and more to those who have not.

If this happens, what level of government would be completely left out of the process? The states! The very level of government meant to stand between the national government and the people!

The Eminent Danger of a Leveling Spirit

James Madison felt this whole balanced system would be destroyed because of this weakness of human nature. He described it this way:

"These [the 'have-nots'] may in time outnumber those [the 'haves'] who are placed above the feelings of indigence. According to the equal laws of suffrage [each person has one vote], the power will slide into the hands of the former. No agrarian attempts have yet been made in this country; but symptoms of a leveling spirit, as we have understood, have sufficiently appeared in a certain quarter to give notice of the future danger."

He then explains that the Founders created the Senate to prevent leveling from occurring:

"How is this danger to be guarded against, on the republican principles? How is the danger, in all cases of interested coalitions to oppress the minority [the 'haves'], to be guarded against?

Among other means, by the establishment of a body, in the government, sufficiently respectable for its wisdom and virtue to aid, on such emergencies, the preponderance of justice, by throwing its weight into that scale. Such being the objects of the second branch in the proposed government [the Senate], he thought a considerable duration [six-year terms] ought to be given to it."

Madison words above explained why the Senate was to guard the property of those who "have" against those who "have-not" but the Senate also protected the people from the very wealthy "haves" who sought power over everybody else.

The original Senate also stands in the way of those who want centralized government

The Founders' formula for the Senate also prevented some of the super-wealthy 'haves' from gaining power by centralizing power in Washington . The Industrial Revolution produced some very wealthy capitalists, a few of whom sought to control the machinery of the national government. In their attempts to do so, the states stood in their way. It was difficult to centralize power in Washington when those pesky states are always there to say "no" to proposals that would usurp power from the states and infringe on states' rights. One of the things these wealthy people did, however, is get control of much of the media in order to influence public opinion. This set the stage for major changes in the structure of the national government. It was dubbed the "progressive" era.

The scheme to rip the states out of the machinery of the national government

Because the state legislatures were the ones who elected U. S. Senators, there were a few charges of irregularities or corruption in the process in a couple of states. This is all the centralized power-schemers needed. When the

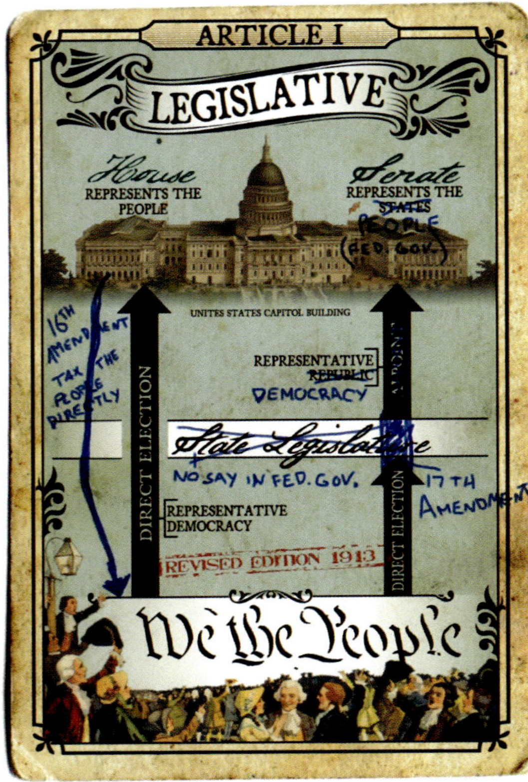

charges of bribery began to surface in some states, the media picked up the stories and cried out to the people, "Do you really want those politicians in your state capitals electing your senators? Wouldn't it be more 'democratic' (a new progressive era term) to let the people elect the senators?" This scenario was the perfect storm to destroy the states' influence in the national government.

When the proposal was made in congress to amend the Constitution to require election of senators by the people, it was first resisted by the Senate. It knew what this would mean—a total destruction of the great states' bulwark of protection of the people. But the media frenzy was too strong and enough senators finally caved to the pressure and Congress approved what was to become the Seventeenth Amendment to the Constitution.

Many of the states also, at first, refused to ratify the amendment, knowing they would be giving up their ability to hold a check on the national government. But once again, enough state legislatures eventually yielded to the pressure and the amendment eventually received the required three-fourths approval of the states to become the Seventeenth Amendment to the Constitution. The states had just given up their trump card to protect the people from powerful influences in Washington; they no longer had real power in the workings of national politics.

The sad result of this destruction of the beautifully balanced, divided, and limited federal system the Founders gave us was to give way to those who so desperately wanted to centralize power in Washington so they could work their power schemes to begin to control nearly every aspect.

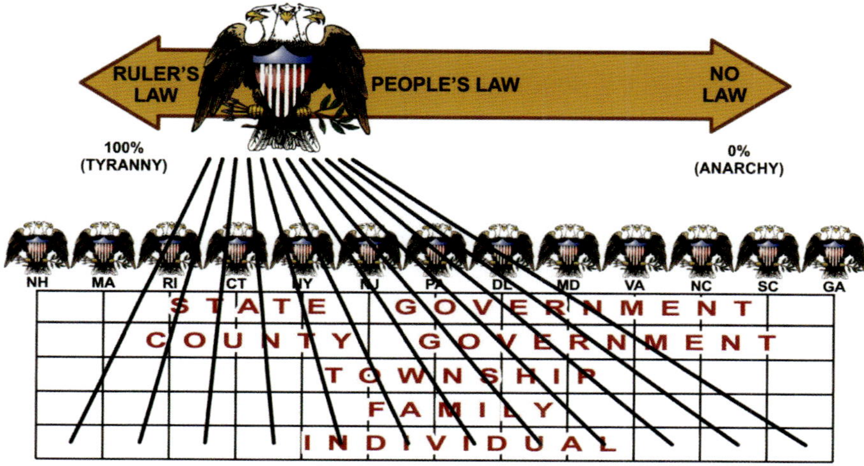

Notice how:

1.   The national government has moved far to the left, usurping more and more power.

2.   Because the state legislatures no longer send their representatives into the U. S. Senate, the states are powerless to protect the people from an overpowering national government.

3.   The national government, with all its agencies, bureaucracies, regulations, and enforcement powers, comes right down into the pocketbooks, homes, schools, and communities of the people; dictating nearly every aspect of life.

4.   The states are left powerless except to pass resolutions and beg Washington, D. C. for mercy.

We, at National Center for Constitutional Studies (NCCS), are convinced that this monstrous power combined will soon crumble from its own weight of unwieldy power. At that time, the millions of freedom loving Americans will be able to restore the beautiful system the Founders gave us. But, of course, Americans must first learn the Founders' marvelous formula for freedom. That is the continuous mission of NCCS.

September 17th is Constitution Day, and It Was Started by an Ohio Mom!

That is what happens when just one woman stands up and speaks out. And when each of us does our small part, we add to the larger picture, like joining pieces in a puzzle of liberty. Each of us holds a piece in the puzzle, and each of us adds to it simply by adding our own little contribution, because it is by small and simple things that great things come to pass. There is no better example of this then the story of one of my heroes—Olga T. Weber.

Olga Weber was an Ohio homemaker who, in 1951, became very concerned that American citizens were taking their freedoms too much for granted. After reflecting on the matter, Olga decided she needed to do something to remind the people of America just how important freedom is. She began distributing copies of the Constitution, the Bill of Rights, flag booklets, and other patriotic leaflets to the local schools, churches, and libraries. Then, in 1952, Olga decided it would be a good idea to establish a Constitution Day to commemorate the signing of the Constitution of the United States. Olga met with Mayor Gerald Romary and members of the Louisville, Ohio city council and shared her idea with them.

On September 17, 1952, Mayor Romary declared the day as Constitution Day in the city of Louisville. It was such a success that Olga decided to approach members of the Ohio General Assembly and ask that Ohio make a statewide designation for Constitution Day. The general assembly thought it a fine idea, and Constitution Day was signed into law by Governor Frank J.

Lausche. Olga's efforts didn't end there, however, she had one more stop—the United States Congress.

In August of 1953, Olga urged the United States Senate to pass a resolution designating September 17-23 as Constitution Week. The Senate and House approved her request, and it was signed into law by President Dwight D. Eisenhower. Today, Constitution Week is nationally recognized, and children all over America celebrate it in their classrooms. The city of Louisville is now known as Constitution Town, and for over fifty years, they have been faithfully celebrating Constitution Week—and all because of an Ohio homemaker named Olga Weber.

I know we're all busy with our homes and families. I know how hard you work and the long hours you keep, but I also know how desperately you want to be heard. I know how deeply you ache for your country and mourn the loss of the society that once supported families, reverenced God, and cherished freedom. I know you long to have those days back, and I know that's why you feel such a need to get involved, and yet, you wonder what you can possibly do to make a difference. But the fact is, it is you who has the greatest influence on society simply by being who you are!

Don't ever sell yourself short. There is no greater place where we have profound influence on the future of our country than in our own homes and families. Nurturing a love of liberty and virtue in the hearts of our children and grandchildren is how we will return to a culture of liberty, civility, and prosperity.

It is not extraordinary people who make this world better. Its ordinary people like you and me who stand up for what's right and do extraordinary things without even meaning to. And that is what makes you extraordinary!

RELATED QUOTES

"Ours is the only country deliberately founded on a good idea."
-John Gunther

"America is much more than a geographical fact. It is a political and moral fact—the first community in which men set out in principle to institutionalize freedom, responsible government, and human equality." **-Adlai Stevenson**

"Democracy and socialism have nothing in common but one word, equality. But notice the difference: while democracy seeks equality in liberty, socialism seeks equality in restraint and servitude." **-Alexis de Tocqueville**

"Americans are so enamored of equality that they would rather be equal in slavery than unequal in freedom." **-Alexis de Tocqueville**

"Collecting more taxes than is absolutely necessary is legalized robbery." **-Calvin Coolidge**

"To live under the American Constitution is the greatest political privilege that was ever accorded to the human race." **-Calvin Coolidge**

"One thing is clear: The Founding Fathers never intended a nation where citizens would pay nearly half of everything they earn to the government." **-Ron Paul**

"Don't interfere with anything in the Constitution. That must be maintained, for it is the only safeguard of our liberties." **-Abraham Lincoln**

"We the people are the rightful masters of both Congress and the courts, not to overthrow the Constitution but to overthrow the men who pervert the Constitution." **-Abraham Lincoln**

"The strength of the Constitution lies entirely in the determination of each citizen to defend it. Only if every single citizen feels duty bound to do his share in this defense are the constitutional rights secure." **-Albert Einstein**

FROM THE FOUNDERS

"I know no safe depository of the ultimate powers of the society but the people themselves; and if we think them not enlightened enough to exercise their control with a wholesome discretion, the remedy is not to take it from them, but to inform their discretion by education. This is the true corrective of abuses of constitutional power." **-Thomas Jefferson**

"There are more instances of the abridgment of the freedom of the people by gradual and silent encroachments of those in power than by violent and sudden usurpations." **-James Madison**

"There is nothing which I dread so much as a division of the republic into two great parties, each arranged under its leader, and concerting measures in opposition to each other. This, in my humble apprehension, is to be dreaded as the greatest political evil under our Constitution." **-John Adams**

Journal

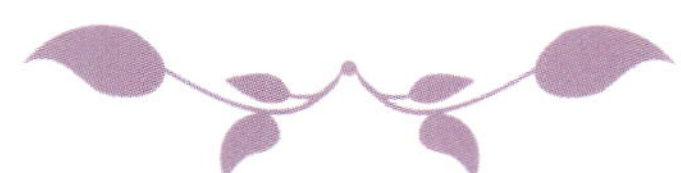

> *"Now this I say, he who sows sparingly will also reap sparingly, and he who sows bountifully will also reap bountifully."*
>
> –Corinthians 9:6

Law of the Harvest

But if any provide not for his own, and specially for those of his own house, he hath denied the faith, and is worse than an infidel.
-1 Timothy 5:8

PREPARATION

To prepare yourself to lead this presentation please review and consider the following material:

- Read "The Pilgrims Experiment" found in the Supplemental Materials of this presentation

- View the video *When the Cold Wind Blows* provided in the Hostess Resource Center on the Moms for America® website www.MomsforAmerica.us

- Read and Review Principles 7 and 25 of the *5000 Year Leap*

- See Bible References—Gen. 41: 54-47 & 47:13-25 (in Story Bible p. 77 & 92) Eccl. 3:13; 5:19, Jer. 29:5; Heb. 11:7

- Review quotes listed in the Supplemental Section of this presentation

PURPOSE

The purpose of this presentation is to introduce the concept of family reliance and escape government dependency. Participants will discover how a free people can use the principles of economics to gain prosperity. The most effective department of health, education, and welfare for the nation begins in the home.

KEY POINTS

- Self-reliance is the opposite of government dependency and is fundamental to preserving liberty

- The burden of debt is as destructive to freedom as subjugation by conquest

- The proper role of government is to provide equal rights, not equal things

Home Assignment

Read excerpt *"Fort Knox"* (link in Cottage Meeting Resources under "Law of the Harvest") Prepare a 2-week menu of foods your family normally eats. Begin a food storage plan with foods you already eat. Visit the Home Reliance resource page linked in Cottage Meeting Resources

Personal Study

Watch video "When the Cold Wind Blows

Read article "The Great Depression According to Milton Freedman"

View Milton Friedman video "Redistribution of Wealth"

Note: Links are in the Cottage Meeting Resource Center under "Law of the Harvest" on the MFA website

Family Enrichment

Family Garden As a family, plan and prepare a small garden or use containers to grow a few vegetables during the growing season. Starting from seedlings and going through the process to harvest is a great way to teach children about being prepared, the importance of work, nurturing plants, and reaping the fruits of our labors. It is also a great opportunity to liken the growing process to nurturing liberty.

MEETING OUTLINE

Welcome

We recommend starting your meeting with a prayer and the Pledge of Allegiance.

Show Video: *When the Cold Wind Blows* (available in Hostess Resource Center)

Read or Review "The Pilgrim's Experiment" with your group. The first colonies in America experimented with Communism. What was the result of this experiment? What were the results when a program of self-reliance and free-enterprise was adopted?

Group Discussion: Principles 7 and 25 of the *5000 Year Leap*

Review highlighted sections of Principle 7 of *5,000 Year Leap* and Vignettes 12.3, 12.13 and 1.6 of *Promises of the Constitution*

> *How does the entitlement philosophy interfere with independence and economic prosperity? What types of laws encourage prosperity?*

> *Why is it wrong to take from the "haves" to give to the "have-nots"?*

> *How did Benjamin Franklin describe counter-productive compassion? What was the Founder's Formula for calculated compassion? (See Principle 7, pages 119-121 and Vignette 7.6 and 12:14 of* Promises of the Constitution*)*

Review highlighted sections of Principle 25 of *5,000 Year Leap*

> *How does the burden of debt interfere with freedom? Does this apply only to individual debt or does it include national debt? What is the remedy for excessive debt?*

> *What can a family do today to become more self-reliant? (Read "Ideas for Becoming a Self-Reliant Family" available in the Supplemental Materials section)*

Summary

Summarize your thoughts on the material covered in this presentation.

- Give the Home Assignment for the next meeting

- Announce date, time and location for next meeting

ADDITIONAL PRESENTATION IDEAS

Proper Role of Government

Read "Not Yours to Give" by Davy Crockett. Review Principles 14 & 15 of the *5000 Year Leap*. Reference the quote by Davy Crockett "We have the right, as individuals, to give away as much of our own money as we please in charity; but as members of Congress, we have not right so to appropriate a dollar of public money.

Preparing in Times of Plenty: If we're prepared, we will not fear

Many people believe preparing for times of want is an act of unfaithfulness, believing that if we prepare, we don't have faith that God will provide for us. This is a complete misinterpretation of faith in the Lord. The Bible clearly testifies of the principle of providing for oneself and storing up for times of want. God helps those who help themselves.

Review Principles 5 and 27 of the *5000 Year Leap*.

Read and Review the following Bible References

- Joseph prepares for the seven-year famine Genesis 41: 33-57

- Parable of the Talents Matthew 25:14-30

- Genesis 3:19

- 1 Timothy 5:8 and 6:19

MINI COTTAGE IDEAS

Mini Cottages are designed especially for moms of preschoolers and moms who work full-time jobs. Moms simply read and/or watch the same materials at home, on their own, then meet together once a week in a playdate or over lunch during the workday to discuss what they read. The articles and videos are short and can usually be read and/or viewed in less than hour. Below are some suggestions to host mini cottage discussions under the "Law of the Harvest" theme.

- Read the story of Joseph in Egypt (Genesis 41:33-57) How can we prepare for times of famine?

- Visit the Home Reliance section of the Moms for America® website.

- Read "The Pilgrim's Experiment" in the Supplemental Materials section of this presentation

- View and discuss the video *When the Cold Wind Blows*

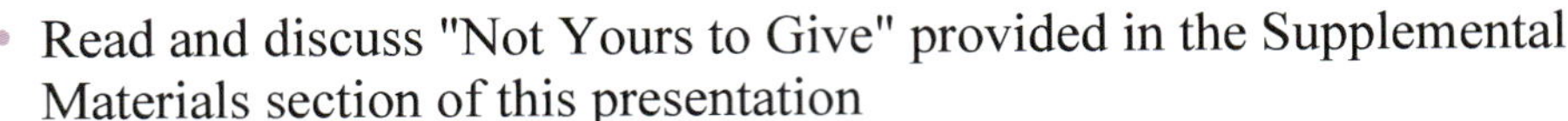

- Read and discuss "Not Yours to Give" provided in the Supplemental Materials section of this presentation

- Discuss ways you and your family can be prepared for difficult times such as natural disasters, increased food costs, loss of job, etc.

COTTAGE MEETING BOOK CLUB

For those who like the book club format, we've compiled a list of great books to help you gain an appreciation and foundational understanding of the concepts presented in "The Law of the Harvest."

The 5000 Year Leap: A Miracle That Changed the World

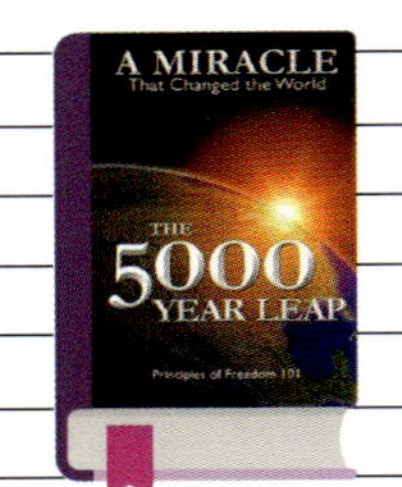

- Review Principles 7 and 25

Promises of the Constitution

- Review the following vignettes: 1.6, 7.6, 8.1, 12.3, 12.13, and 12.14

Warning to the West by Aleksandr Solzhenitsyn

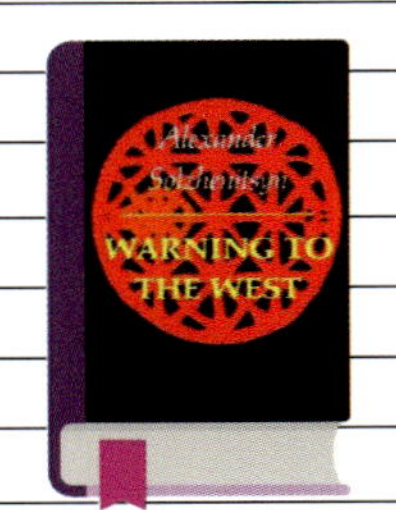

"Can one part of humanity learn from the bitter experience of another or can it not?"

During 1975 and 1976, Nobel Prize-winner Aleksandr Solzhenitsyn, who spent years in the Communist Gulag, embarked on a series of speeches across America and Britain that would shock and scandalize both countries. His message: the West was veering towards moral and spiritual bankruptcy and, with it, destroying the world's one hope against tyranny and totalitarianism.

From Solzhenitsyn's warnings about the allure of communism, to his rebuke that the West should not abandon its age-old concepts of 'good' and 'evil', the speeches collected in *Warning to the West* provide insight into Solzhenitsyn's uncompromising moral vision. Read today, the message of his speeches remains as powerfully urgent as when Solzhenitsyn first delivered them.

"Is it possible or impossible to warn someone of danger...to assess soberly the worldwide menace that threatens to swallow the whole world? I was swallowed myself. I have been in the dragon's belly, in its red-hot innards. It was unable to digest me and threw me up. I have come to you as a witness to what it is like there, in the dragon's belly."   -Aleksandr Solzhenitsyn

My Side of the Mountain by Jean Craighead George (great family read aloud)

Every kid thinks about running away at one point or another; few get farther than the end of the block. Young Sam Gribley gets to the end of the block and keeps going—all the way to the Catskill Mountains of upstate New York. With only a penknife, a ball of cord, forty dollars, and some flint and steel, he intends to survive on his own. With his wits as his greatest tool for survival, he sets up house in a huge hollowed-out tree. With a falcon and a weasel for companions, Sam learns about courage, danger, and independence during his year in the wilderness—a year that changes his life forever.

In a spellbinding, touching, funny account, Sam learns to live off the land and grows up a little in the process. Blizzards, hunters, loneliness, and fear all battle to drive Sam back to city life. But his desire for freedom, independence, and adventure is stronger. No reader will be immune to the compulsion to go right out and start whittling fishhooks and befriending raccoons. (Available through your public library and through Amazon)

Stories of the American Frontier (Freedom Series volume from Libraries of Hope)

A pioneer is "one who goes before, as into the wilderness, preparing the way for others to follow." Those rugged, daring men and women who braved unknown territories, for the most part, remain unnamed. These stories remind us the price that was paid for the comforts of life we now enjoy. You will see the world they faced through their eyes and words. You will also be given another face of the Indians. The stories that are most often told are stories of brutality and fierceness. Lesser told are the stories of their brave and noble chiefs and their words of honor and faith. Those stories, also, need to be told and remembered. Includes a sampling of stories taken from journals, diaries and letters and other sources (Available at Libraries of Hope www.LibrariesOfHope.com). The stories collected in this book make great little bedtime stories or stories to share at the dinner table to spark great conversations.

COTTAGE MEETING FOR KIDS

Cottage Meeting for Kids is a liberty promoting program for the entire family and focused on children from preschool to teens. It is full of great stories and fun activities to help children gain a love of liberty. Families can join together each month for an Activity Day to share the concepts they've learned and enhance them through group activities. Here are some ideas to promote the concepts presented in "Law of the Harvest." You can find additional ideas, outlines and activities on the Moms for America® website under "Cottage Meetings for Kids."

- Watch the video *When the Cold Wind Blows* and discuss ways you and your family can be prepared for difficult times such as natural disasters, increased food costs, loss of job, etc.

- Create a home storage rotation log, making a list of the items you use most

- Play *Monopoly* together as a family. Another great game is the *Game of Life*. This is a great way to teach children the value of money, savings, spending, etc. They will need to learn to make choice and prepare for unforeseen circumstances when they land on a property or are sent to jail.

- Read *My Side of the Mountain* with your children

- Read or tell the story of Joseph In Egypt and how he prepared for famine in times of plenty

Book & Movie List

Suggested books and readings for children all ages to nurture a love of liberty in the home.

Tuttle Twins Book Series
by Connor Boyack

The Thieves of Tyburn Square
by Dave Jackson

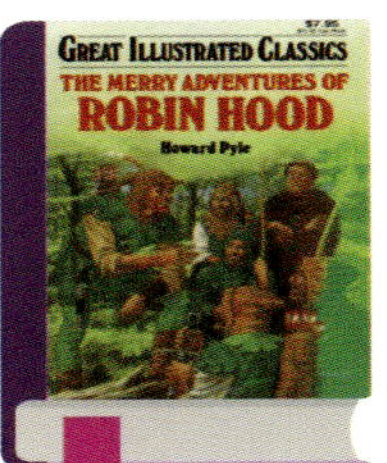

The Merry Adventures of Robin Hood
by Howard Pyle

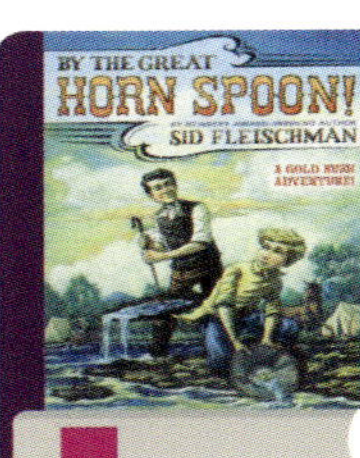

By the Great Horn Spoon
by Sid Fleischman

My Side of the Mountain
by Jean Craighead George

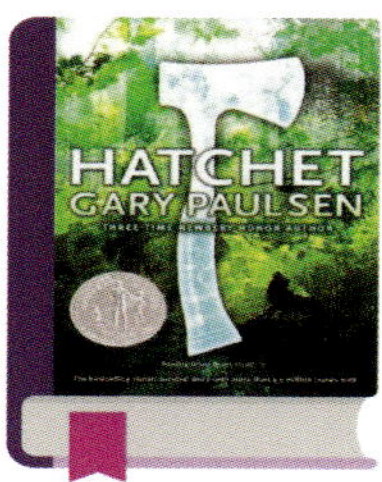

Hatchett
by Gary Paulsen

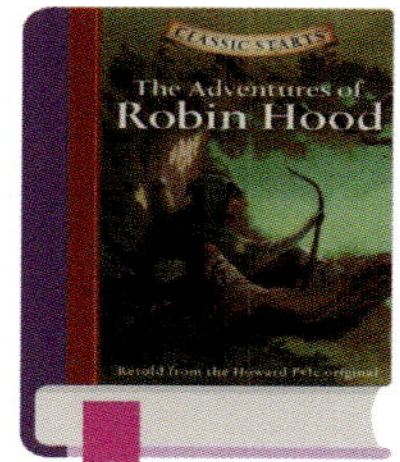

Adventures of Robin Hood
by Howard Pyle and John Burrows

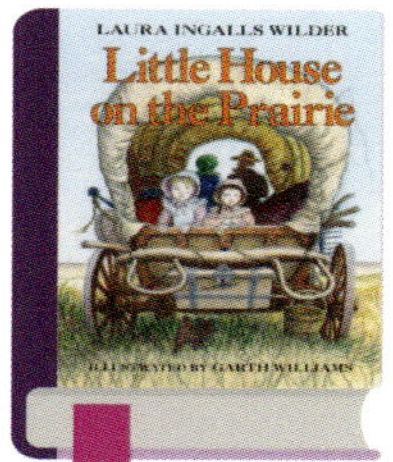

The Little House Series
by Laura Ingalls Wilder

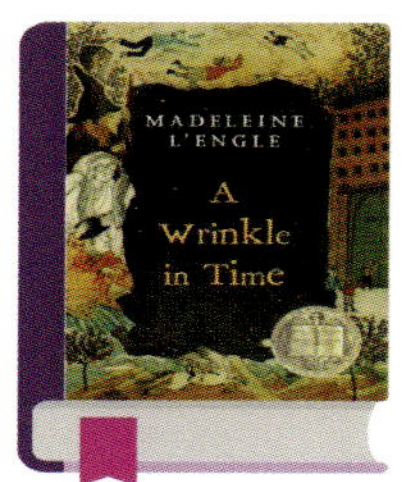

A Wrinkle in Time
by Madeleine L'Engl

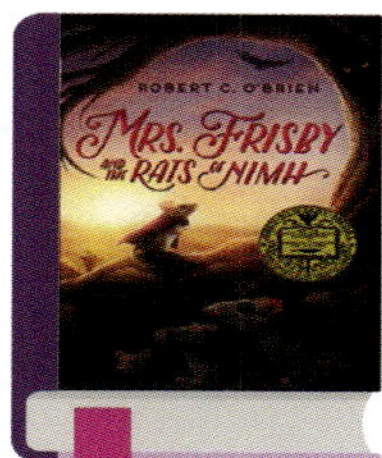

***Mrs. Frisby
and the Rats of Nimh***
by Robert c. O'brien

The Secret of Nimh
1982

Robin Hood
1973

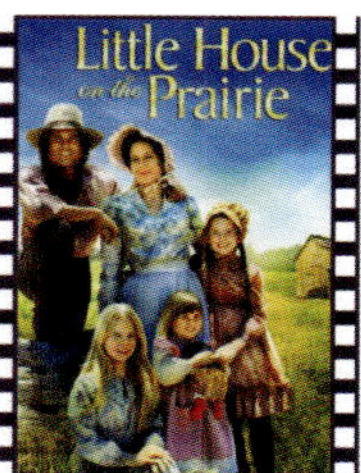

Little House on the Prairie
1974-1983

My Side of the Mountain
1969

A Wrinkle in Time
2003

The Pilgrim's Experiment

From the very beginning of our nation, we were a unique people. We were unique because we came to America to seek a better life. America was a new frontier. It was a place where new things could be tried, and the survival of the Colonists who came here depended on trying new things. The old things just didn't work in the New World, and God never intended them to.

The people of America had an intimate knowledge of the Bible, which told them who they were, what their rights were, and from whence those rights came. They believed that not only could they govern and provide for themselves but that, according to God, they were expected to.

It was the pilgrims who first introduced the concept of freedom to America, for it was they who discovered it. The experiences they had in that little colony were a living tutorial on the principles and blessings of freedom, the responsibility to maintain it, and the prosperity that flows from it. One might wonder why the Plymouth Colony faired so well so quickly when the Jamestown Colony struggled with want and starvation for so long. Why was it that the Pilgrims were able to make peace with their Indian neighbors and the Jamestown colonists were constantly at war with them?

The reason is rooted in each colony's purpose for coming to the new world. The Jamestown colonists came seeking gold. The pilgrims came seeking freedom to worship. The matter of purpose may seem like insignificant trivia to us, but when you understand the history of the colonies, you realize just how much that difference made in the establishment of America and freedom itself.

The people in both colonies had been brought up in the same European feudal system. Both came from the same country. But the purpose with which the Pilgrims came made them more desirous to treat each other as equals. The Jamestown colonists came with their feudal classes with every intention of establishing a colony with those same classes firmly in place. The Lords and nobles expected the

peasants and crew to do the work building homes, planting fields, and searching for their illusive gold. Their job, of course, was to govern and reap the fruits of the underclass's labors.

That may have worked out fine in England, but in America, if everyone didn't work, everyone starved. That was a lesson that took the Jamestown colonists many tortuous years of war and hunger to realize, and when they didn't have enough food, they just took it from the Indians, which escalated their miseries even further. But the Pilgrims struggled as well. They too faced death and starvation, so why did their colony succeed so well so quickly when the Jamestown colony suffered for decades? The answer is human energy.

The Pilgrims came to America seeking freedom, but they also knew they needed order. You don't just start a colony with no kind of organization or law. So, before they even set foot on land, the Pilgrims organized a government with the signing of the Mayflower Compact—a document that guaranteed just and equal laws to govern all residents of the community, regardless of their religious convictions. The concepts contained in the Compact were all based on Biblical reasoning, which the Pilgrims had become very familiar with as they read the Bible together with their families every day.

The first thing the Pilgrims did when they landed was build a common house where the people could worship and gather. Once that was done, they began building individual homes and planting crops. Everyone worked together as a community. No one owned anything, but the community owned everything. Everyone was given a job to do for the community. Those who were designated to do laundry did the laundry for the entire community, just as those who did the planning, building, and cooking. Everything came from the community, everything went to the community, and everyone received an equal share. It was, in fact, the first experiment in Christian Communism. It seemed the perfect expression of brotherly love. Why wouldn't the pilgrims, who were such devout witnesses of Christ, want to serve their neighbors in this way? But the Pilgrims learned very quickly that their communal idea could not sustain their fledgling colony.

William Bradford, who became Governor of the Colony, explained the results of their experiment in his diary. He said young able-bodied men, who were perfectly fit to work, complained that they were expected to spend their time and strength to work for other men's women and children with no compensation whatsoever. They felt it was terribly unjust. What incentive did they have to put in a hard day's work? So, the women started feigning sickness and there was a sudden epidemic of "bad backs" among the men. Everyone received an equal portion of food and goods regardless of how much work they did, so why would they work harder? Why would they work at all?

The result of their experiment was less production, which led to less rations to share. While it wasn't the same kind of society that Jamestown had established, the results were just as devastating. Half of the Pilgrims died during the first winter, including William Bradford's wife. He witnessed firsthand what a costly and destructive mistake their experiment in collectivism had been. The Pilgrims learned a valuable lesson from the experience. They realized that socialism gave no incentive to the most creative and industrious among them to work any harder than anyone else. Collectivism had prevented the exercise of personal motivation. It had stifled human energy!

So, after dabbling in collectivism, socialism, and communism, the colonists decided to try a new experiment—self-reliance. With the aid of their Indian neighbors, they learned how to produce better crops and harvest more fish. They completely did away with their communal disbursements by assigning all members private property rights of land as well as the right to profit from their own industry. What happened next was a sudden robust release of human energy that proved to all of Europe you could make a good home in America. It was the first experiment in Christian Capitalism, and it was a huge success! The Pilgrims became more industrious than even they imagined they could. They planted more corn, built more homes and churches, opened shops, organized trade and, true to the word their word, paid off the London sponsors who had made their journey to America possible.

So, what made the difference? Why did the Pilgrims succeed so well in their experiment with Capitalism and fail so miserably under their

experiment with Communism? In each instance the Pilgrims had a Christian heart and purpose; in each, they had a will to survive, but in the first they were totally okay with others providing for their survival, and in the second, they worked like dogs to provide for their own. So, what changed? Was it a desire to turn a profit? Was it fear of starvation? No. It was because now they had a personal interest and personal stake, and suddenly, they cared.

The Pilgrims had no problem being slothful when it was for "the community's" benefit; but when the responsibility for their own family's survival was put square on their shoulders, and they knew their family would benefit from their own labors, they immediately had a deep desire to give it everything they had. Their work had a purpose, and it became very personal—it became a matter of the heart. There is no greater incentive than that. Their hearts were infused with a desire to succeed, and Human Energy sprang forth at mammoth proportions, blessing not only their own families but the entire colony. Johann Goethe once said, "If everyone swept his own porch, the whole town would be clean." The Pilgrims swept their own porches, so to speak, and the whole colony thrived.

So the purposes for which the Plymouth and Jamestown colonies operated is not just insignificant trivia; it is, in fact, profoundly relevant. While Jamestown continued for decades to rely on Europe for supply ships for their survival, Plymouth became a source of supplies for Europe. It was the success of Plymouth, not the establishment of Jamestown, which initiated the "Great Puritan Migration" leading to the rapid colonization of America. It literally was a matter of the heart.

Human Energy is directly related to the heart. Seeking riches and fame can only take you so far. If you are truly going to extend your human energy to its greatest degree, it has to become a matter of the heart. And it is to the heart that we, the authors, wish to speak.

We have been told over and over that there is an energy crisis in America—in the world, for that matter—and we, at Moms for America, wholeheartedly agree. We are in the worst energy crisis ever—a Human Energy Crisis! We live in a nation where We the People govern, We the People produce, We the People create, but there is a serious lack of creation, production, and governing being done on our part. Why? Because we have lost our incentive. It is no longer personal. Human energy is the energy output from the heart, and too many hearts have become cold.

As previously stated, there is a direct correlation between human energy and the heart. When our heart is filled with truth, virtue, and beauty, the outpouring of our energy in our time, talents, and the choices we make reflects what is in our hearts. When we are inspired by a story, a song, a piece of art, or the recognition of a truth, we have a greater desire to do better, to be better, to work harder. Or in other words, we increase our human energy. When human energy increases, we see a rise in knowledge, wisdom, compassion, innovation, joy, peace, enlightenment, selfless service, discernment, and true education—as free men and women seek for a better life.

The opposite of inspire is to hinder, deter, depress, or discourage. When these things are present, the energy output of the heart decreases and we see a rise in depression, anger, selfishness, fear, grief, apathy, and shame. When people are governed by fear, they are reactive to their external environment—they become more irritable, explosive, and oversensitive and we see an increase in addictions, obsessions, and greed.

Is that not what we are seeing in the world today?

American Author David Starr Jordan has stated:

"If the experiment of government by the people is to be successful, it is you and such as you who must make it so. The future of the Republic must lie in the hands of the men and women of culture and intelligence, of self-control and of self-resource, capable of taking care of themselves and of helping others. If it falls not into such hands, the republic will have no future.... The problem of life is not to make life easier, but to make men stronger, so that no problem shall be beyond their solution....The remedy for oppression is to bring in better men who cannot be oppressed."

The human will is the strongest energy in the universe. It is time we release it and put an end to the debilitating energy crisis once and for all.

Ideas for Becoming Self-Reliant

Our Founding Fathers knew that home and family life sets the tempo for society. Whatever happens in the home is carried into the community. If there are strong, peaceful family relationships, there will be a strong, peaceful society. On the other hand, if the family is in turmoil, those problems are carried directly into society and create problems no government can manage. When families are prepared and work together to become self-reliant, our entire nation benefits.

We become self-reliant through obtaining sufficient knowledge, education, and literacy; by managing money and resources wisely, being spiritually strong, preparing for emergencies and unforeseen circumstances (such as job loss), and by having physical health and social and emotional well-being. Below are some ideas to help your family become more self-reliant.

- Create a basic first-aid kit

- Prepared a 72 hour emergency kit

- Try a new recipe with a food item that has a long shelf-life. Such as wheat pancakes, oatmeal, home made tortillas, rice and beans, etc.

- Prepare a small garden space or use containers to grow a few vegetables during the growing season

- Avoid debt: spending less than you make is essential to financial security; avoid debt as much as possible and when you do need to go into debt for essential items, such as a home, or education, pay off the debt as soon as possible

- Use a budget: keep a record of monthly income and expenses and determine how to reduce what you spend on non-essentials; when you have and use a budget, you are much more likely to spend wisely and ensure your family's needs are met before wants are addressed

- Have a cash reserve (it is recommended to have a minimum of $200.00 in cash on hand and a cash savings equivalent to 3 month's pay)

- Begin a food storage plan with foods you already eat and determine the shelf-life of the ingredients required for the meals your family eats most often. How long can you store these ingredients before they go bad? Are there some complete menus where all the necessary foods can be stored for several months?

Davey Crockett: Not Yours to Give

PUBLISHED IN HARPER'S MAGAZINE IN 1867, AS WRITTEN BY JAMES J. BETHUNE, A PSEUDONYM USED BY EDWARD S. ELLIS

The events that are recounted here are true, including Crockett's opposition to the bill in question, though the precise rendering and some artistic liberty has been taken..

One day in the House of Representatives, a bill was taken up appropriating money for the benefit of a widow of a distinguished naval officer. Several beautiful speeches had been made in its support. The Speaker was just about to put the question when Davy Crockett arose:

"Mr. Speaker—I have as much respect for the memory of the deceased, and as much sympathy for the sufferings of the living, if suffering there be, as any man in this House, but we must not permit our respect for the dead or our sympathy for a part of the living to lead us into an act of injustice to the balance of the living. I will not go into an argument to prove that Congress has no power to appropriate this money as an act of charity. Every member upon this floor knows it. We have the right, as individuals, to give away as much of our own money as we please in charity; but as members of Congress we have no right to appropriate a dollar of the public money. Some eloquent appeals have been made to us upon the ground that it is a debt due the deceased. Mr. Speaker, the deceased lived long after the close of the war; he was in office to the day of his death, and I have never heard that the government was in arrears to him.

"Every man in this House knows it is not a debt. We cannot, without the grossest corruption, appropriate this money as the payment of a debt. We have not the semblance of authority to appropriate it as a charity. Mr. Speaker, I have said we have the right to give as much money of our own as we please. I am the poorest man on this floor. I cannot vote for this bill, but I will give one week's pay to the object, and if every member of Congress will do the same, it will amount to more than the bill asks."

He took his seat. Nobody replied. The bill was put upon its passage, and instead of passing unanimously, as was generally supposed, and as, no doubt, it would but for that speech, it received but few votes and, of course, was lost.

Later, when asked by a friend why he had opposed the appropriation, Crockett gave this explanation:

"Several years ago, I was one evening standing on the steps of the Capitol with some other members of Congress when our attention was attracted by a great light over in Georgetown. It was evidently a large fire. We jumped into a hack and drove over as fast as we could. In spite of all that could be done, many houses were burned and many families made homeless and, besides, some of them had lost all but the clothes they had on. The weather was very cold, and when I saw so many women and children suffering, I felt that something ought to be done for them. The next morning, a bill was introduced appropriating $20,000 for their relief. We put aside all other business and rushed it through as soon as it could be done.

"The next summer, when it began to be time to think about the election, I concluded I would take a scout around among the boys of my district. I had no opposition there, but as the election was some time off, I did not know what might turn up. When riding one day in a part of my district in which I was more of a stranger than any other, I saw a man in a field plowing and coming toward the road. I gauged my gait so that we should meet as he came to the fence. As he came up, I

spoke to the man. He replied politely but, as I thought, rather coldly.

"I began: 'Well, friend, I am one of those unfortunate beings called candidates, and-'

"'Yes, I know you; you are Colonel Crockett, I have seen you once before and voted for you the last time you were elected. I suppose you are out electioneering now, but you had better not waste your time or mine. I shall not vote for you again.'

"This was a sockdolager…I begged him to tell me what was the matter.

"'Well, Colonel, it is hardly worth-while to waste time or words upon it. I do not see how it can be mended, but you gave a vote last winter which shows that either you have not capacity to understand the Constitution or that you are wanting in the honesty and firmness to be guided by it. In either case, you are not the man to represent me. But I beg your pardon for expressing it in that way. I did not intend to avail myself of the privilege of the constituent to speak plainly to a candidate for the purpose

of insulting or wounding you. I intend by it only to say that your understanding of the Constitution is very different from mine; and I will say to you what, but for my rudeness, I should not have said, that I believe you to be honest….But an understanding of the Constitution different from mine I cannot overlook, because the Constitution, to be worth anything, must be held sacred and rigidly observed in all its provisions. The man who wields power and misinterprets it is the more dangerous the more honest he is.'

"'I admit the truth of all you say, but there must be some mistake about it, for I do not remember that I gave any vote last winter upon any constitutional question.'

"'No, Colonel, there's no mistake. Though I live here in the backwoods and seldom go from home, I take the papers from Washington and read very carefully all the proceedings of Congress. My papers say that last winter you voted for a bill to appropriate $20,000 to some sufferers by a fire in Georgetown. Is that true?'

"'Well, my friend; I may as well own up. You have got me there. But certainly nobody will complain that a great and rich country like ours should give the insignificant sum of $20,000 to relieve its suffering women and children, particularly with a full and overflowing Treasury, and I am sure, if you had been there, you would have done just as I did.'

"'It is not the amount, Colonel, that I complain of; it is the principle. In the first place, the government ought to have in the Treasury no more than enough for its legitimate purposes. But that has nothing to do with the question. The power of collecting and disbursing money at pleasure is the most dangerous power that can be entrusted to man, particularly under our system of collecting revenue by a tariff, which reaches every man in the country, no matter how poor he may be, and the poorer he is, the more he pays in proportion to his means. What is worse, it presses upon him without his knowledge where the weight centers, for there is not a man in the United States who can ever guess how much he pays to the government. So you see, that while you are contributing to relieve one, you are drawing it from thousands who are even worse off than he.

"'If you had the right to give anything, the amount was simply a matter of discretion with you, and you had as much right to give $20,000,000 as $20,000. If you have the right to give to one, you have the right to give to all; and, as the Constitution neither defines charity nor stipulates the amount, you are at liberty to give to any and everything which you may believe, or profess to believe, is a charity, and to any amount you may think proper. You will very easily perceive what a wide door this would open for fraud and corruption and favoritism, on the one hand, and for robbing the people on the other. No, Colonel, Congress has no right to give charity.

"'Individual members may give as much of their own money as they please, but they have no right to touch a dollar of the public money for that purpose. If twice as many houses had been burned in this county as in Georgetown, neither you nor any other member of Congress would have thought of appropriating a dollar for our relief. There are about two hundred and forty members of Congress. If they had shown their sympathy for the sufferers by contributing each one week's pay, it would have made over $13,000. There are plenty of wealthy men in and around Washington who could have given $20,000 without depriving themselves of even a luxury of life. The congressmen chose to keep their own money, which, if reports be true, some of them spend not very creditably; and the people about Washington, no doubt, applauded you for relieving them from the necessity of giving by giving what was not yours to give. The people have delegated to Congress, by the Constitution, the power to do certain things. To do these, it is authorized to collect and pay moneys, and for nothing else. Everything beyond this is usurpation and a violation of the Constitution.

"'So you see, Colonel, you have violated the Constitution in what I consider a vital point. It is a precedent fraught with danger to the country, for when Congress once begins to stretch its power beyond the limits of the Constitution, there is no limit to it, and no security for the people. I have no doubt you acted honestly, but that does not make it any better, except as far as you are personally concerned, and you see that I cannot vote for you.'

"I tell you I felt streaked. I saw if I should have opposition, and this man should go to talking, he would set others to talking, and in that district I was a gone fawn-skin. I could not answer him, and the fact is, I was so fully convinced that he was right, I did not want to. But I must satisfy him, and I said to him:

"'Well, my friend, you hit the nail upon the head when you said I had not sense enough to understand the Constitution. I intended to be guided by it, and thought I had studied it fully. I have heard many speeches in Congress about the powers of Congress, but what you have said here at your plow has got more hard, sound sense in it than all the fine speeches I ever heard. If I had ever taken the view of it that you have, I would have put my head into the fire before I would have given that vote; and if you will forgive me and vote for me again, if I ever vote for another unconstitutional law, I wish I may be shot.'

"He laughingly replied: 'Yes, Colonel, you have sworn to that once before, but I will trust you again upon one condition. You say that you are convinced that your vote was wrong. Your acknowledgment of it will do more good than beating you for it. If, as you go around the district, you will tell people about this vote, and that you are satisfied it was wrong, I will

not only vote for you but will do what I can to keep down opposition, and perhaps, I may exert some little influence in that way.'

"'If I don't,' said I, 'I wish I may be shot; and to convince you that I am in earnest in what I say, I will come back this way in a week or ten days, and if you will get up a gathering of the people, I will make a speech to them. Get up a barbecue, and I will pay for it.'

"'No, Colonel, we are not rich people in this section, but we have plenty of provisions to contribute for a barbecue and some to spare for those who have none. The push of crops will be over in a few days, and we can then afford a day for a barbecue. This is Thursday; I will see to getting it up on Saturday week. Come to my house on Friday, and we will go together, and I promise you a very respectable crowd to see and hear you.'

"'Well, I will be here. But one thing more before I say good-by. I must know your name.'

"'My name is Bunce.'

"'Not Horatio Bunce?'

"'Yes.'

"'Well, Mr. Bunce, I never saw you before, though you say you have seen me, but I know you very well. I am glad I have met you and very proud that I may hope to have you for my friend.'

"It was one of the luckiest hits of my life that I met him. He mingled but little with the public but was widely known for his remarkable intelligence and incorruptible integrity and for a heart brimful and running over with kindness and benevolence, which showed themselves not only in words but in acts. He was the oracle of the whole country around him, and his fame had extended far beyond the circle of his immediate acquaintance. Though I had never met him before, I had heard much of him, and but for this meeting, it is very likely I should have had opposition and had been beaten. One thing is very certain, no man could now stand up in that district under such a vote.

"At the appointed time, I was at his house, having told our conversation to every crowd I had met and to every man I stayed all night with, and I found that it gave the people an interest and a confidence in me stronger than I had ever seen manifested before.

"Though I was considerably fatigued when I reached his house and, under ordinary circumstances, should have gone early to bed, I kept him up until midnight talking about the principles and affairs of government and got more real, true knowledge of them than I had got all my life before.

"I have known and seen much of him since, for I respect him—no, that is not the word—I reverence and love him more than any living man, and I go to see him two or three times every year; and I will tell you, sir, if every one who professes to be a Christian lived and acted and enjoyed it as he does, the religion of Christ would take the world by storm.

"But to return to my story. The next morning, we went to the barbecue and, to my surprise, found about a thousand men there. I met a good many whom I had not known before, and they and my friend introduced me around until I had got pretty well acquainted—at least, they all knew me.

"In due time, notice was given that I would speak to them. They gathered up around a stand that had been erected. I opened my speech by saying:

"'Fellow citizens—I present myself before you today feeling like a new man. My eyes have lately been opened to truths which ignorance or prejudice, or both, had heretofore hidden from my view. I feel that I can today offer you the ability to render you more valuable service than I have ever been able to render before. I am here today more for the purpose of acknowledging my error than to seek your votes. That I should make this acknowledgment is due to myself as well as to you. Whether you will vote for me is a matter for your consideration only.'

"I went on to tell them about the fire and my vote for the appropriation and then told them why I was satisfied it was wrong. I closed by saying:

"'And now, fellow citizens, it remains only for me to tell you that the most of the speech you have listened to with so much interest was simply a repetition of the arguments by which your neighbor, Mr. Bunce, convinced me of my error.

"'It is the best speech I ever made in my life, but he is entitled to the credit for it. And now I hope he is satisfied with his convert and that he will get up here and tell you so.'

"He came upon the stand and said:

CROCKETT MAKING A CHARACTERISTIC CANVASS.

"'Fellow citizens—It affords me great pleasure to comply with the request of Colonel Crockett. I have always considered him a thoroughly honest man, and I am satisfied that he will faithfully perform all that he has promised you today.'

"He went down, and there went up from that crowd such a shout for Davy Crockett as his name never called forth before.

"I am not much given to tears, but I was taken with a choking then and felt some big drops rolling down my cheeks. And I tell you now that the remembrance of those few words spoken by such a man, and the honest, hearty shout they produced, is worth more to me than all the honors I have received and all the reputation I have ever made, or ever shall make, as a member of Congress.

"Now, sir," concluded Crockett, "you know why I made that speech yesterday.

"There is one thing now to which I will call your attention. You remember that I proposed to give a week's pay. There are in that House many very wealthy men—men who think nothing of spending a week's pay, or a dozen of them, for a dinner or a wine party when they have something to accomplish by it. Some of those same men made beautiful speeches upon the great debt of gratitude which the country owed the deceased—a debt which could not be paid by money—and the insignificance and worthlessness of money, particularly so insignificant a sum as $10,000 when weighted against the honor of the nation. Yet not one of them responded to my proposition. Money with them is nothing but trash when it is to come out of the people. But it is the one great thing for which most of them are striving, and many of them sacrifice honor, integrity, and justice to obtain it."

RELATED QUOTES

"Most of the major ills of the world have been caused by well-meaning people who ignored the principle of individual freedom, except as applied to themselves, and who were obsessed with fanatical zeal to improve the lot of mankind-in-the-mass through some pet formula of their own....the harm done by ordinary criminals, murderers, gangsters, and thieves is negligible in comparison with the agony inflicted up human beings by the professional 'Do-Gooders', who attempt to set themselves up as gods on earth and who would ruthlessly force their views on all others—with the abiding assurance that the end justifies the means."
-Henry Grady Weaver, The Mainspring of Human Progress

"I wish it need not have happened in my time," said Frodo.

"So do I," said Gandalf, "and so do all who live to see such times. But that is not for them to decide. All we have to decide is what to do with the time that is given us."
-J.R.R. Tolkien, The Fellowship of the Ring

"Liberty means responsibility. That is why most men dread it."
-George Bernard Shaw

"Ask not what your country can do for you; ask what you can do for your country."
-John F. Kennedy

"Property is the fruit of labor—property is desirable—it is a positive good in the world. That some should be rich, shows that others may become rich, and hence is just encouragement to industry and enterprise. Let not who is houseless pull down the house of another; but let him labor diligently and build one for himself, thus by example assuring that his own shall be safe from violence..."
-Abraham Lincoln

"Collecting more taxes than is absolutely necessary is legalized robbery."
-Calvin Coolidge

"And that food shall be for store to the land against the seven years of famine, which shall be in the land of Egypt; that the land perish not through the famine." **-Genesis 41:36**

FROM THE FOUNDERS

"The multiplication of public offices, increase of expense beyond income, growth and entailment of a public debt, are indications soliciting the employment of the pruning knife."
-Thomas Jefferson

"[A] wise and frugal government... shall restrain men from injuring one another, shall leave them otherwise free to regulate their own pursuits of industry and improvement, and shall not take from the mouth of labor the bread it has earned. This is the sum of good government."
-Thomas Jefferson

"These are the times that try men's souls. The summer soldier and the sunshine patriot will, in this crisis, shrink from the service of their country; but he that stands it now, deserves the love and thanks of man and woman. Tyranny, like hell, is not easily conquered; yet we have this consolation with us, that the harder the conflict, the more glorious the triumph. What we obtain too cheap, we esteem too lightly. Heaven knows how to put a proper price upon its goods; and it would be strange indeed, if so celestial an article as Freedom should not be highly rated."
-Thomas Paine

"To take from one, because it is thought his own industry and that of his fathers has acquired too much, in order to spare to others, who, or whose fathers, have not exercised equal industry and skill, is to violate arbitrarily the first principle of association, the guarantee to everyone the free exercise of his industry and the fruits acquired by it."
-Thomas Jefferson

"Industry pays Debts, Despair increases them."
-Ben Franklin

"A wise and frugal government, which shall restrain men from injuring one another; shall leave them otherwise free to regulate their own pursuits of industry and improvement."
-Thomas Jefferson

"We must not let our rulers load us with perpetual debt. We must make our selection between economy and liberty or profusion and servitude."
-Thomas Jefferson

"A departure from principle becomes a precedent for a second; that second for a third; and so on, till the bulk of society is reduced to mere automations of misery, to have no sensibilities left but for sinning and suffering... And the fore horse of this frightful team is public debt. Taxation follows that, and in it's train wretchedness and oppression."
-Thomas Jefferson

"I think we have more machinery of government than is necessary, too many parasites living on the labor of the industrious."
-Thomas Jefferson

"It is incumbent on every generation to pay its own debts as it goes. A principle which if acted on would save one-half the wars of the world."
-Thomas Jefferson

"Equal rights for all, special privileges for none."
-Thomas Jefferson

"History records that the money changers have used every form of abuse, intrigue, deceit, and violent means possible to maintain their control over governments by controlling the money and its issuance."
-James Madison

"The democracy will cease to exist when you take away from those who are willing to work and give to those who would not."
-Thomas Jefferson

"I, however, place the economy among the first and most important republican virtues, and public debt as the greatest of the dangers to be feared." **-Thomas Jefferson**

"Does the government fear us? Or do we fear the government? When the people fear the government, tyranny has found victory. The federal government is our servant, not our master!"
-Thomas Jefferson

"Experience hath shewn, that even under the best forms of government those entrusted with power have, in time, and by slow operations, perverted it into tyranny."
-Thomas Jefferson

"A true patriot will defend his country from its government. "
-Thomas Jefferson

"Children should be educated and instructed in the principles of freedom." **-John Adams**

If ye love wealth better than liberty, the tranquility of servitude than the animated contest of freedom, go from us in peace. We ask not your counsels or arms. Crouch down and lick the hands which feed you. May your chains sit lightly upon you, and may posterity forget that you were our countrymen! **-Samuel Adams** (though this quote may seem harsh, it gives a clear indication of how passionate the founders were about freedom)

"If men through fear, fraud or mistake, should in terms renounce and give up any essential natural right, the eternal law of reason and the great end of society, would absolutely vacate such renunciation; the right to freedom being the gift of God Almighty, it is not in the power of Man to alienate this gift, and voluntarily become a slave."
-John Adams

"Since the general civilization of mankind, I believe there are more instances of the abridgment of the freedom of the people by gradual and silent encroachments of those in power than by violent and sudden usurpations." **-James Madison**

Journal

"Children are the living messages we send to a time we will not see."
-Neil Postman

Raising a New Generation of Patriots

The boys [and girls] of the rising generation are to be the men [and women] of the next, and the sole guardians of the principles we deliver over to them.

-Thomas Jefferson

PREPARATION

To prepare yourself to lead this presentation please review and consider the following material:

- Read "Mother's Garden" and "The Urgent Need to Teach the Constitution to the Rising Generation" found in the supplemental materials of this presentation.

- View the video *Raising A Generation of Patriots* provided in the Hostess Resource Center on the Moms for America® website www.MomsforAmerica.us

- Review Principles 23 and 26 in the *5000 Year Leap*.

- Review the quotes provided in the supplemental materials section.

PURPOSE

The purpose of this presentation is to introduce activities and learning experiences that can be used to teach the next generation. Whether your family participates in public school, private school, or home school, this presentation will boost your confidence in educating and inspiring the next generation about the principles of liberty.

KEY POINTS

- Education in a free Republic includes religion, morality, and knowledge

- Parents have the sovereign stewardship to guide their children's educational journey

- A free society cannot survive as a Republic without a broad program of general education in civics, liberty, and patriotism

Home Assignment

Watch the *"Thomas Jefferson Education"* Videos Series (in Cottage Meeting Resource Center) If possible, retain a copy of the book *A Thomas Jefferson Education* by Oliver DeMille and read prior to the next meeting

Personal Study

Read *A Thomas Jefferson Education* by Oliver DeMille (other excellent books in this series are *The TJED Home Companion* and *TJED for Teens*)

Family Enrichment

Gather with other families to start a Cottage Meetings for Kids group. There are fun activities that go along with each presentation in the Cottage Meeting Resource Guide as well as additional resources we recommend for raising patriots.

MEETING OUTLINE

Welcome & Gathering

We recommend starting your meeting with a prayer and the Pledge of Allegiance.

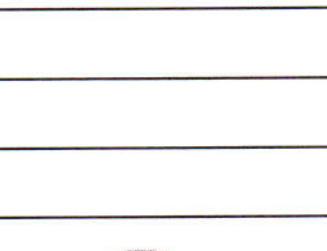

Show Video: *Raising A Generation of Patriots* (available in Hostess Resource Center)

> *Who is responsible and accountable to God for the education of the next generation? What power and influence does a parent have over the education of a child? (See Psalms 78: 1-8) How does what is taught and nurtured in the home impact society?*

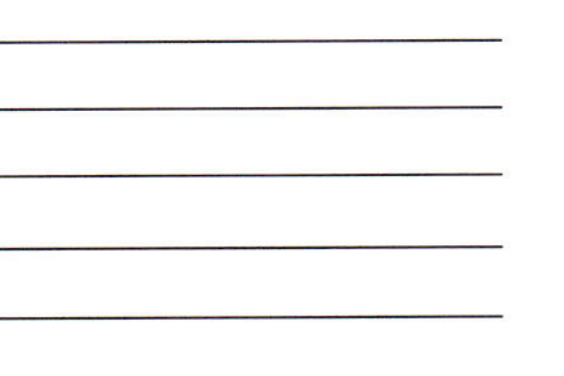

Group Discussion

Reference and review the highlighted sections of Principles 23 and 24 from the *5000 Year Leap* when leading the discussion.

> *Parents have a God-given right to guide their children's educational journey. What boundaries must government's work within as they seek to provide education opportunities for citizens? (see Principle 26)*

> *How did the Founder's propose to educate the general population? Why were local school boards successful? What did early educational curriculum include? (See Principle 23)*

> *What is the Northwest Ordinance and what did it require be included in public school curriculum? (See Vignette 7.8 from Promises of the Constitution)*

Read & Discuss "A Mother's Garden" (available in the Supplemental Materials section)

> *What can parents do in their own homes to educate their families in the principles of liberty? (See Vignettes 13.4, 13.5, and 13.7 from Promises of the Constitution)*

Summarize "The Urgent Need to Teach the Constitution to the Rising Generation" (available in the supplemental materials section of this presentation)

> *What educational options and opportunities are available to families? How can we teach and promote the principles of liberty and a free society in our home? What resources are available to us?*

Summary

Summarize your thoughts on the material covered in this presentation.

- Give the Home Assignment for the next meeting

- Announce date, time, and location for next meeting

ADDITIONAL PRESENTATION IDEAS

Raising George Washingtons

Read and Discuss "Raising George Washingtons" (available in the supplemental materials section of this presentation) What is the difference between a politician and a statesman? How can parents raise a statesman? How can we be statesmen ourselves? (visit the hostess resource center for ideas, suggestions, and other resources to consider)

Parents Must Become the First Line of Defense, devoting time and effort to teaching our children that America is a good country and to teach them about American heroes and history. We can front-load liberty loving values through strong association and participation in the 4th of July and Memorial Day activities. We need to teach our children how liberty and personal responsibility are linked and how tyranny can evolve without them. We can't preserve what we don't know we have.

MINI COTTAGE IDEAS

Mini Cottages are designed especially for moms of preschoolers and moms who work full-time jobs. Moms simply read and/or watch the same materials at home, on their own, then meet together once a week in a playdate or over lunch during the workday to discuss what they read. The articles and videos are short and can usually be read and/or viewed in less than hour. Below are some suggestions to host mini cottage discussions under the "Raising Patriots" theme.

- Read and Discuss "Coming Full Circle" provided in the supplemental materials section of this presentation

- Read and Discuss "The Urgent Need to Teach the Constitution to the Rising Generation" provided in the supplemental materials section of this presentation

- Read and Discuss "Raising George Washingtons" provided in the supplemental materials section of this presentation. What is the difference between a statesmen and a politician? How do we raise statesmen in our homes? How can we be statesmen ourselves?

COTTAGE MEETING BOOK CLUB

For those who like the book club format, we've compiled a list of great books to help you gain an appreciation and foundational understanding of the concepts presented in "Raising A New Generation of Patriots."

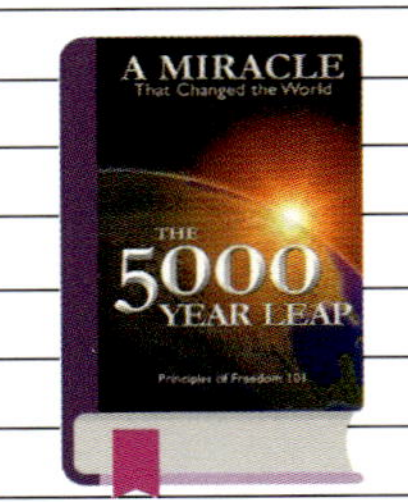

The 5000 Year Leap: A Miracle That Changed the World

- Review Principles 23 and 26

Promises of the Constitution

Review the following vignettes:

- Read vignettes 13.3, 13.4, 13.5, 13.7, and 13.8

A Thomas Jefferson Education by Oliver DeMille

Is American education preparing the future leaders our nation needs or merely struggling to teach basic literacy and job skills? Without leadership education, are we settling for an inadequate system that delivers educational, industrial, governmental, and societal mediocrity? In *A Thomas Jefferson Education: Teaching a Generation of Leaders for the Twenty-first Century*, Oliver DeMille presents a new educational vision based on proven methods that really work! Teachers, students, parents, educators, legislators, leaders, and everyone who cares about America's future must read this compelling book.

My America Storybook

This 12-book series comes in hard copy and audio. The link to the books and audios are in the Hostess Resource Center.

COTTAGE MEETING FOR KIDS

Cottage Meeting for Kids is a liberty promoting program for the entire family and focused on children from preschool to teens. It is full of great stories and fun activities to help children gain a love of liberty. Families can join together each month for an Activity Day to share the concepts they've learned and enhance them through group activities. Here are some ideas to promote the concepts presented in "Raising a New Generation of Patriots." You can find additional ideas, outlines and activities on the Moms for America® website under "Cottage Meetings for Kids."

- *Vacation Liberty School* is a great program to use with the kids to promote patriotism; the link to the book with a 7-day program is available in the Hostess Resource Center and Cottage Resources

- Read to, or have the Children listen to, *My America Storybook*; link is the Hostess Resource Center and Cottage Resources

- Have a fun day of patriotic songs, crafts, and activities with other families

- Read and discuss as a family *The Bulletproof George Washington* by David Barton; another great book is *George Washington: The Man Who Would Not Be King* by Stephen Krensky

Book and Movie List

Suggested books and readings for children all ages to nurture a love of liberty in the home.

Rush Revere Series
by Rush Limbaugh

Freedom Series
Published by Libraries of Hope

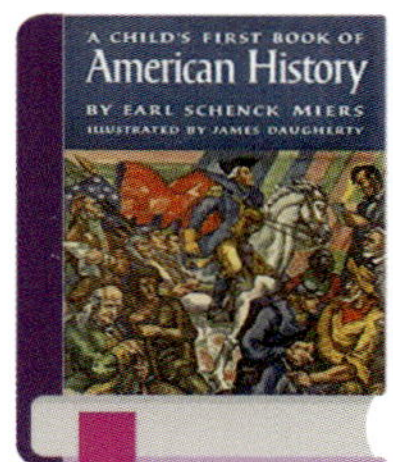

A Child's First Book of American History
by Earl Schenck Miers

What Does It Mean to Be An American
by Rana Di Orio and Elad Yoran

When Washington Crossed the Delaware
by Lynn Cheney

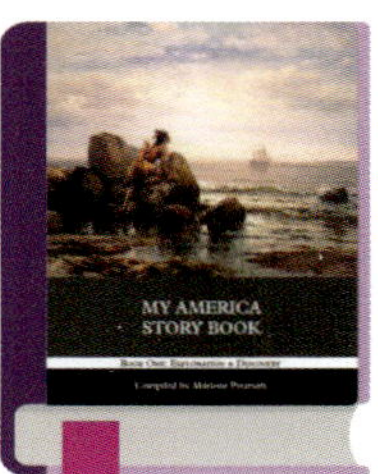

My America Storybook
(books 1-12)

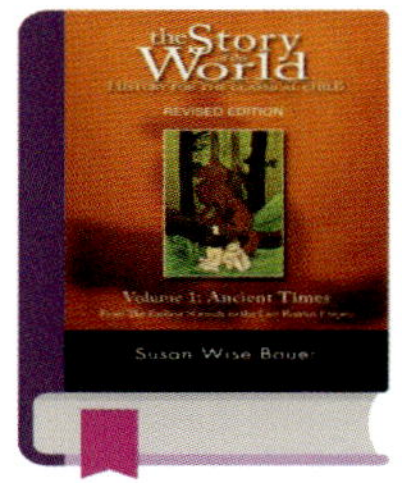

Story of the World
by Susan Wise Bauer

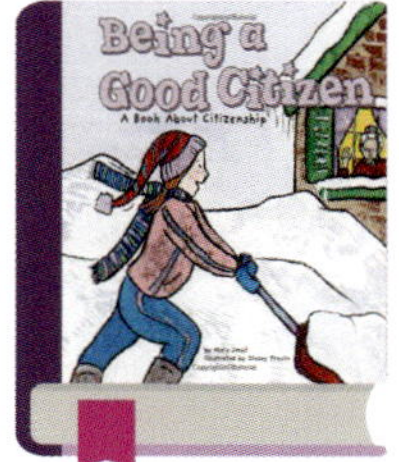

Being a Good Citizen
by Mary Small

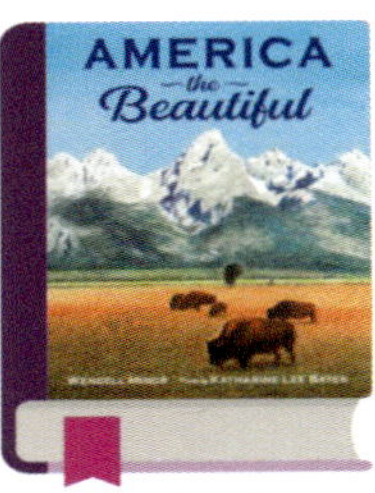

American the Beautiful
by Wendell Minor

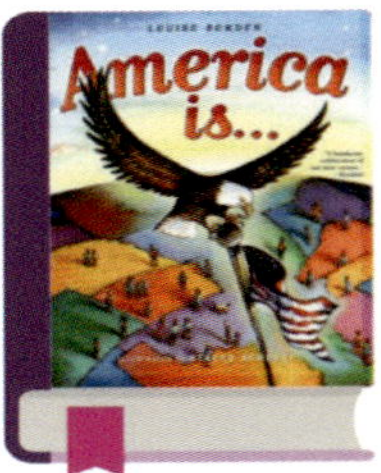

America Is…
by Louise Borden

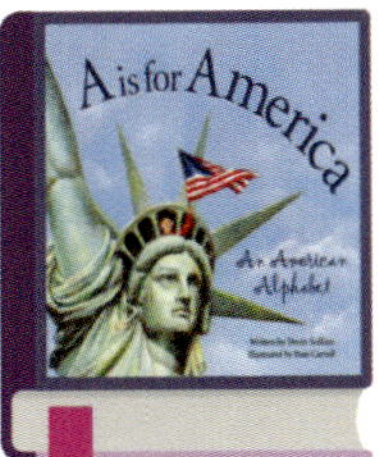

A Is for America
by Devin Scillian

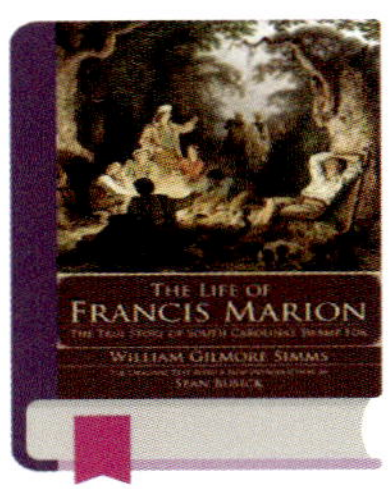

***The Life of Francis Marion:
The True Story of
South Carolina's Swamp Fox***
by William Gilmore and Sean Busick

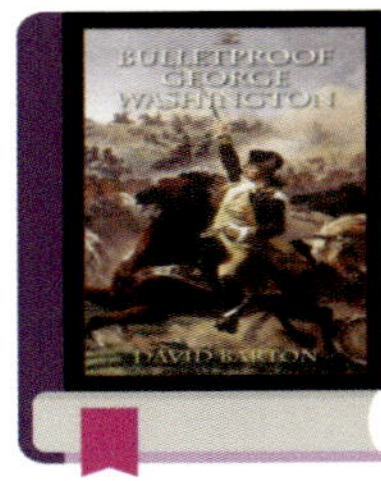

***The Bulletproof
George Washington***
by David Barton

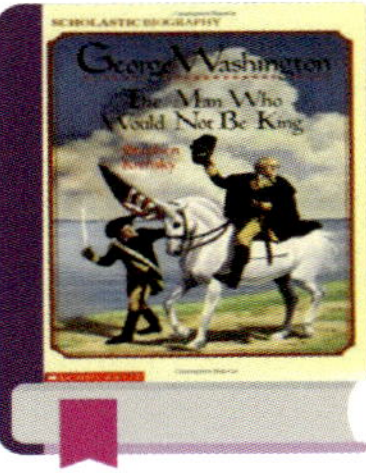

***George Washington:
The Man Who
Would Not Be King***
by Stephen Krensky

***The Glorious American
Songbook***
compiled by Cooper Edens

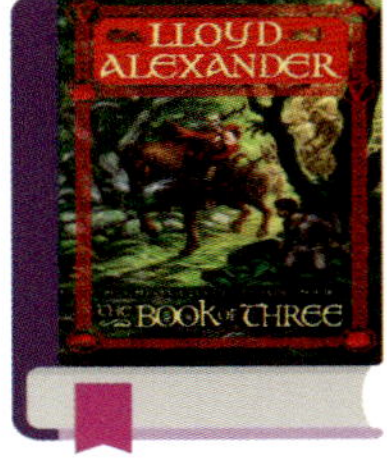

The Book of Three
by Lloyd Alexander

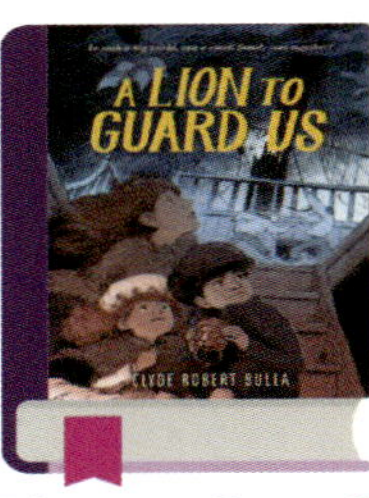

A Lion to Guard Us
by Clyde Robert Bulla

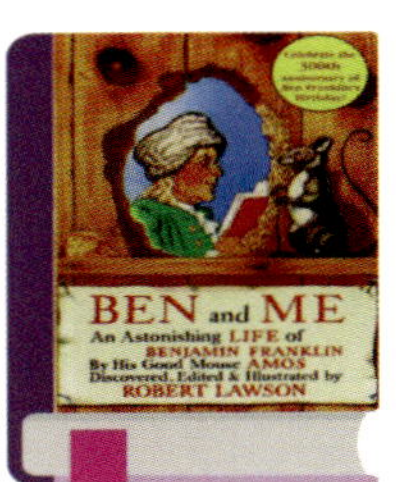

Ben and Me
by Robert Lawson

Toliver's Secret
by Esther Wood Brady

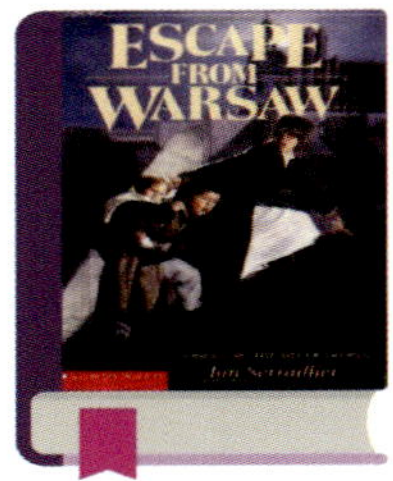

Escape from Warsaw
by Ian Serraillier

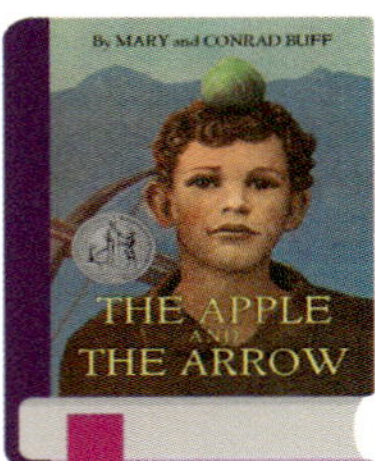

The Apple and the Arrow
by Conrad Buff

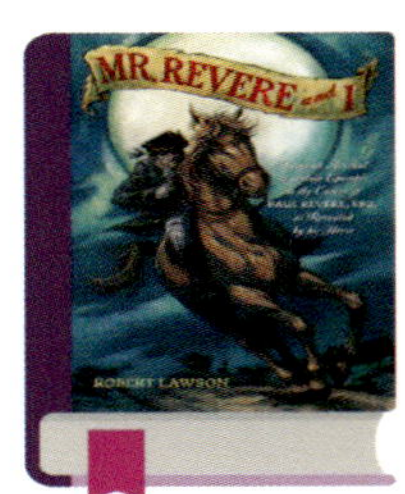

Mr. Revere and I
by Robert Lawson

***The Girl Who
Wore Freedom***
2020

SUPPLEMENTAL MATERIALS

A Mother's Garden

Several years ago, when my children were still young, they gave me a beautiful gift. They made a picture of a flower pot with each of their precious faces filling the center of each flower in the pot. It was just a simple little gift. It didn't take a lot of time and cost next to nothing, but it has become a priceless treasure that I keep on my wall and look at again and again to remind me of the garden I am nurturing in my home—the most important garden I will ever grow. And the most remarkable thing about what I see when I look at the picture is not just how much my children have grown, but how much I have grown in the gardening process.

Mother's Garden
May 2000

By far, I would have to say the most valuable lesson I have learned is just how important I am in my children's lives. As they have grown and started families of their own, I have witnessed first-hand just how important—and critical—our influence is, not just for their own welfare, but for the destiny of our very nation. What we teach our children today will determine the policies, voters, and candidates of tomorrow. We are painting the future picture of America every day through the lives of our children—and there is no more important work we will ever do. Something else I have discovered, much to my deepest dismay, is while we were once able to count on schools, media, and the community at large to help support our efforts in raising our children, today, we cannot.

I have been completely disheartened to see, not only what are our children are being taught in school, but what they are not. While our classrooms and schoolbooks were once filled with the stories of great patriots, miracles, and the principles of liberty that lead to good citizens, today, they are filled with stories of why America is not so great. Instead of raising patriots, our schools are graduating future citizens who have no love or respect for their country.

While it is true there have been many forces working against us feverishly trying to destroy this last bastion of hope for the world, in the end, we are the keepers of the flame—not the schools, not Congress, not the media. If our schools aren't teaching our children about America's history and heritage, then we need to be. If the media is not going to present truth and facts, then we need to. It is not the government's job to raise and teach our children; it is ours. We cannot count on others to do our job for us. The schools and churches are a support and resource for us as parents, not a replacement. If that resource is not supporting us, and is even going so far as to contradict everything we are teaching our children, and all the things we want them to know, then it is our job to change it, replace it, or counteract it.

Weeding the Garden

Anyone who has had any experience in gardening knows how hard it is to control weeds. If you are not consistently dedicated to pulling the weeds, they will soon overrun your garden—especially after a hard rain. You must battle the weeds at the root if you want to keep ahead of them, and you need to be especially diligent with stubborn weeds as they can quickly choke the life out of your plants. We need to use the same skills and principles in weeding our Liberty Gardens.

When I started Gardening and began assessing the influences in my children's lives, I realized that one of the greatest threats to my little Garden were the schools our children were attending. I was astonished at the kinds of books in their libraries, the absolute falsehoods I found in their history books, and the constant underlying messages of "parents just don't understand you." I couldn't believe how many things our children were learning in school that were

going directly against everything I wanted them to know and value.

I know many parents who have come to this realization and, like me, wondered what they could possibly do about it. I mean, our children have to go to get an education, right? Some concerned parents have chosen the "change" route and tried to make the system better by helping to choose curriculum, rewrite textbooks, get involved in the PTO, volunteer in their children's classrooms, and even run for school board. Other parents have chosen the "replace" method and chose private school, charter school, or homeschooling. Still others have gone the "counteract" route and work very hard to provide strong positive influences that will counteract the destructive ones. I have tested all three methods.

I served on the PTO, volunteered in my children's classrooms, and even ran for school board. I served on the school site council where I had direct input on classroom curriculum and where school funds were spent. I tried

to change it. But it didn't take long for me to realize that the current system was too well established and too deeply entrenched to change. At the pace things were "changing," our children would be having children before I would see any real change. Don't get me wrong, I'm all for making things better for the future, but my children were *my* future. I wanted the best influences for them now, and time was running out. So that brought me to the "replace" option.

We tried it all—private school, charter school, and homeschool. And while the final decision our family prayerfully came to was homeschooling our children, I quickly realized that it is not for everyone. I also realized that even if you homeschool, you still have the constant threat of noxious weeds creeping in on your tender plants. The fact is, it doesn't matter where your children go to school, what matters is that we, as parents, are engaged in their lives and doing all we can to create positive influences—and become the greatest positive influence we can ourselves.

From my experience in trying all three options, I can tell you that the most valuable lesson I have learned is that, regardless of how you decide to formally educate your children, "counteracting" is the most successful and effective tool in weeding our Gardens. It is so successful that, in time, you can establish every gardeners dream—an almost weed-free garden.

I read a story once about a church leader who went to visit one of their small congregations that had been cut off from the rest of the world behind the Iron Curtain for years. He was very concerned for the youth of the congregation because he said, "strange ideologies were taught and pernicious doctrines promulgated every day in the schools and in the captive press. Every day the children listened to the doctrines, philosophies, and ideals their teachers related."

Knowing the reality of the old saying "constant dripping will wear away the hardest stone," he feared the children would be swayed by the "constant dripping" they were receiving. When meeting with the parents, he asked about their children. "Do they retain their faith?" he asked. "Are they not overcome by the pressure of their teachers? How can you be sure they will not leave the simple faith in God?"

The parents responded, "We mend the damaged reservoir each night. We teach our children positive righteousness so that the false philosophies do not take hold. Our children are growing in faith and righteousness in spite of almost overwhelming pressures from outside."

The church leader shared the experience he had with these devoted families saying, "Even cracked dams can be mended and saved, and sandbags can hold back the flood. And reiterated truth…expression of love and parental interest can save the child and keep him on the right path."

I have read many stories of families who had been trapped behind the iron curtain for years being taught godlessness, and yet, when that iron curtain collapsed, thousands of families emerged with their faith intact because their parents tended and nurtured their Gardens.

The Powerful Influence of Parents

The first thing the communists did when they raised that curtain was to purge the country of religion. They closed churches and outlawed worship, but they could not destroy the faith of the people; the parents shared their faith and taught their children so carefully at home that the false teachings and propaganda they received from school rolled off them like water off a duck's back.

This is the power and influence we have as parents. And this is the influence the destroyers of liberty and virtue fear most. Two of the most vicious destroyers of liberty and virtue—Joseph Stalin and Adolf Hitler—knew this. Stalin said, "Education is a weapon whose effects depend on who holds it in his hands and at whom it is aimed." Stalin went to great lengths to limit the influence parents had on their children. Hitler used the same tactics when forming the Hitler Youth programs and instituting youth sports programs on Sundays so the children couldn't go to church and be influenced there.

Religion was highly frowned upon and even outlawed under Nazi rule. Oh, they were allowed to keep their churches open, but they were stripped of all authority and influence and were dictated what would be taught and when. The teaching of God and prayer in schools—even Catholic Schools— was forbidden. One day, children were attending catholic school reciting the Lord's prayer to the Crucifix, and the next day, the Crucifix was replaced with the Nazi flag and the children were reciting "Heil Hitler!"

Why do you think Hitler worked so hard to create a division between

parents and their children? He even went so far as to encourage and reward children for spying on their parents and reporting any infractions of "the rules." He made every effort to turn their parents into the enemy. Why? Because he knew he was investing in his own future. "He, alone, who owns the youth," Hitler declared, "gains the future."

The strategy of Hitler and Stalin was simple—take away the parents, the churches, and individual thought and you have the people. Hitler and Stalin went straight to the children and taught them what they wanted them to know and believe. They created as many barriers as they could to any and all influences that contradicted their influence—especially the parents. We face the same powerful forces today. But, like those who emerged from the iron curtain with their faith intact, we too can—and must—emerge a strong, confident, moral, and free people, and it all begins with a few tiny seeds planted in the tender hearts of our children.

Just like those children from the Soviet Union, our children our being taught "strange ideologies and pernicious doctrines" every day. They hear it at school. They see it in the media, in their music, on TV. Every day, our children are listening to doctrines, philosophies, and ideals that are directly contrary to everything we stand for—and they hear it over and over, like "constant dripping." But if we tend our Gardens and teach our children carefully at home, then they will grow in liberty and virtue in spite of the almost overwhelming pressures from outside. I know this is true. I have witnessed it firsthand.

The two things destroyers of liberty fear most are faith and parents. Combine the two—faithful parents—and you have the greatest and most powerful weapon against tyranny. Hitler clearly recognized this. He lamented, "It is always more difficult to fight against faith than against knowledge." It is also much harder to propagate a lie when you have been infused with truth and taught how to recognize it. Hitler's strategy was "make the lie big, make it simple, keep saying it, and eventually, they will believe it." Our strategy needs to be teach the truth, teach with love, reinforce it with stories, and they will embrace it!

While elections, public policy, and government oversight are important things to participate in, it is so vitally important that we remember what matters most. The greatest and most important contribution we can make in preserving liberty is what we give the future from the Gardens we are planting in our own homes today.

Raising George Washingtons

BY KIMBERLY FLETCHER

Contains excerpts from *WOMEN: America's Last Best Hope*

A few years ago, I had a conversation with a friend who had asked about Moms for America. I shared our mission with her which is "to foster an understanding, love, and respect for America's history and heritage, her founding principles and values, her legacy and destiny, and build a nation of informed

citizens and devoted patriots one woman and one family at a time."

My friend then looked at me and said, "Oh, I didn't know it was political. I don't get involved in politics." I was quite surprised by her comment and confused as to how she thought preserving freedom and building a nation of informed citizens was political, and she went on to explain that politics was too cynical and petty, full of mudslinging and accusations. "I just don't get involved in that," she said.

Again, I was confused because political mudslinging has nothing to do with the mission and purpose of Moms for America. As I conversed further with my friend, I realized that the reason she, like so many Americans—particularly Christians— don't get involved in elections, public policy issues, or even defending liberty and the Constitution because we are confusing civic responsibility with politics, and they are *not* the same thing. I have (based on my own personal experiences) compiled some definitions to clarify the difference.

Politics is a product of pride, worldliness, and a lust for power. That is why so many of us cringe when we hear the word "politician" and look down our noses on the profession as beneath us—and it is. But politics is not what I am addressing here—civic responsibility is, and there is a difference.

Civic responsibility is that duty which every American has as a citizen of this country to respect the law, preserve the U.S. Constitution, be involved in our communities, safeguard the Republic, watch over our government, and seek out and elect good leaders to represent us. Politics is the result of what happens when not enough of us fulfill that duty.

So that leads us to the perpetrators of politics—the politicians!

A Politician is a person who lusts for power, is obsessed with self-importance, and motivated by greed. Politicians have been groomed in politics. They learn the artful craftiness of deceit, the clever tactics of scheming to get gain and win votes, and the cunning methods of distraction, distortion, denial, and blame shifting. Politicians will say and do whatever it takes to keep and add to their power. They are motivated by self-preservation and personal gain and put their own interests above the people they serve. Politicians will vote for anything they feel benefits them, regardless of how their constituents feel or whether or not it is in the best interest of the country. Politicians are self-serving individuals who hold little regard for God or country and feel no loyalty or affection for the people they serve. Not very Christ-like attributes, are they?

A statesman, on the other hand, is a person of integrity and high moral character, who possesses a strong desire to serve others, recognizes his/her imperfections, and strives to overcome them to be the best person he/she can be. Statesmen have been trained in humanity. They learn the moral code of right and wrong, the positive attributes of honesty, humility, patriotism, accepting responsibility, and the selfless standards of love thy neighbor, the golden rule, and country before self.

Statesmen are people of faith who believe in a supreme being and a future state of rewards and punishments. They research issues carefully and do their best to vote in the best interest of the Republic and the people they represent—even if it means losing votes.

Statesmen cherish freedom and liberty, have a deep affection and concern for those they serve, and feel a profound sense of duty and loyalty to their Country. They live their faith, reverence God, and respect the faith of others.

Now that you've read these definitions, I want you to ask yourself—do you want politicians serving in Congress or Statesmen? What about city councils, school boards, the media?

I think you would agree that we need Statesmen in all spectrums of society—in our schools teaching our children, in the media presenting the news, in our elected offices serving the people. And if this is what we want, then we need to begin with us. We need to be statesmen, and we need to be raising statesmen in our homes.

Do you want your children to be Politicians or Statesmen? If your answer is politician, then just keep

sending your children out to the world every day to be taught and influenced by politicians. But if you want your children to be Statesmen, then you must become a greater influence in your children's lives to combat the insurmountable influences raging against them from a world of degeneracy, deceit, and corruption.

George Washington proclaimed, "All I am I owe to my mother. I attribute all my success in life to the moral, intellectual, and physical education I received from her." What an endorsement that is! George Washington was the great and humble man he was because of the influence of his dear mother. That is the power of our influence today.

If we want our children to be Statesmen, then we have got to be that influence in their lives. If we want them to know their history and heritage and develop a love of country, we need to be instilling it in them because they aren't getting it anywhere else. Our children aren't born with a love and respect for America and liberty simply because they are born here. We need to teach and inspire them by the things we read to them, the experiences we provide for them, and most of all, by our example.

If our children are patriots, it is because we raised patriots in our homes. If our children know and understand the Constitution, it is because we taught them. If our children embrace freedom and love their country, it is because we instilled that love in them through our own examples.

Barbara Bush once said, "Our success as a society depends not on what happens in the White House, but what happens inside your house."

So we must decide, here and now will, our house be a house of Politicians or a home full of Statesmen? If America is to survive with all the beauty that made her great, then we need to be raising George Washingtons in our homes. That is the greatest contribution we can make to liberty and our beloved country.

We are the hope of the future. What we build in our homes today will be the foundation for tomorrow. We must stay firmly rooted in the principles and values that made America great because while the rest of the world is grooming politicians, we are raising George Washingtons!

The Urgent Need to Teach the Constitution to the Rising Generation

BY EARL TAYLOR
PRESIDENT, NATIONAL CENTER FOR CONSTITUTIONAL STUDIES

The other day, I was speaking to a young friend of mine who attends one of the local high schools. He was reviewing with me the classes in which he was currently enrolled. One of them was Advanced Placement American Government. I asked him to tell me about what the class was learning and the methods employed by the teacher. He said the main assignment was that each student had to bring a current issue to class. Three or four issues would then be chosen, which would be the basis of the discussion that day in class. He said

there quickly develops several different opinions strongly expressed by members of the class as they try to convince others of their point of view. I asked him if the teacher gives any input. To which he replied: "Oh no, the teacher says he doesn't want to influence our minds with his opinions. He merely wants us to be able to convince others of our position. But we have some pretty good discussions."

I asked him if the teachers taught any underlying principles of good government to the class. He said no. I asked him if the teacher expected you to read and study the writings of the founders and to learn their reasoning on important issues. He said no. I asked him if he felt there was a serious study of the Constitution itself. Again, he said no.

As our conversation ended I thought to myself how sad it is to have the opportunity to do some valuable teaching and have such great influence over young inquiring minds—only to see it squandered in opinions and rhetoric. And somehow, this passes the requirement for studying the Constitution in high school.

Studying the Constitution becomes a Requirement in 43 States

In 1926, Samuel P. Weaver, a member of the Spokane, Washington Bar Association, outlined the growing concern for stronger teaching of the Constitution after World War I:

"The gospel of the Constitution began to be proclaimed during the period immediately following the World War. Prior to that time the schools taught American History and civics, and in connection with those courses sought to train the students in the mechanics of government. After the war, however, when our national safety was threatened by the rapidly spreading danger of Communism, by the questioned loyalty of groups of foreign-born citizens and the

ignorance and indifference of many others, leaders of political thought fostered a movement for a more general, uniform, and effective teaching of the Constitution. Under the leadership of the American Bar Association and other patriotic organizations, forty-one states [by 1926] have enacted statutes requiring the Constitution to be taught in the schools."

My own state of Arizona was one of the 43 states that eventually adopted legislation requiring the teaching of the Constitution. The Arizona Revised Statute 15-710 mandates: *"all public schools in the State which are sustained or in any manner supported by public funds shall give instruction in the essentials, sources and history of the United States Constitution,.. and instruction in American institutions and ideals.." And if that isn't enough, our state law further declares to public school teachers that "Willful neglect or failure ... to observe and carry out the requirements of ARS 15-710 is sufficient cause for dismissal..."* (ARS 15-508)

By the end of the decade of the 1920s, 43 states had been persuaded to pass new laws, or emphasize old ones, requiring instruction about the Constitution in the schools. Even Congress became involved; in 1925, the U. S. House of Representatives, by a vote of 162 to 29, passed this resolution:

It is interesting to note that national emergencies, concerns about foreign presence in our country, and warlike threats to our nation always bring us to reexamine our teaching of the Constitution. It is as though Americans innately know that answers to our problems lie in that document. With the events of September 11, 2001 emblazoned on our minds, we are once again asking ourselves how well we are really teaching the rising generation the correct "essentials, sources and history of the United States Constitution."

A National Report Card on Teaching the Constitution

Mr. Weaver later gave an assessment as to the teaching of the Constitution in the schools. While his remarks are many years old, his description accurately describes our situation today:

"The Constitution should be taught as a separate course of study. This recommendation has met with the approval of the teaching profession. Many teachers and educators say there is no time in the present organization of the school system to allot for a separate course in the Constitution of the United States, and that the only way they can teach it is incidentally in connection with courses in history and civics. For example, in South Carolina, it is a part of the history course; in California, it is a part of the course in civics. In many states, it is reported as a part of both of these courses. In Missouri, it is taught only incidentally. In almost all of the states, it is taught by reference only. While no one will deny that the teaching of history and general civics offers many opportunities to impress the lessons of patriotism and good citizenship, yet all of us should readily understand that the fundamental principles of our constitutional government cannot be taught in this manner. The Constitution, being the source of all powers of our national government, should be emblazoned on the minds of every citizen with a distinctness that time cannot obliterate, and this can only be done when it is presented clearly and unobscured in its original setting and outlines.

"As a general rule there is little effort to teach the development of the Constitution, or to uncover the foundation upon which our constitutional structure rests. For example, there is no clear or adequate explanation of its development through colonial charters, state constitutions, the Declaration of Independence, Articles of Confederation, Ordinance of 1787, and other important instruments of government. Its kinship to the common law is not referred to in any text. Its relation to the customs and the commercial and social conditions existing at the time of its adoption are not adequately discussed. Its application and growth to meet critical conditions at the different periods of our history and at the present time have not been illustrated or explained.

"Some of the texts have abandoned the method of discussion used by Justice Story, Judge Cooley, and other eminent authors, and have adopted a method of their own, For example, two texts do not contain the Constitution except in the appendix. One author has reclassified the clauses of the Constitution and grouped them under divisions selected by him, under the theory that the high school student must be content chiefly with the study of selected topics. Some of the texts contain references and questions that are frivolous:

1. what is meant by gerrymander;

2. what is a filibuster;

3. what is a lame duck;

4. can a lame duck be appointed to office;

5. why did Mr. Bryan resign from Mr. Wilson's cabinet?

While these questions relate in a general way to the administration of our government, can they be said to inspire in the student an unfaltering devotion to the Constitution? Do they impress upon his mind and heart the great truth uttered by the immortal Gladstone: "The American Constitution is the most wonderful work ever struck off at a given time by the brain and purpose of man"?"

Mr. Weaver discusses the fact that most high school textbooks are poorly written and factually incorrect. He then raises the question as to who should prepare the texts for this purpose. He continues:

"It is not necessary that the authors be lawyers, but they must understand the law and its many distinctions. The Constitution is a legal document, and no person can explain it intelligently unless he has a clear conception of the history, meaning, growth, and

application of the principles upon which it rests. Almost all of the present texts reveal a lack of legal appreciation on the part of the authors, which makes them fail to accomplish the purpose desired.. The author to be successful must have the following qualifications:

1. he must be thoroughly trained in the law;

2. he must understand methods of teaching;

3. he must understand the methods used in writing textbooks;

4. he must be able to analyze the Constitution, its background, its meaning, and its application to conditions arising since its adoption; he must have the time, industry, and ability to devote to the work."

Mr. Weaver gave suggestions as to what a great textbook on the Constitution would contain. Among other things he included:

1. It should orient our Constitution among other constitutions in the world

2. It should trace the development of the great principles of the Constitution from their English and American origins

3. It should explain how these principles were built into our present constitutional structure by the Constitutional Convention and the conventions of the original thirteen states

4. It should analyze the Constitution section by section and paragraph by paragraph. It is difficult to improve upon the clear, logical arrangement of the scholars of the Constitutional Convention

5. It should explain the meaning of all the provisions of the Constitution and all legal and unfamiliar terms and phrases so that students become familiar with the framework and the powers of our national government from the great instrument which is their fountain source

It should illustrate how the Constitution, through the legislative, executive, and judicial branches, has been interpreted and applied to meet new conditions as they have arisen during all periods of our history so that students can understand the timeless nature of this marvelous document.

The Instructional Materials of NCCS Meet all of these Requirements

How grateful we are to the talented and gifted founder of the NCCS, W. Cleon Skousen, who meets and exceeds all of Mr. Weaver's requirements to author Constitutional textbooks and whose published works meet the requirements to be called great textbooks on the Constitution.

In our present national crisis, as in the 1920s, there is an increase of interest in good, constitutional government. Hopefully, the [NCCS] resources will prove to be a turning point back to America's sure foundation. Other than learning to serve the God of this land, is there any greater service we can do for the rising generation than to see they are taught about the marvelous and miraculous document called the Constitution of the United States?

Journal

RELATED QUOTES

"Our concern isn't about the flames of freedom which burn in our generation. The concern is that in the upcoming generation, the fire has never been kindled." **-Vaughn J. Featherstone**

"We would impress upon the minds of our readers this grand truth, and would that we might thunder it into the ears of all mankind, that a nation is but a magnified home." -
CE Sargent, Our Home

"When you look into the eyes of your children and grandchildren, when you picture their greatness and potential, do you feel that they are getting the education that is up to par with who they were born to become?" **-Oliver DeMille, A Thomas Jefferson Education**

"Children are the living messages we send to a time we will not see." **-Neil Postman**

"..the founding American generations did something that almost no others have ever done. They read the fine print! They taught their children to read bills, laws, court cases, legislative debates, executive decrees, and bureaucratic policies. They read them in schoolrooms and at home....They said they would consider their children uneducated if they didn't read such things." **-Oliver DeMille, How to Destroy the Constitution**

"There is a beautiful parallelism between the condition of woman in her domestic life, and the character of a nation." **-Edward D. Mansfield**

"You, today, are writing on the yielding tablets of their hearts and minds the preface to the next volume of our nation's history. America should fear the disloyalty and contention of the fireside more than the nefarious plots of scheming politicians." **-CE Sargent**

"Even the smallest person can change the course of the future." **- J.R.R. Tolkien**

"Ours is the first experiment with a true republic. If we fail in this experiment, if our government falls, the world will hear the echo of that fall till the end of time as a dismal, warning sound." **-CE Sargent**

"The future doesn't belong to the faint-hearted. It belongs to the brave." **-Ronald Reagan**

"Your boys [and girls] are soon to take the reins of this high mettled steed, America. A nation's only hope is in them, and their only hope is in

you; and the instruments which God has put into your hands with which to fit them for this high office, are the influences of the home."
-CE Sargent

FROM THE FOUNDERS

"The boys [and girls] of the rising generation are to be the men [and women] of the next, and the sole guardians of the principles we deliver over to them."
-Thomas Jefferson

"The best means of forming a manly, virtuous, and happy people will be found in the right education of youth. Without this foundation, every other means, in my opinion, must fail."
-George Washington

"When tyranny becomes law, rebellion becomes duty."
-Thomas Jefferson

"The issue today is the same as it has been throughout all history, whether man shall be allowed to govern himself or be ruled by a small elite."
-Thomas Jefferson

"Freedom had been hunted round the globe; reason was considered as rebellion; and the slavery of fear had made men afraid to think. But such is the irresistible nature of truth, that all it asks, and all it wants, is the liberty of appearing."
-Thomas Paine

Journal

Journal

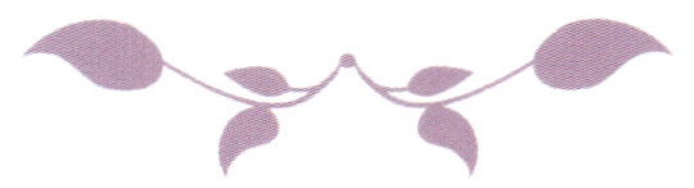